RAVENS IN THE STORM

A PERSONAL HISTORY OF THE 1960S ANTIWAR MOVEMENT

Carl Oglesby

Scribner

New York   London   Toronto   Sydney

SCRIBNER
A Division of Simon & Schuster, Inc.
1230 Avenue of the Americas
New York, NY 10020

First Scribner hardcover edition February 2008

SCRIBNER and design are trademarks of
Macmillan Library Reference USA, Inc., used under license
by Simon & Schuster, the publisher of this work.

For information about special discounts for bulk purchases,
please contact Simon & Schuster Special Sales:
1-800-456-6798 or business@simonandschuster.com.

Book design by Ellen R. Sasahara
Text set in Apollo MT

Manufactured in the United States of America

10   9   8   7   6   5   4   3   2   1

Library of Congress Cataloging-in-Publication Data

ISBN-13: 978-1-4165-4736-5
ISBN-10:   1-4165-4736-3

And it came to pass at the end of forty days,
that Noah opened the window of the ark which he had made:
And he sent forth a raven, which went forth to and fro,
until the waters were dried up from off the earth.

—Genesis 8:6–7

Contents

Acknowledgments

IN VARIOUS WAYS, the following people were of great help to me in completing this book and seeing it into print: Ross Altman, Paul Booth, Helen Garvey, Susan Kahn, Michael Locker, Don Miller, Elizabeth Rimanoczy, and Kathleen Silver. Colin Robinson was in every sense the writer's dream editor.

A Note on Memory

I OFFER THIS BOOK not as a history but a memoir, as my memories of what I heard people say and saw them do. My aim is to convey the spirit of the time and my impressions of the people I shared it with.

This said, I have enjoyed some rather unique aide-mémoires. Invaluable in my reconstructions have been the more than four thousand pages of Federal Bureau of Investigation (FBI), army intelligence, State Department, and Central Intelligence Agency (CIA) files released to me decades later as a result of suits under the Freedom of Information and Privacy acts (FOIA), suits in which I was superbly represented by the masterful James Lesar, Esq., surely the world's champion FOIA attorney.

My FOIA files allow me to recover the details of my life in the hot part of the sixties to a level of detail that otherwise would have been impossible. The CIA even took the trouble to assemble a list of every one of the several dozen addresses I have lived at back to the date of my birth, half of which I had forgotten about. Oddly, its one mistake is that it has me visiting North instead of South Vietnam in 1965. Thanks to the great concern these federal agencies took in me, I can pick almost any date in the period from the summer of 1965 through 1970 and tell you exactly where I was and what I was up to. Not even my mother cared so much.

As to my characterizations of the people with whom I shared these events, I do not believe that I have allowed myself the least liberty as to what I took to be their real views and attitudes. And most of the passages of explicit dialogue are based on notes I made at the time or articles that others or I published soon after the event. But I do not claim that the dialogues I present here are verbatim. I have verified the few contemporary passages with their sources, but I was not tape-recording my life during the sixties. Except for some especially memorable phrases and some words that found their way into news reports, the specific language of these conversations surely differed in some degree from the language I recall and have put on the page. The mise-en-scene and substance are, however, as I recall them.

On Birds

THE HAWK BECAME the warrior's definitive symbol early in the 1800s, when senators John Calhoun of South Carolina and Henry Clay of Kentucky led the so-called War Hawks, a coalition of southern and western states supporting aggressive westward expansion and the War of 1812.

Fully at one with the spirit of the original War Hawks, the hawks of the Vietnam War period saw the Viet Cong of South Vietnam as the puppets of North Vietnam, and North Vietnam as the puppet of either the Soviet Union or China. Southeast Asia, the hawks believed, was a sphere of American interest, and holding on to South Vietnam was therefore vital to American security, if only because of the domino effect. Hawks believed that the situation demanded that we intervene militarily against the Viet Cong to contain the spread of communism.

The dove has a much longer pedigree as the symbol of pacifism because of its role in the story of the Great Flood.

By returning to the ark after its first release, the dove told Noah that the flood still covered the earth. By returning after its second release with an olive branch, it told Noah that the waters were receding. And by not returning at all after its third release, it told him that peace was returning to the earth.

But the movement against the Vietnam War was not fundamentally a pacifist movement—a point of importance to me because, as I recount in this book, I played a leadership role in this movement. Most of us who flocked in opposition to the war did not do so because we oppose all wars on principle, as the true doves do, but because we opposed the Vietnam War in particular. Our study of the war persuaded us that the hawks badly misread the Vietnamese insurgency and failed to make a valid case for intervention. We were for the most part not pacifists.

Certainly I was not. Indeed, as late as the summer of 1965, when the war was still a "police action" and just starting to become an issue for the American people, I was still proud to be a professional hawk with a solid job in the defense industry.

I was not a dove.

Nor was the first creature to leave the ark.

We commonly overlook the raven in our retelling of the story of the Great Flood, perhaps because its moment comes and goes so quickly and is presented so completely without comment.

The raven enters the story in the eighth chapter of Genesis, verses 6 and 7:

> And it came to pass at the end of forty days,
> that Noah opened the window of the ark which he had made:
> And he sent forth a raven, which went forth to and fro,
> until the waters were dried up from off the earth.

The next verse, chapter 8, verse 8, brings the dove into the story: "Also he sent forth a dove from him, to see if the waters were abated from off the face of the ground."

We read no more of the raven in Genesis. It reappears in four later books, always fleetingly, but always with an intriguing role in an important story:

- When the prophet Elijah draws the wrath of wicked King Ahab, God sends Elijah for safety into the wilderness "to be fed bread and meat by the ravens" (I Kings 17:6).
- When Job, hurt and confused, questions God's goodness in afflicting him so horribly, God interrupts him with a long string of thundering rhetorical questions, beginning, "Where wast thou when I laid the foundations of the earth?" and ending, "Who provideth for the raven his food?" (Job 38:41)

- In Proverbs 30:17, God promises that "the eye that mocketh at his father, and despiseth to obey his mother, the ravens of the valley shall pick it out."
- Urging his disciples to hold on to their faith in a dangerous time, Jesus says, "Consider the ravens: for they neither sow nor reap, which neither have storehouse nor barn; and God feedeth them" (Luke 12:24).

So I suggest that the raven is a better bird than the dove for those of us who flew against the hawk.

We opposed the war for empirical, practical reasons that were specific to the Vietnam War itself. We studied the war, the history of Vietnam, and the formation of American policy. These studies convinced us that the reasoning behind the hawks' demand for military intervention was deeply misguided.

We drew the hawks into public debate wherever and whenever we could. We gave the hawks every opportunity to respond to our critique of their beliefs about Vietnam and the increasingly violent intervention they were leading the United States into.

As the public debate progressed, we became more and more confident that the hawks' case for war was founded on a gross misreading of Vietnamese history as well as of American security needs. We argued that the hawks' stubborn insistence on constantly escalating the level of violence, despite the war's appalling costs in blood and treasure, reflected nothing nobler than the hawks' blindness to their own errors.

We recognized a duty—yes, a patriotic duty—to take our beliefs about the war to the larger American public and to insist that the hawks meet us for open debate in the public forum. Despite the hawks' contemptible efforts to call our patriotism into question for having the audacity to challenge their beliefs, we pursued them into their very aeries to demand that they respond to our bill of particulars.

Unlike the dove, we left the security of the ark and never went back to it.

Like the raven, we took to the storm.

To my tale.

PART 1 | Taking Off

1 | The Blue Badge of Clearance
Ann Arbor, 1963

I WOKE UP early that morning with my mind set on getting to work as soon as possible. One cup of instant coffee heated while I pulled on my standard work uniform of gray slacks, white shirt, red tie, and blue jacket, with my blue ID badge clipped to the lapel, careful not to awaken Beth or any of our three kids. A few quick gulps, then I hopped into my red Alfa Romeo ragtop and roared out of Ann Arbor's Sunnyside Street for the five-mile drive on the still-empty freeway to my place of work, Bendix Corporation's Systems Division (BSD).

BSD was a defense contractor, and I was the supervisor of the company's technical-editing section, made up of about thirty tech editors and about sixty tech typists. We were frantic that morning to get the last parts of a fifteen-hundred-page proposal edited, typed, proofed, corrected, and integrated with hundreds of schematics and diagrams coming over from the art department, okayed by the engineers, and sent off to the printer in time to make the air force's hard-and-fast deadline.

We were bidding to design and build a satellite communication system. It was the biggest job we had ever bid on, and corporate headquarters badly wanted us to win it. It would mean lots of work not only for BSD but also for many of Bendix Corporation's twenty-seven other divisions.

There had already been serious schedule slippages because the engineers, as was their wont, kept redesigning components. *We* couldn't get a deadline extension from the air force because then our rival bidders would bitch for more time, too. So all the delays upstream of my department cut into my group's time for editing and final typing. We just had to do it.

I'D BEEN IN the tech-editing dodge in the defense business a little more than six years, first at Goodyear Aircraft Corporation in Akron, where I grew up, and then for the next four years at BSD in Ann Arbor. I could hardly tell an ohm from an amp, but I was strong on verbs and nouns. I was good at rendering engineers' prose into Standard English without giving undue offense, and I was good at working under pressure and meeting hard deadlines. The year before I'd been promoted to supervisor of my section and given a nice raise. Beth and I were buying a comfortable three-bedroom ranch-style house with a spacious backyard and a two-car garage on grassy, well-kept Sunnyside Street. Beth was as busy as I was, with daughter Aron in the second grade, daughter Shay in playschool, and son Caleb toddling along behind.

If one of us was already a radical of any kind, it was Beth. She called herself a socialist and held strong views on early education grounded in the writings of A. S. Neill and Dr. Benjamin Spock, heroes in our house. "Give kids love and freedom," she said, "and they'll find their own discipline." I was with her on civil rights and child rearing, but socialism seemed to me a bit over the top, a way to bury social problems under a federal bureaucracy. We enjoyed tweaking each other about it. I couldn't imagine a better mother for our kids.

And maybe I was living a crypto-radical side life in that I spent most of my evenings at my basement desk quietly writing angry-young-man plays or hanging out at the University of Michigan billiards room to shoot pool with a Brooklyn poet and close friend, Jerry Badanes, whom I'd met in a modern-poetry class taught by the poet Donald Hall. Beth and I also socialized with Frithjof and Taya Bergman, he an exciting young Austrian philosopher who taught a four-star class on existentialism and she a fine dancer in the Martha Graham style. It was in Bergman's class that I fell for the great anti-Communist radical Jean-Paul Sartre.

There was also something just a touch radical in getting so avidly into folk music, although the real allure of it was that you could sing without knowing how to. I got my first guitar and learned a few of the easier chords.

But when morning came I was happy to kiss Beth and the kids good-bye and head off for Bendix, joyful to be in my Alfa, as ultimate in middle-class extravagance as Beth's Austin Minivan was in socialist utility. I was the first in my family to work in a white collar, happy to be an upwardly mobile Everyman with a mortgage and a few dreams.

The only thing at all distinctive about my uniform was the badge I wore.

This was a blue-bordered, plastic-laminated ID badge clipped to my lapel or shirt pocket. The standard full-front mug shot on it showed a young white guy staring soberly into the camera through plastic-framed glasses and with a skinny Anglo face, brown hair combed in a standard part. Well, and a short goatee. For 1963, maybe that was a bit advanced.

As such portraits go, mine wasn't too bad. It showed well enough what the person wearing that badge was supposed to look like. It wasn't the worst way to get an identity. A blue badge meant that the FBI had cleared you for Secret. In the social hierarchy of classified knowledge, blue stood between the low-level clearance of green and the higher level, which was red, denoting a kind of middle class of military secrets. Almost all of our work was blue.

MY JOB WAS a hot spot, always under time pressure, and I loved it. By late 1963, I had worked for about four years as a technical editor in Systems's publications department, the last year as section supervisor. Our work area was often chaotic, with engineers yearning to make last-minute changes in press-ready copy, and tech typists yearning to go home for the day. But I was always glad to rise to the challenge of it and was proud of my blue badge. I worked hard, got nice raises, and was given time off to finish my BA at the University of Michigan, making the time up in the evenings and on Saturdays.

My mother was enthusiastic about this middle-classing of my life, but my father approved only grudgingly. If this house on Sunnyside was what college could get you, well, okay, maybe my mother was right, but he still worried about a job where your tool was a mere blue pencil. He had been happier during my days on the breaker mills in the rubber factory. To him, that was a real job, something you did in a factory with a big machine. "You think you can handle that white collar?" he said. "Ain't that a pretty long leap?"

But he and my mother had made much longer leaps themselves, both leaving the South for the North, he escaping the hardscrabble life of a small cotton farm near Cowpens, South Carolina, she from a drunkard father working for the coal mines, sometimes in Alabama, sometimes in Tennessee. Both had run north from their roots during the Depression, both in flight from a poverty that I can scarcely imagine.

My father was born in 1904 and raised without schooling on a forty-acre cotton farm near Cowpens, the first of eight boys among the dozen kids in his family. He spent much of his early life behind the family mule and a plow. He hated it but felt obliged to stay for the family's sake. Sometime in the late 1920s the family sent him to Akron, where a distant relative could get him in at Firestone. His mission was to earn a factory worker's big pay and send a lot of money back home.

He met my mother there in 1934, and they were soon married, he at thirty, she at twenty. Then the Depression reached his plant, he got laid off, and we moved to Kalamazoo, where my mother's three sisters had resettled from Tennessee. One of them put us up until Dad found a job as a mixer at a small cinderblock ink plant, Kelly Ink Factory. It was low-paying but steady work at a machine that poured two colors of oily ink together into a huge iron vat and stirred them slowly with an iron ladle until they had become one. He took me to work with him one day to show me what true colors looked like. They were deeply saturated and shiny, with a heavy, gravylike consistency, colors that reached the back of your eye. We found our own place to live, a three-room cottage near Millwood School, where I started kindergarten. I was six and in first grade when the Japanese hit Pearl Harbor. Dad heard the rubber shops were hiring again, so we moved back to Akron. He got a job at

Goodyear and stayed there for the rest of his working life. Somewhere along the line he accepted an invitation to become a Mason, but never joined anything else besides the Akron local of the United Rubber Workers Union, which was obligatory because Goodyear was a closed shop. He didn't like the union because he thought it just put more bosses in your life, but he was glad to have the job and he always voted Democrat. He and my mom split when I went away to college. They had stayed together in mutual agony so I could have a happy home. He retired at sixty-five and went back to Cowpens to die of emphysema and lung cancer a few years later.

My mother, Alma Loving, also had made big leaps to keep ahead of poverty. She was the third of four daughters born to a coal miner who moved his family around a lot in Alabama and Tennessee, going where the mines were hiring and drinking a lot of moonshine. He died when she was in her teens, but she and her sisters all finished high school and all fled to the North to find work. She went to Akron because an uncle's family offered her room and board. She worked as a dime-store clerk. In 1949, as I was starting high school, we moved to Ghent, a village north of Akron, first to be caretakers on an estate and live rent-free in the caretakers' house, then moving to another place nearby when Mom declared it odious to do another woman's housework. In tears at the kitchen table one evening, she said to my father, "I'd have thought you had more pride than to make your wife wash another man's dirty shorts."

My mother did her best to make up for my father's constant pout. She was involved in my schooling from the start, several times president of the PTA, excited when I showed signs of being an adept student because she saw education as the way out of the coal miner's life she'd grown up with and the factory worker's life she was living. She went back to clerking at a dime store in Akron so I could use the scholarship I'd won to Kent State.

I discovered the stage there in my sophomore year when my debate partner and I tried out for the roles of the two lawyers in John Galsworthy's *Justice,* which were major cameo roles—just one scene, but big, fat speeches. Gary and I got only bit parts, but I was hooked and promptly left the speech department for the Green Room. In another year I played the lead, John Proctor, in Arthur Miller's *The Crucible*. Later I discovered a taste for Shakespeare and played Macbeth in the first Greater Akron Summer Shakespeare Festival. But Miller's play put the bug's bite so deep in me that I had to drop out of school and split for the Apple to see what I could do about it. I played one Off-Broadway role. I was the wicked sheriff in an antisegregation play called *Mississippi* by a pill-popping freak named Richard Davidson, who had not bothered to finish the script before going into rehearsals and who came to rely on me for a line here and there, so that my bit part became the second lead. It was enough to persuade me that it was more fun to be the playwright than the actor, so I went back to Kent to see if I could settle down and start writing in earnest.

Beth Rimanoczy, from Cleveland, a smart, bright grad student at Kent, an English major who knew her Beowulf, small-framed and strong, glamorous when she wanted to be but happiest in jeans telling me what was wrong with people who liked capitalism and T. S. Eliot, also was ready to settle down. Both of us came from broken homes, hers of the middle class in Cleveland. I think both of us wanted to show our parents how they should have raised us. We spent three months getting to know one another, easily got through the parental introductions, and got married in 1956 in a minimal ceremony in a small Unitarian church, she in a white gown and veil. Both of us wanted children, and soon. The first of our three kids was born on our first wedding anniversary. Once Beth was pregnant, my part-time job at Sam's Pizza Shop no longer paid enough, so I started looking around.

The job at Sam's was hard to leave. For one thing, the shop was right below our walk-up apartment on Water Street across from the railroad depot and the Mahonning River, so there were no to-and-from hassles. For another, we got a lot of free pizzas. But most important, Sam's had become the meeting place of a group consisting of myself and seven or eight other lit-school part-time beatnik types who often collected there to talk about poetry, jazz, the issues of the day, and what we could do to embarrass the campus frat rats—for example, by sponsoring an inter-fraternity greased-pig wrestling contest. We called ourselves the Macedonians after the classical foes of the Greeks. It was my first dalliance with radical activism.

But now Beth and I needed more income, so I got a job at one of Akron's rubber plants. I worked in a three-man crew running a line of breaker mills that refined crude rubber brought to us in smoking slabs.

The money was all right, and Dad was proud of me because I had finally cut out what he had regarded as college crap and gotten a real job, the kind that he had held for more than twenty years. The money beat Sam's, but it was eight hours, six days a week of hard, dangerous work, constantly in an intimate physical relationship with heavy, fast-spinning mill drums. And despite my best efforts in the shower room, I brought home such a stench of hot rubber that Beth could barely stand to be in the same room with me. I started looking for something better suited to a skinny intellectual type.

I lucked out through a Macedonian comrade, Don Thomson, and landed a job at Goodyear Aircraft as a tech editor. Goodyear had just won a big contract and needed to staff up its pubs department quickly. And so, on the strength of Thomson's recommendation and a good interview, Goodyear overlooked my lack of a degree and gave me a shot. I had a gift for nitpicky editing and working in a hurry, so I did well despite having been defeated by high-school physics.

About a year into the job, something astonishing happened. The Margo Jones Theater in Dallas called to say it wanted to produce a play I'd sent them, *Season of the Beast,* the first of three I had written in my basement. *Season of the Beast* was an old-fashioned melodrama taking a blast at the Bible Belt fundamentalism that had almost caught me as a teenager. When it opened, the Dallas reviews were friendly, but the town fathers sensed something they didn't like about the play and sent a committee of six men to check it out. They all sat together in a back row, arms folded, didn't applaud at the end, and left quickly as a group. On the basis of their subsequent report, the town fathers ordered the theater to close the production and fire the director, Ramsey Burch. The theater resisted, and the dispute got into the papers. This drew the attention of theologian Thomas Driver of Union Theological Seminary, who wrote an admiring article about the play, and Brooks Atkinson, esteemed critic of *The New York Times,* who thought the play was drivel but wrote a long review of it because of the uproar it had provoked. Certainly I couldn't complain of being ignored.

BETH AND I were reasonably contented in the eighth year of our marriage. We had three delightful kids to raise: Aron, Shay, and Caleb. We were buying what we thought of as our starter home, a one-story three-bedroomer in a Dick-and-Jane neighborhood. We had scores of good friends, engineers from Bendix and poets and philosophers from the university, and we were delighted to throw them together in sometimes sexually liberated parties. Yes, it was the sixties, and we were glad to be a part of all that.

Tech editing in the defense industry was not a bad money job for an aspiring playwright with a family and a mortgage. I was proud to be entrusted with a few of my country's military secrets, and also proud to win the University of Michigan's Hopwood Prize in 1962 for my plays. I was at cruise speed, and life felt good. Of course, the outer world could be frightening. Along with all the young poets and missile engineers, the coffee-shop folk singers, and my golf and pool buddies, the dancers, actors, and apprentice dharma bums who were our friends, Beth and I worried about the Bay of Pigs crisis and the missile crisis and the missile-gap crisis and the Berlin Wall crisis and the civil-rights crisis. But the Ann Arbor scene was rich, and we both felt good to be part of it. And I felt good to be part of America's national defense.

BUT MY BROOKLYN poet friend Jerry Badanes kept bugging me about my job. "So when're you gonna stop killing people?" he would ask me every so often, more or less gently.

It was easy for me to laugh him off. I wasn't ashamed of my job. On the contrary. I had no problem with the idea that Free America needed military strength to contain Stalinism. I was a mild social liberal but a foreign-policy conservative, and not just because my job made it convenient.

I had grown up like that. As a high-school senior in Ohio I'd won a national contest in original oratory with a ten-minute speech titled "Peace or Freedom," arguing that it was one or the other and that the time to get pushy with the Soviets was now, while we, the good guys, still had the nuclear advantage. The nine other kids who made the final round in Denver that year, 1953, had all written speeches saying how good peace was, and I was the only one saying that if the cost of peace was freedom, it wasn't worth it.

Ten years after that, in 1963, it seemed perfectly normal to me that I should spend my days helping to bring new instruments of destruction into being, then spend my evenings and weekends hanging out with the local poets and writing melodramas of good and evil. I saw not the least irony, bad faith, false consciousness, or self-contradiction in any of this. Yes, I sympathized with organized labor and with the civil-rights movement, and I believed that our government should help the poor. I had sympathy for Cuba's revolution because Batista had been such a beast, but I also heartily agreed with JFK that those Soviet missiles had to go.

ONE DAY late in 1963, my department at BSD was at full speed on a huge proposal to the air force. Engineers with loosened collars and sweaty brows were everywhere among us, their plastic pocket protectors bulging with pens and pencils of every color.

"Just this one last change to a printer-ready wiring diagram," one would say, "and we will definitely win the job. Without it, the air force guys will know that we have no idea how these things work." Engineers must be taught this speech in school.

We all knew we would be working around the clock through the weekend.

My office was tucked into one corner of a big room filled with desks and editors, right next to another big room where all the tech typists were. I had just called Beth to tell her I would be late getting home. Beth said, "Did you hear the news?"

"I don't need any news," I said.

"The president's been shot," she said. I was fixed on getting the management proposal to the printer. It took me a second to get focused.

"The president," Beth said with a gentle, plaintive stress. "President Kennedy. Down in Texas, in a motorcade through Dallas."

One of our editors, Peggy, was standing in the door of my office. She could tell I had just heard. "There's a radio on in the art department," Peggy said.

I told Beth I would call her back and followed Peggy through the typing room, where the news was just beginning to register. The clatter of the typewriters was trailing off. People were looking up from their work with puzzled smiles, as though expecting this to be a bad joke and waiting for the punch line.

The art department was in a big room filled with drafting tables and illustrators and little groups of harried engineers. One of our part-timers was a college student who worked mostly at night alone and was therefore allowed to keep a little radio for company. He now had it turned on. Everyone had stopped work to listen.

It was well past one o'clock. The shooting was less than an hour old. Information was still scanty. Walter Cronkite repeated the basics. Both JFK and Texas governor John Connally had been seriously hurt and were at Parkland Memorial Hospital. No one knew who did it.

My first thought was that it must have been one of the nuts who had shut down my play in Dallas six years before. My second thought was that this would take care of the 1964 election all right, because now JFK would be unbeatable. I had liked Kennedy since first growing aware of him in the 1960 presidential election, and for all the ordinary reasons: his wit, grace, youth, sexy wife, energy, the sense he conveyed so effortlessly of speaking for a new generation.

Along with two or three thousand others, I had stayed up into the wee hours the night of October 1, 1960, after the first Kennedy-Nixon TV debate, to cheer for Kennedy when he came to spend the night on the Michigan campus. It was after two in the morning and I was far to the back of the crowd when suddenly the TV lights went on up front and JFK materialized on the steps of the Student Union to make the very brief speech in which he announced his intention to create the Peace Corps. A plaque memorializes the spot.

I was close to the young teachers and grad students at Michigan who had conceived the Peace Corps idea, notably Eddie and Judy Guskin, who had helped run a pilot project in Thailand that year. By 1960 a strong wind had already sprung up in that generation, a freshening restlessness that was not yet angry or rebellious and that could still go either way, into the system or out of it, but in either event with its own agenda. The civil-rights movement and the folk-song revival and later Bob Dylan and the Beatles infused culture with politics and politics with culture in a way that had not been seen here since the 1930s. Young middle-class white people were picking up on the civil-rights high and starting to dance with their whole bodies in an erotic and yet innocent, free-form way, bored with the gray-flannel quietism of the 1950s and no longer intimidated by the so-called Silent Generation that had come before them. They were looking to claim a share in America on terms still to be worked out but to be their own.

JFK seemed alone among the politicians of that moment in sensing that this energy was good, a force to be welcomed, one that bore his own soul with it. His speech late that night in Ann Arbor helped convince my friends and me that the spirit of young America would find a place in the world of the New Frontier.

And now the voice above the static on the radio stopped, paused, and then in a deeply altered tone, with great solemn dignity, announced, "Ladies and gentlemen, the president of the United States is dead."

The radio cut immediately to the *Eroica*'s funeral march. We all stood separately silent, then one by one began to stir. I heard the phone ring in my boss's office. From the half of the conversation I could hear, I could tell it was the outside printer wanting to know if this was going to affect our deadline. I heard my boss say that we had to assume it would not. In that case, the printer wanted to know when the next delivery of press-ready text was coming because he had to schedule his crew. My boss called me over to ask for an estimate, and I mumbled something. Then an illustrator came up to ask in a soft voice for clarification of an editing mark on a wiring schematic. A typewriter, then another, resumed their clatter in the typing room. We were all dazed but had to go on.

Bits and pieces of the event came drifting in over the next few hours. Governor Connally had been hit in the shoulder but would survive. A Dallas policeman named J. D. Tippit had been killed in what seemed a related incident. Acting on a phoned-in tip, the Dallas police had arrested an ex-Marine named Lee Harvey Oswald in a theater a few hours after the shooting.

It must have been four o'clock before I had an errand on the other side of the building and happened to look out a front window. The flag was still flying at full staff. That's an oversight, I thought. Somebody should straighten that out.

I called the guard shack. A security guard named Julio answered, a Cuban refugee from Castro whom I'd come to know pretty well. I used to work nights a lot in those days to make up for time I spent in class, and Julio would stop by on his rounds for a friendly little argument about Castro. He would call Castro a dirty Commie. I would call Batista a dirty fascist. He would laugh and pretend amazement that the FBI had ever cleared a guy like me.

"Oh, Carlos," he would say, shaking his head, "I think I better arrest you! You got to be some kind of Commie spy!"

I liked him. I had not yet heard the term *gusano,* or worm, Castro's term for the other side. Julio wasn't a worm. He just didn't buy Castro's deal. I wasn't sure I did either, but if the alternative was a scumbag such as Batista, then, hey, I thought, give the guy a chance.

I called Julio now because he handled the flag.

"Gate," he said.

I told him who it was and said, "You know, the flag ought to be at half-staff. Don't you think you ought to lower it?"

There was a pause. Then he said, "Oh, no, Carlos, I couldn't do that without an order from Tony."

By Tony he meant his boss, our personnel director, a round, jovial man in his middle forties whom I enjoyed watching shank his drives in the company golf league. Tony's office was in the front of the building. I told my secretary, Jean, that I'd be back in a few minutes.

Tony was on the phone in his office and I waited outside for him, glad for the quiet in that end of the building. Soon he came out and said, "What's up, kid?" He didn't seem shaken by the afternoon's events. "How's the big proposal coming? You going to make the deadline?"

"Yeah, I think so, as usual," I said. "But listen, I was wondering, shouldn't we lower the flag?"

"Lower the flag?" He smiled expectantly, as though waiting for the punch line.

"You know, out of respect for the president?"

He stiffened. His face darkened. "Why are you asking me this?"

"Well, I talked to Julio about it, and he said he had to get his orders from you."

"Orders to do what?"

"To lower the flag, Tony." I couldn't believe he didn't know what I was talking about. I said, "You *have* heard that President Kennedy's been killed?" He just looked at me. "Or maybe you haven't?"

"I've heard," he said.

"Well, don't you agree that it would be correct protocol? To lower the flag to half-mast? To show, you know, mourning and respect? That sort of thing?"

"I don't know anything about that," he said. "I'd have to get instructions from Detroit."

He meant corporate headquarters. "What's Detroit got to do with it?" He gave me a sideways look with a little smile of disbelief. "You've got to be kidding me," he said.

I said, "It's not the company's private flag, is it?"

He gave me a wry smile and a shrug. "You've got me there, kid. Somebody paid for it, I guess." He turned back into his office.

"All right, what if the GM says to lower it?"

"Look," he said with a little laugh, "if you want to bother Russ about a thing like this, be my guest."

I said, "Shit, Tony," and turned to go.

"But, Carl, if you want my advice," he said, "you'll forget about it. It's not your call."

I considered forgetting about it. It seemed an empty gesture. And maybe Tony was right and it wasn't my call. Nobody in the world was going to ask what I had done personally to get that particular flag lowered to half-staff on the day JFK was shot and killed.

The GM's office was right above Tony's on the next floor. Its rooms were carpeted and wood-paneled and graced by well-groomed secretaries whose desks sat behind big potted plants. That part of the building always had a cool, serene atmosphere to it, and it seemed especially quiet at that moment. I saw the three executive secretaries at the far end of the hall headed for their last break of the day. The door to the GM's office was ajar and I could hear male voices inside, the tinkle of ice cubes in a glass, then quiet laughter. Through the door I could see several of the executives around the GM's work table, all of them wearing red badges. There was a bottle of Chivas Regal on the table. They each had a glass. I had never seen that before. I knew that the GM had a little refrigerator off his main office, but I had never seen liquor in the building.

Turning away before they saw me, I went straight back to my office and was glad to find the work frenzy getting back up to speed. It was a kind of solace. I embraced it and stopped thinking about flags and flagpoles and protocols for the dead.

Beth and the kids were asleep when I got home late that night and were still asleep when I got up early Saturday morning to head back to work.

The flag at Bendix was at half-staff the next day. Detroit must have spoken in the night. The *Eroica* funeral march was still everywhere on the radio. I sat in my car for a bit in the almost-empty parking lot, had a little private moment, shook it off, made sure my blue badge was securely clipped to my jacket pocket, then walked through the gate with a sober nod to Julio. I was relieved to find the proposal in a mess and needing me to focus on pulling it back together.

We were still at work the next day, Sunday, when we heard that Oswald, after telling the police he was "just the patsy," had himself been shot and killed while in police custody by a Dallas nightclub owner named Jack Ruby, but we kept at our task and somehow got the proposal delivered on time Monday morning. The air force project officer congratulated us on it and told us that we would be asked to bid on similar jobs about to be put out to contract.

And future jobs there would be. Where I worked, at least, the change from Kennedy to Johnson could hardly have been more dramatic. The defense industry as a whole had begun to worry about the New Frontier. First, JFK had campaigned with a get-tough line toward Castro's Cuba, but then, after the Bay of Pigs, had turned away from it. Castro was left standing. Then JFK goofed around on his defense budget, which did not keep pace with the defense establishment's idea of our national-security needs.

A little worse than typical was our experience with a combined air force–navy contract to design and build the Eagle missile system, our biggest and most glamorous project.

The Eagle was to be carried by the next-generation fighter, at that point in its design history still designated TFX, for tactical fighter experimental. The TFX was in fact so very experimental that basic design characteristics were still being debated. Zealous in pursuit of "cost-effectiveness," JFK and his defense secretary, Robert McNamara, believed that one basic fighter could be designed to satisfy the needs of both the air force and the navy, thus allowing for economies of scale in production. But each service wanted its own dedicated fighter and kept insisting on features it knew the other could not live with.

For example, as our project engineers were trying to nail down the requirements for mounting the missile under the airplane's wing, the Defense Department still couldn't say whether the wing would be fixed or variable.

The air force wanted the TFX to have a fixed, swept-back wing because this would give it greater speed and maneuverability and more pounds for armor. Fewer complicated moving parts would make it cheaper to build, more reliable, and easier to service.

The navy wanted an aircraft with a wing that the pilot could vary in flight from a swept-back configuration for high speed to a spread configuration for the low speed needed to land on an aircraft carrier.

This difference was important to us as the missile contractor because our design had to include a way to mount the missile under the airplane's wing, and basic details of the mount's interface would obviously differ depending on whether the wing was movable or fixed.

Somebody in Kennedy's Defense Department, probably McNamara, the original "cost-effectiveness" man, decided that it made no sense to push ahead with the design of a wing-mounted missile before resolving basic design questions about the wing itself. So our contract was canceled.

The day we got the news was a gloomy day at BSD. No one was inclined to see canceling the Eagle as the reasonable thing to do. I saw friends of mine, guys I played golf with, pound their fists on their desks and curse JFK about it.

Maybe this is why the red-badge guys at Systems might have shed few tears for JFK, might even have seen the coming of the more hawkish Johnson as a kind of blessing, even as something to celebrate, though privately, of course, with a quiet scotch rather than with loud champagne and with a flag at full mast.

2 | Stumbling on Vietnam

Ann Arbor, 1964

THE MILITARY COUP attempted and suppressed in Saigon in November 1960, about a week after JFK's narrow, even questionable victory over Richard Nixon, seemed to have a comic-opera quality to it, the sort of thing that happened in faraway places with strange-sounding names.

As with many of us, my first sense that something on the grim side of comic might be going on in Vietnam dawned in January 1963, with the Battle of Ap Bac. This was the first major victory by the Viet Cong over units of the army of the Republic of South Vietnam. Until Ap Bac, the VC had limited itself to guerrilla-style engagements in which it would strike by surprise at times and places of its own choosing, then quickly melt into the general population or the jungle before Saigon's regular forces could reach the scene.

But at Ap Bac, the VC had stood its ground and prevailed against a South Vietnamese division ten times its size and fighting with the support of U.S. airpower, including helicopter gunships and Special Forces advisers in combat roles.[1]

People generally started paying a bit more attention to the emerging picture of a corrupt Saigon regime hopelessly isolated from the Vietnamese people and seemingly content to let the United States do its fighting for it.

Then, sometime in the spring of 1964, our interest at Systems Division sharpened when we won two contracts from the army: Jungle Canopy and Jungle Relay. We called them our Tarzan projects. Neither was explicitly targeted on Vietnam, but we all knew they were headed for Southeast Asia.

The problem the Jungle Relay system was to solve was that combat units could easily lose radio contact when they were operating with a hill or a ridge between them. The Jungle Relay system was a transmitter-receiver, or transceiver, packaged inside a dropsonde, a slender tube about four feet long. The dropsonde would be released on a small parachute from a low-flying helicopter over the target area, generally the crest of a ridge. The dropsonde would be fitted with a mechanism like the ribs of an umbrella that opened as the dropsonde was falling. These ribs were meant to snag the device in the treetops, the higher the better. Once it was in place, the transceiver's antenna would pop out, enabling it to function as an automatic communications-relay station for units operating on either side of the ridge, receiving signals from one unit and transmitting them to the other.

The environmental expertise we built up with Jungle Relay led to our other Tarzan project, Jungle Canopy, which addressed a completely different kind of tactical problem. Enemy forces operating in a rain forest could escape detection from the air by hiding under the palm trees, the canopy. The thought arose that the most straightforward way to deal with this was simply to spray the enemy's trail areas with a powerful herbicide such as Agent Orange. Then the question became how to adjust the nozzles on the dispensing mechanism: to produce a liquid stream, raindrops, a foggy mist, an aerosol, or a dry powder. What size of drops or droplets or particulates of mist would be best for burning off the big leaves at the tops of the palm trees? What size would work best for the undergrowth?

So two of my golf buddies, Harry and Paul, went down to Panama to make camp for a few weeks in a jungle that closely resembled the jungles of Southeast Asia. There, they installed sensors at several heights, from the treetops down to the undergrowth and on the ground. Then they helped the army outfit a helicopter with a dispensing mechanism something like the sort of thing used for crop-dusting, so it could fly over the test area at a low altitude and dispense a variety of chemicals through adjustable nozzles in a range of droplet and particle sizes. The sensors that Harry and Paul had installed in the jungle below would tell them what types and sizes of payload reached what levels of growth.

A much more pungent whiff of our police action in far-off Southeast Asia came wafting my way when word went around the plant that someone was in town recruiting for an outfit called Trojan Engineering. The big bosses would normally view an outside recruiter as the next thing down from Stalin, but for some reason our management was cooperating with this guy. It was coffee-break gossip that the Trojan rep had even been allowed to look through our personnel records. Then my boss told me that the Trojan man was interested in interviewing me and that I should feel free to talk to him. So out of curiosity and the lure of a gigantic salary, I called the phone number my boss had given me.

A guy with a gruff voice answered on the first ring.

"Trojan Engineering," he growled. "State your name and purpose."

I told him my name and where I worked and said, "I hear you're looking for tech writers, and that's my line."

"Are you willing to spend some time in another country under arduous and sometimes hazardous conditions?"

My interest quickened. "Well, for the right pay, sure."

"Meet me at the Pretzel Bell in an hour."

"How will I recognize you?"

"Don't worry about it. Just be there on time." Click.

And indeed he was unmistakable, not at all a P-Bell type, a tall, dark, hook-nosed, rawboned man of about forty with close-cropped black hair, piercing black eyes, and dressed in a well-tailored business suit. He had the look of a man on the run, constantly glancing behind him and talking in low, raspy bursts.

"Call me Jones," he said, his handshake firm and abrupt.

We ordered coffee and got right down to business.

"Well, Oglesby," he growled, "I hear you run a mean blue pencil."

"I can tell a verb from a hole in the ground," I said, trying lamely to sound sort of tough myself. "Where'd you hear a thing like that?"

"I've got my sources," he said.

"I'm intrigued."

"Forget intrigue," he said, checking his watch. "I hear you like your mother. Is this true?"

I stared at him uncomprehendingly a moment, then said, "I love my mother, Mr. Jones." I didn't know yet that mother was a nickname for the CIA. "Where'd you hear a thing like that?"

"I ask the questions, son," he said.

At about that point I began to sense that something a little odd was going on, though I didn't have a clue what it was. I figured it couldn't hurt to play along for a while. "Well, Mr. Jones," I said, "in that case, fire away."

"Are you willing to live apart from your family for several weeks at a time?"

"If it would help us buy the house, I'm pretty sure we could handle it."

"You like tigers?"

That stopped me again. I stared at him. He checked the door. "What," I managed to say, "like in 'burning bright'?"

"An English major, huh?" he said.

I was surprised that he caught the allusion to Blake. He didn't seem to be a guy who would read a lot of poetry. "You hold it against me?" I said.

"We all have our flaws," he said. "What about elephants?"

"Elephants are very big with me, Mr. Jones."

"Do you know of any problems that an investigation of you for top-secret clearance might turn up?"

Wow! Red-badge knowledge! I started wanting this job. "You will find no problems with me," I said. "But tigers? Elephants? Is this job with the circus?"

"Some might say so," he said without a smile. "Would you be willing to work in a rain forest, sometimes around the clock, for months at a time?"

"Would I get an umbrella?"

"Umbrellas make good targets," he said, "but we could work something out."

"Targets?"

He looked over his shoulder, then right into my eyes. "How would you feel about getting shot at sometimes?"

I didn't blink. Now I really wanted this part. "Could I shoot back?"

"You would be fully supported."

"Well, I'm an adventurous type. I could see it. But work on what?"

He sat back, releasing some of the tension, but didn't take his eyes away. "Field progress reports for an arm of the government," he said. "The pay would be several times what you make in your current job."

"How do you know what I make?"

He ignored my question. "There'd be a substantial signing-on bonus," he said, "several thousand bucks, and a big per diem add-on for in-country time, plus hazardous-duty pay. You would get an open-ended leave of absence from your current position and be taken back when the tour is over, with continuing seniority."

"Sounds great," I said. "So where is this rain forest you're talking about?"

He looked over his shoulder again, then leaned closer, again fixing me with his stern eyes. An inner voice started whispering, *Watch out,* but I told it to shut up.

In his low, gravelly voice, Jones said, "You ever hear of a joint called Cambodia?"

My enthusiasm for the job became more complex. I'd been thinking Panama, maybe Colombia. I rolled it around for a moment, then said, "Let me look it up and get back to you."

"No, I'll get back to you," he said, and called for the check.

But he never did. I never got my red badge. I still wonder what might have happened if he'd called again. Among my several roads not taken, this one ranks high. True, my chicken side was saying watch out for this guy. But then, my fear of cowardice is also great. And I was already thinking there might be a good play in it, so who knows? If Jones had shown me a hoop, I'd probably have jumped.

BETH AND I had some friends over for dinner not long after my Trojan moment, among them a young Michigan anthropologist named Merrill

Jackson. Merrill had been raised in Vietnam as the son of missionaries. I told him about my meeting with the man from Trojan, thinking he would be amused, but he was not amused.

"This is about Indochina," he said right away.

"How could you know a thing like that?"

"It just means we're taking up where the French left off."

"So what?" I said.

"That's not the place for us to fight a war," he said.

"Not even a little war? A guerrilla war?" I said.

"Especially not a guerrilla war."

"But we've got to go where the Russians are, right?"

"Russians?"

"Oh, Merrill, come on."

"The Vietnamese rebels are not being run by the Russians."

"They're Reds, aren't they?"

"What communism means in Southeast Asia, Carl, is not what it means in the West. The Vietnamese revolution is nationalist. It's a war for national independence."

If I'd heard it from someone else, I'd have easily dismissed it as the same old same old. But I knew Merrill. He wasn't a Red. He was a devout Catholic, and he knew Vietnam from the ground up. And from the top down, too, since he had been a member of an ad hoc committee secretly organized by intimates of JFK in the summer of 1963. Its purpose had been to reassure high officials of the Catholic Church, chiefly Cardinals Bea and Koenig of Austria, that the welfare of South Vietnam's then head of state, Ngo Dinh Diem, a Catholic, as well as of Vietnamese Catholics generally, would be protected even though Diem was about to be removed from power.

I had been impressed. "You had known beforehand that JFK was going to remove Diem?"

"Yes," said Merrill, "along with everybody else in Saigon and Washington. And Rome and Paris and London."

I had no idea what Merrill was talking about. I was still a red-blooded Middle American who thought it was cool to wear a blue badge to work and fly around with some hawks. Vietnam was nothing to me but an obscure place on the map. And I was terrific at leaving my job at the office. If I wanted to brag about something I was writing, it would be whatever was cooking in the way of a new play.

The one time I did have something of my work life to bring home and show off, I got it stuffed in my face by one of my closest friends.

I had written what the trade calls a "facilities brochure," a flashy document of thirty-two pages printed in full color on heavy, glossy paper. Its purpose was to convince potential customers that they should look to BSD as a prime contractor. It was received with great sounds of satisfaction at corporate headquarters in Detroit, and my boss said I would get a nice raise and that he'd heard a VP mention a bonus.

It was unclassified, so I brought a copy home to show my friends. All but one of them said all the right things. The exception was Jerry Badanes.

Jerry had told me he wrote poetry, and I had confessed the like to him. We immediately started showing one another our stuff. We also both liked to shoot pool, and we spent many hours dissing the New Critics in the billiards room at the Michigan Union. Jerry was in his late twenties when we met, about my age, and, like me, a married lit major who had come to Michigan by a wandering path. We became friends on some law of opposites. He was a burly, dark-eyed, heavy-featured guy, my first Brooklyn Jew. I was a blue-eyed, fair-skinned, brown-haired guy, as goy as a guy could be, Jerry's first bardic innocent from the hinterlands of small-town Ohio. We would either totally confuse one another or make it to brotherhood, and finally we did not confuse one another. His Brooklyn Jewishness, the way he fused a lusty voice with little cracks of despair and irony, the way he had come to distrust poetry and rely on it at the same time and therefore would have to be a teacher of poetry whose main lesson would be that poetry could not be taught—these were not stranger or more fascinating to me than my combination of Midwestern team-spiritedness with what he strangely and without explaining himself called my "burnt-cork mind" was to him. In trying to explain Jewishness and Brooklyn to me, Jerry started seeing himself in a new way, I think, just as I began seeing myself in a new way in trying to explain small-town Ohio to him. He was a piece of a lost puzzle, and I was a puzzle with lost pieces. We were grateful to have each other to be incomplete with.

Jerry and his wife and young daughter had come out to Sunnyside for dinner one evening. Our wives had taken our kids to the movies. At a certain point, completely on impulse, I handed him a copy of my big-hit Bendix brochure. "By the way, check this out," I said.

"What's this?" he said.

"My latest potboiler."

He flipped quickly through the pages, then tore it right in half.

"Jerry!"

He tossed the two halves aside in a gesture of contempt. "I don't want to see this kind of crap from you," he said quietly with a look of distaste on his heavy features.

"Man, what are you talking about?" I said.

"Why do you want to remind me that you do this?"

"What's so terrible about working for a living, Jerry?"

"Whores work for a living," he said with a little shrug.

I couldn't believe it. I was embarrassed and hurt and pissed off. Who the hell was he? Couldn't he just say something nice and move on? Couldn't he see that we all have to put in some time on the street?

"It's a good piece of tech writing, Jerry," I said.

He shrugged and said quietly, "So what if it's good? If it is good, then it's good for the bad guys, right?"

"What do you mean by 'bad guys'?"

"And if it's bad, then it's bad for *you*, no? Either you lose or you lose. So what can I tell you?"

I started to defend myself but realized that I didn't want to, that I hadn't really been attacked. Jerry had just confronted me with a question of my own that I was trying to run from. Good poets do that.

I DIDN'T REALLY start stumbling out onto the slippery slope, didn't start seriously thinking that what was happening in Vietnam was part of my own life, until sometime in the early summer of 1964 when I got a call at my office from an assistant professor of political science at the

University of Michigan, a guy about my age named Dick Cady. He surely does not know it, but more than anyone else, more even than Jerry or Merrill or the man from Trojan, it was Cady who put me on the path to the door that I couldn't resist opening, little stopping to wonder what I might do if things got crazy and the door locked shut behind me.

I knew Cady through my job at Bendix, where he was an occasional consultant to our arms-control and disarmament department, a group whose main purpose seemed to be proving that arms control and disarmament were threats to our national security.

JFK had come to the presidency with a promise to close a missile gap that had proved nonexistent, but with a concurrent interest in disarmament, an interest whetted by his need to keep the liberals aboard his coalition. He had quickly set up the Arms Control and Disarmament Agency. One of ACDA's purposes was to get our defense industry thinking about whether it might be possible, lacking on-site verification, to know for certain whether the folks in the USSR were keeping any promises they might have made about beating their swords into plowshares. Another was to get our own defense industry to look into phasing itself into nondefense lines of work.

No one I knew at BSD thought that the Cold War would ever end without some heavy shooting. But if there were contracts to be had for looking into the possibility of disarmament, then we would be as happy as the next guy to bid on them. Besides, how better to prove that the goal of mutual disarmament was a dangerous chimera than by conducting technical studies on verification?

So, early in 1962, BSD announced formation of a new department to specialize in such studies. To make sure nobody got the wrong idea, the company named a rough-riding retired soldier, Colonel Joe Coffee, to head it. And then, as if to show on the other hand that the army itself had no problem with academic values, Coffee reached out to Michigan's political science department for the help of a bright young assistant professor to help us ensure that our studies were correctly designed. This is why young green-badged Cady showed up in my office one day late in 1963 with a report needing to be ushered through the publications process.

Cady and I knew some of the same people on campus, we were about the same age, both liberals, and became good, if casual, friends. And so it was that one day in the summer of 1964, Cady was confident enough of my politics to ask me if I would donate some off-hours help to a new congressional candidate whose campaign team he had joined, one Wes Vivian, a Democrat.

Vivian was, in fact, one of the *New* Democrats, as they were called, in that he had supported the late Kennedy and the New Frontier's programs on civil rights, poverty, and federal aid to education. Vivian, said Cady, also was voicing some doubts about the growing American involvement in Vietnam.

Normally in those days, working for a Democrat in the Ann Arbor district was a sure way to waste your time. A hard-right Republican named George Meader, heavily backed by local real-estate interests and with the quiet blessings of the university, had held the seat for fourteen years and seemed to have made the job a lifetime sinecure.

"But 1964 is starting to feel different," Cady said. He was a short, solid, bright, intense man with sharp eyes. First, he said, this was because the reaction to JFK's assassination had given Democrats, especially northern ones, an edge of sentiment that completely changed the normal political balance between Democrats and Republicans. "The elections this year," he said, "will be a national tribute to the memory of JFK."

Second, he said, it looked as though the GOP was going to nominate Barry Goldwater to run against President Johnson. "This doubles the advantage of being a Democrat."

Cady studied with political scientists at the university's Institute for Social Research, the ISR, which produced high-tech analysis of up-to-the-minute political polls. The ISR's most recent results confirmed Cady's hunch that a strong tide was running in favor of the Democrats.

"So if George Meader is ever going to be beaten," said Cady, "this is the year to do it. All the Democrats have to do is put up a reasonably attractive candidate of moderate views who is unassailably anti-Communist and smart enough to run a strong campaign without making major mistakes. Johnson's coattails, the Goldwater effect, and the national mourning for

JFK will do all the work. In our district, all a Democrat needs to do in order to win is to not beat himself."

I could see why Cady thought Vivian tailor-made to knock off Meader for the Democrats. Wes Vivian was founder and president of a defense lab across the road from BSD called Conductron, so he was armored against the sort of Red-baiting that Meader liked to pull. Not even Meader could outflank him to the right on defense issues. Had it not been for his sympathy for the civil-rights movement and federal aid to education, Vivian might hardly have seemed liberal at all.

To start with, Vivian-staffer Cady was not looking for much from me. The candidate needed a polished campaign brochure, something to billboard his political assets on shiny paper. Cady was part of the committee of volunteers Vivian had formed to put such a brochure together. This committee had produced a first draft. What Cady wanted from me was an editorial once-over and some work with an illustrator getting it ready for the printer. If Cady had pitched me rather passionately on the desirability of getting Vivian elected, that was because he needed to get this work done for free. I saw this, but the job wouldn't take long, it was something different, and I liked Cady and what he was telling me about Vivian. So I told him I'd do it.

The job took a Sunday afternoon and came out well. The candidate was pleased. Cady introduced me to him and a few others on his campaign team. Vivian asked me to take part in a series of staff discussions to help him refine his positions on the issues of the day. I thought this would be fun. There seemed to be some smart people in the group. I liked the feeling of being part of a political campaign. And my bosses at BSD let me know it would be good for us all if I were a friend of the man likely to be our district's new congressman.

It was at an issues-committee meeting one evening, the third or fourth I'd attended, that Vivian raised the question of the war in Vietnam.

"Or is it really not a war?" he asked the dozen or so of us gathered in his living room. "Is it instead just a police action? What should we call it? And if Meader decides to make an issue of it, what should we say?"

Somebody needed to do a little library work and draft a position paper. Who wanted to volunteer to do this? Nobody did. *We* all thought we had more amusing ways to waste a weekend. But since I was the writer in the crowd, Wes asked if I would sketch something out.

Well, why not? It shouldn't take that long. Maybe I'd do a good job and win a little prestige. And what if Vivian were elected? It couldn't hurt to have a real, live U.S. congressman feel a bit indebted to me. So sure, I could do it. Just take a weekend to read up a little and crank out a few pages, right?

It took me a Saturday morning in the library to realize that I didn't know a thing about Vietnam. That afternoon in the UM stacks, I ran into my own version of the problem that Secretary of Defense Robert McNamara would encounter three years later, and which he tried to cut through by ordering the study that resulted in the Pentagon Papers.

And I, too, in effect, turned to the Pentagon in the form of Colonel Joe Coffee, who ran BSD's arms-control department, the guy Cady did his consulting work for. It was Cady who told me I should go talk to him. Colonel Coffee was a ramrod of a man in his late fifties with graying black hair that he slicked down and combed straight back. He liked to snap his fingers as he marched down the hall. His reputation was that of a fierce ultraconservative who would bite your head off if you even looked at him from the left. Yet Cady was a dishwater liberal, as was the candidate for whom I was to write this thing. Why would a liberal like Cady send me to a guy like Coffee for advice on Vietnam?

Cady shrugged the question off. "The colonel knows the literature on the Cold War as well as anybody at the university. He's a totally straight guy. He's right here. And he's told me he likes your work."

So I called up Coffee's office to see if he had half a minute. He told me to come on down.

"I need a good source book on the history of the Cold War, Colonel," I told him, "especially the cold war in Asia. I need something that just says what happened and when it happened and why. I haven't got forever to study it, and I need to not fall into the hands of somebody with an ax to grind."

Colonel Coffee did not ask for another word. Like a doctor writing out a prescription, he made a note on a slip of paper and handed it to me across his desk.

"You may think it's a trifle left-wing," he said, "but this is an honest book, and it will tell you what you need to know."

I thanked him and left, not in the least suspecting that I was about to have my worldview shattered.

The good right-wing colonel had put me onto what was then one of the most important works in the canon of Cold War revisionism, Vanderbilt historian Dena F. Fleming's two-volume tome first published in 1961, *The Cold War and Its Origins, 1917 to 1960*. Writers such as Gabriel Kolko, Richard Barnet, William Appleman Williams, and Noam Chomsky would later fill in the story with a greater command of detail on particular issues. And some critics argued that Fleming depended too much on journalistic sources in assembling his narrative. Yet there was nobody quite like him for establishing the detailed sequence of events in which the Cold War was born and had its being.

And that was Fleming's purpose: to set forth clearly what came first and what followed, for as he often repeats throughout his book, "what came afterwards cannot have caused what came before." What made Fleming's book seem so powerful to me was the effort he made to see events from the Soviet standpoint as well as the Western. Fleming did not make this effort because he was a Communist or had the least sympathy for Stalin, but because, in the era of nuclear weapons, he was concerned that mistaken perceptions of the other side's intentions might trigger a belligerent move that could easily prove irreversible and catastrophic. We had all just lived through the Missile Crisis of October 1962, so I had no trouble seeing what Fleming meant.

I can't imagine coming across this book in any other way. These were the days in which I read "literature"—novels, plays, poetry, criticism, philosophy—and little else. But now I was on an assignment that required a body of historical knowledge. So I needed to learn what Fleming had to teach. If the United States was going to war in Vietnam because of an Asian cold war imposed upon us by Red China, as was the conventional wisdom of the time, then I needed to know what the cold war in Asia was about and what Vietnam had to do with it. And this not only because the candidate Vivian needed a position paper but also because my job at Bendix, even if only remotely, made me an active part of the Vietnam expedition.

The whole episode—drawing the assignment, reading Fleming, finding the counterarguments, drafting the paper for Vivian—took about two weeks. During that time the candidate passed word through Cady that he wanted me to write the paper in the form of a speech. Cady also told me not to try to second-guess Vivian but to write it the way I would want to give it myself.

After I had finished, I brought the speech along to a meeting with the candidate and a group of his supporters. I was asked to read it. The core passages ran as follows:

"The ugly war grows dimmer in its origins, our commitment to it more obscure in its purposes. Witness after witness before the Senate Foreign Relations Committee makes it clear that the only possible victory for the United States in Vietnam is a victory over the South Vietnamese people themselves—who are as hungry as ever though we spend $2 million there every day—and that even so cruel a victory is ultimately untenable.

"Our leaders are far from informative. They seem willing to talk about *how* we might win there, but the important questions are really: What do we want to win, and why do we want to win it? Above all: In the name of what vision of history and the common human good has the United States committed its power?"

There was, of course, the question of the influence of Red China, which was the question that aroused my bravest sallies. It is easy to forget, so much farther down the road, that the perception of an expansionistic Red China was once the centerpiece of the argument favoring our Vietnam expedition. My crash course in the history of the Cold War had taught me to see this perception as a grave mistake. So I wanted the candidate to say:

"North Vietnam is no more dependent upon Red China than American intervention has forced it to be. Indeed, as with the parallel case of

Cuba and the Soviet Union, North Vietnam only disappears into the control of the Red Chinese to the extent that American policy succeeds in depriving it of alternatives."

And then there was the question of our South Vietnamese allies:

"Our counterinsurgency war, justified in the name of democracy, takes a few privileged Vietnamese oligarchs as our friends and turns the Vietnamese people as a whole into our enemies. And if it sounds like doctrinaire radicalism to say this so bluntly, that's too bad because it is still a fact. Our generals know it. Our reporters know it. Our politicians know it. The Soviet Union and China know it, and so do France and Britain. Besides the ordinary American citizens who think they voted for peace and yet find themselves paying for the helicopters and the napalm and sending their puzzled sons off to kill and to bleed in an utterly alien land, who indeed does *not* know it?"

And as to the diplomatic complexities of finding a solution:

"The problem of Vietnam *is* not complex at all. It is only made to seem so by those who have no real interest in solving it. All that is necessary to solve the problem of Vietnam—and besides this very easy solution there is no other solution at all—is simply for the United States government to direct its military forces to leave Vietnam as gracefully and as promptly as they can."

I looked up from reading this text aloud to the living room and saw right away that it had not made a really big hit. The candidate's face wore a frowning smile.

"Gee, Carl, I can't deliver a speech like that," Vivian said mildly. "The Democratic Party doesn't believe that and neither does President Johnson, the Congress, the American people, or most of the experts I know. And I'm pretty damned sure that I don't believe it either. So I am certainly not going to say anything like that. What made you think I would go for appeasement?"

I was surprised and embarrassed. I tried not to be defensive. "Well, it's just some language," I said, "just a set of talking points."

"What made you think I'd go for such a defeatist line?" the candidate said with a smile. Then he joked, seeming pleased with himself, "Gee, is it something I'm doing?" People in the room laughed uneasily. I threw in a little nervous chuckle of my own. "No," I stammered, "it's, well, it's just how I came out feeling about the war."

He smiled again and said, "I had no idea we had any radicals around here." A chuckle went around the room.

I felt a flash of embarrassment. What the hell was so radical about thinking the government had its pants on backward in Vietnam? Foolish lies were foolish lies, weren't they? But I tried to keep cool.

"The chances are good, Wes," I said, in what I hoped was a forgiving, professional tone, "that you'll end up thinking as do I that this Vietnam expedition is a big mistake. But I can see you're not there yet. So I'll thank you for the experience and wish you luck and get out of your hair." And I got up to leave.

"Oh, no, Carl," everyone said in a chorus aimed at making me feel appreciated, and I sat down again. But it was a comeuppance, and I went home stung by it. I made Beth listen to my harangue.

"Is the prowar side just trying to close off the debate?"

"What debate?" she said.

"Are all the pols just trying to make us shut up and do as we're told?"

"At least," she said, "you don't have to work for a prowar politician." She was right. I wasn't looking for things to do. My play *The Peacemaker* was scheduled for production that fall by Michigan's drama department. So, now that Vivian and I were no longer comfortable with each other, I begged off his campaign team and spent my spare time getting the play ready. The 1964 election came and went as though behind my back, though I could hardly help noticing that Vivian handily knocked off Meader in the great LBJ landslide of that year without saying much of anything about Vietnam. Johnson's effectiveness as a social liberal and the extremism of the GOP candidate, Arizona senator Barry Goldwater, made it easy to overlook Johnson's sharp escalation of the air war. Maybe he would at least keep the troops out.

Famously, once elected, he started sending them in, despite the growing chaos this was bringing to South Vietnam. Still, Vietnam was on the other side of the world. It was too bad for the Vietnamese as well as for the increasing numbers of American troops who were being sent there to carry out an increasingly ambiguous mission, but what could a guy like me do about that?

By Election Day, I was spending all my spare time at rehearsals, immersed in the make-believe of the stage. It was because of that play that my last blundering steps onto the stage of the antiwar movement came about.

THE PEACEMAKER was about the famous Blue Ridge Mountains feud between the McCoy family of Kentucky and the Hatfield family of West Virginia, a feud that had its bloodiest years in the 1880s, after the Reconstruction period.

I'd gotten the idea for the play from running across a folk song about those "feudin' mountain boys" in a collection and being struck by the way it treated the feud as a comedy. It hit me that those were, after all, real people shooting real bullets at each other. What was it all about? I found some histories, saw some interesting characters, started sketching scenes, and pretty soon the play was in production at the university.

One day that fall, my good friend and literary boon companion George Abbott White came out to Sunnyside to pick up a copy of the play. George was the editor of the UM's literary magazine *Generation*. He planned to print the play in his next issue, which would come out the week the play was running. We started talking about the elections and my fling with Vivian, by then a congressman-elect. George asked to see the thing I'd written for Vivian on Vietnam. He read it on the spot and said he thought it should be printed in the same issue as the play.

Great, I thought. My fiery polemic wouldn't be altogether wasted. I spent half an hour with it, changing a few sentences to put it in the form of an open letter to the victorious candidate.

The Peacemaker opened, ran its scheduled week, got nice reviews and good crowds, then closed. And one unseasonably warm December day a few days after, as I was fooling with a shutter in the front yard, Beth came to the window to say I had a call.

The guy had a high, nasal voice and a singsong, rapid manner of speech. "Hi, Carl, my name is Roger Manela, and I'm a grad student in sociology at the university. I saw your play the other night, and I bought a copy of *Generation* and just read it over. I wanted to tell you how much I enjoyed it."

Before I could get past thanks, he went on, "But you know, what really struck me was that letter of yours on Vietnam. I'm a member of SDS, and I'm assuming from your letter that we have a common political viewpoint. I'm wondering why I haven't met you around campus."

"What's SDS?"

He paused. "You've never heard of SDS?"

"Afraid not."

"It stands for Students for a Democratic Society."

"Oh? And what's that?"

"I'm surprised you don't know about us," he said. "It's a national group. It was founded here a couple years ago. Could I come out and fill you in?"

"Uh . . ."

"Because to judge from your letter about Vietnam, I think you'll be interested."

The Sunday calm of the neighborhood was soon broken by the roar of a black Harley-Davidson, with Roger, bareheaded, astride it in a brown leather jacket. And with that, the chain of coincidences that led my family and me from Sunnyside Street to the thick of the sixties was complete.

3 | The Joy of Movement
Kewadin, 1965

ROGER MANELA was a burly, round-faced, olive-skinned guy in his early twenties, already balding, with a friendly, energetic manner, alert brown eyes, and a bright, ready grin.

Beth and I sat down for coffee with him in the kitchen and talked a little about profs we both knew. Then Beth said, "All right, so what's this SDS? And why do we want to know?"

Roger laughed. "SDS stands for Students for a Democratic Society," he said. "And I think you want to know because, to judge from Carl's piece against the war, we seem to be on the same side."

"Meaning the three of us, or what?" Beth said.

"Meaning, you know, the three of us and SDS."

I could see that Beth was a little miffed by Roger's assumption that her views were the same as mine. He didn't know her yet. I wanted the United States to negotiate with the Viet Cong, whereas she'd have probably been happy to see the VC storm Washington. But she let it pass with a little grimace to me. Beth and I thought we hadn't heard of SDS, Roger guessed, because the UM chapter went by the name of Voice, a campus political party that was constantly being written up in the *Michigan Daily* for its habit of making its views known in campus demonstrations.

SDS had chapters at about forty schools. It had about two thousand members.[1] It was strongest in the Northeast, but it had been born in Ann Arbor and was growing fast in the Midwest. A related group in

California, the Free Speech Movement, had led an angry fight against the witch hunts of the House Un-American Activities Committee. SDS was almost wholly white and northern but had fraternal ties with two organizations working mainly in the South, the mostly white Southern Student Organizing Committee and the mostly black Student Nonviolent Coordinating Committee.

"What's the so-called New Left?" said Beth.

"That's us, SDS, plus the FSM and SNCC," said Roger, "and a few other small groups of activists."

"What's new about it?"

"Well, mainly, there hasn't been much of any Left around for a while," Roger said with a laugh, "so any Left at all would be new. There's more to it than that, but if you asked ten of us what that is, you'd get ten different answers." Roger's version was that the New Left was new in that it was not socialist. In the eyes of a generation raised on George Orwell, big government seemed too much the suspect of choice in contemporary crime to be trusted as the manager of social progress.

"I think our most basic idea," he said, "is that there's no final outcome to social progress. So we concentrate on how decisions are made. We believe in a radical form of democracy, something like populism. Our main goal is to get people involved in making the decisions that affect their lives. We call this participatory democracy."

The New Left also rejected the standing idea that student activists could only have an impact through alliances with the Democrats or organized labor. "With industry moving into high-tech, the university is a more and more important part of the production process. Students are part of this new proletariat, an important constituency in their own right."

SDS had begun its life as the student auxiliary of the League for Industrial Democracy, a small, fiercely anti-Communist group strategically committed to trade-union politics. But the LID's student auxiliary had started moving away from its parent organization in 1962, when it became SDS. Besides organizing students around campus issues, its main project since then was an attempt to organize the urban white poor, a group that the Old Left discounted as a lumpen proletariat, too fragmented and alienated to bring into politics. "But if the black poor can be politicized," Roger said, "so can the white poor. We want to build an antiracism coalition with black activist groups."

All this was argued out in a pamphlet called "The Port Huron Statement," adopted by the SDS as its manifesto at its convention in Port Huron, Michigan, in 1962. Roger gave us several printed copies of it and asked us to give the extras to our friends. In accepting them to pass out, presto, Beth and I had joined SDS. In actually passing them around, we had become organizers, too. We had stepped out onto the slippery slope.

So young SDSers started trekking out to Sunnyside Street to tell us upwardly mobile Oglesbys more about the new stirrings in the land and to explain to us gently why I should quit a well-paying job in the defense industry and plunge my family into the uncertainties of direct action on behalf of noble causes.

In the next few weeks, Roger set up meetings between us and SDS's national president, Paul Potter. Then we met its founding president, Tom Hayden, chief author of the "Port Huron Statement." Then came Todd Gitlin, a former president and one of its key national strategists. Then came Rennie Davis, the director of ERAP, SDS's major organizing project.

ERAP stood for "Economic Research and Action Project." It was an experimental program to see if racially mixed poor neighborhoods might respond to New Left organizing efforts. A volunteer staff of several score college students had spent the summer organizing around community issues in ten cities across the United States. It was funded at the peanut-butter level by grants from the United Auto Workers and the Stern Family Fund.   •

ERAP's basic aim was to confront the question that was central to the Left's predicament in all the advanced countries: Where could it find somebody to love it? In view of what seemed the irreversible co-optation of the industrial workforce, the New Left appeared to have no constituency. How could it ever achieve its goals if it couldn't find a base of support beyond the campus?

"Well, maybe such a base could be assembled from the white urban poor," said Roger one spring weekend at the Oglesbys' backyard picnic table. "If the white poor could be organized," said Roger, "then the campaign for a better society and, you know, a more peaceful world might take on some substance."

"And this is what you call an interracial movement of the poor," Beth said.

"Doesn't it make sense?" said Roger with his signature excited grin. "I mean, as a minimum, this would make the poor more interesting to the Democrats. Maybe all the poor need to form such a bloc is a little help from their middle-class friends. If we get some numbers outside the campus, maybe we can start shoving the system around."

"Are you talking about violence?" said Beth.

"SDS is absolutely committed to nonviolence," Roger said.

"King's a hero in our house," Beth said, "but what's run into more violence than the civil-rights movement?"

"Sure," he said, "but you can't avoid that, can you? And as we build the movement and poor whites learn how to band together politically in their own cause, we think they'll come to see that their real interests lie in forming alliances with similar groups in the black community. This can happen. We're starting to see it happen. We students just have to pitch in with what we have to give."

"Which is what exactly?" I said.

"Some political perspective," said Roger. "Some organizing skills. A sense of how the system works. No?"

"So you guys know how the system works?" said Beth. Roger laughed. "Actually, we're working on that."

EARLY IN 1965, SDS held an ERAP organizers' conference in Ann Arbor. Beth and I put up a houseful of ERAPers and went to a few meetings. We were moved by the commitment and energy we saw, not to mention the volubility: no Silent Generation here!

At our breakfast table the last morning of the conference, one of the SDSers, a young woman named Carol, said to us sweetly, "So when do you plan on turning around?" Dumb stares from Beth and Carl.

"Plan on turning around?" Beth said with a little chuckle.

"You know," said Carol. "When are you going to drop the Sunnyside bit and come run with the movement?"

Pause. "We've got three kids to think about," Beth said.

"That's what I mean," said Carol.

MY FIRST STAB at New Left theorizing came about by accident, as did virtually everything else that happened in this period of sudden change.

SDS's organizing philosophy was to use anything at hand that might work to get people talking together about political issues. Once the SDSers found out about my interest in the stage, they encouraged me to give them some ideas on how theater might be used "to build the movement," a phrase I quickly got used to hearing. I had never thought about the political dimension of theater before except in connection with the plays of Brecht and Lorca, who were distant textbook figures to me. But once I got past thinking I didn't know anything, a few possibilities did occur. For example, maybe organizers could help neighborhood people stage street skits to dramatize their complaints. My memo was printed in a mimeographed ERAP newsletter late in 1964. Nothing ever came of it, but it was my first bit of writing for SDS. Another followed soon. I still didn't know what to write after *The Peacemaker*. All my plays had been set in remote rural scenes, and I felt a need to get past that, to come to today's city, to move from melodrama to irony. Perhaps to move from my father's life to my own.

But I couldn't find a nice, complicated, citified story, so I decided to quit worrying about it for a while and write up my notes on Vietnam, something to bring together what I had learned and had come to believe about the war since taking on the Vivian assignment. It turned out to be an essay of a few thousand words, and I had no idea what to do with it.

While I was working on it, New York SDSers created a big stir when they tried to buy space in the subway system to put up a poster showing a frightened, badly burned Vietnamese child and bearing the message "Why are we burning, torturing, killing the people of South Vietnam? Get the facts. Write SDS."

The subway authority refused to accept the poster, but the furor brought in a good many requests for "the facts," and my paper turned out to be what SDS had ready to copy and send out. So it became SDS's first formal statement on the war.

For about ten years by then I'd been laboring my damnedest to write a warning about the threat of religious fundamentalism, working in dramatic form. It seemed to me that the best way to show the damage that religious fundamentalism could do was to put it on the stage. But despite several good productions, I had to admit that not a lot had happened. Now I'd stopped laboring at that sort of thing long enough to scribble one piece of political criticism, and it had gone straight into print as the SDS position paper against the war and been immediately reprinted by several journals, widely commented on, and picked up for a few anthologies.

Was there a lesson here? Or was it a warning?

IN FEBRUARY 1965 Beth and I decided, as our new SDS friends had encouraged us, to "turn around." I would leave Bendix. We would become full-time SDSers. SDS would help me find funding for some sort of movement-related job. Beth and I had no idea where this would take us, but she was even more strongly for it than I was. When I asked how we meant to take care of our children, she said, "Carol was right. I don't think we can take care of them the way we want to if we don't do this."

The first all-night teach-in on the Vietnam War was held that March at the University of Michigan, starting at midnight and running until dawn. It was soon repeated on hundreds of campuses across the country and overseas, ultimately to establish the teach-in as a basic form of academic protest. The idea of the teach-in did not crystallize all at once. The initial thought was that the UM teachers, no more than half a dozen at first, would pick a certain class day, stay off campus, meet their students in their homes, and talk about Vietnam instead of the regular subject.

Left unchallenged, this act might have come and gone with scarcely a ripple, but it caught the eye of the conservative state legislature in Lansing, which exploded in fury. And since the University of Michigan was in part supported by the state, this explosion was seen on campus as a serious event.

Suddenly the planned action, reported wrongly as a faculty strike, was being debated in all the papers. In just a few days, the faculty group grew from half a dozen to upwards of fifty.

The larger faculty group was less militant than the smaller core of original organizers, who might well have told the legislature where to put it. But the larger group wanted to avoid a wounding confrontation between the university and the state of Michigan.

The professors went into committee mode and soon came up with an alternative proposal. First, they would hold the special Vietnam War sessions in their classrooms. Second, they would provide a platform for all views, making sure that the government's position was well represented. And third, the key detail: they would hold the sessions at night. This nicely preempted the university's objection that teachers ought not to proselytize when they were supposed to be teaching and the legislature's objection that students ought to have a choice as to whether they wanted to be proselytized.

Another key detail: by analogy with the sit-in movement, the teachers would call the event a teach-in.

The university administration got behind this plan immediately, hailing it as a compromise in the best academic spirit. The state house people, their demands apparently met but in fact merely circumvented, could only sit down and shut up.

Four days before the teach-in, in the ballroom in the Student Center, a poetry reading was to be given by my buddy Jerry Badanes and a grad-student friend of ours, Gus Lardas. They asked me to introduce them. Jerry, Gus, and I agreed to make the reading the occasion of a statement against the war and a pitch for the teach-in. We wanted to get the English majors interested.

The reading was packed, and our statement made a considerable impact. Typically apolitical students and teachers were starting to see the war as something they should care about. I became part of the teach-in program since by this time I knew enough about Vietnam to enter the debate, my hurried self-education on behalf of the Vivian campaign having given me a good leg up. The teach-in was my first experience of defending in public, against all comers, the view that the Vietnam War was a mistake, all the more terrible for being so unnecessary. I was surprised to discover that the prowar faculty experts seemed to know even less about Vietnam than I did.

The teach-in was a major success. Over the next several days, its key organizers were deluged by calls from campuses all over the country. People wanted our list of speakers. They wanted to know how we had handled this or that problem. By the end of the semester, similar teach-ins had been held at more than a hundred schools, and early that summer in Washington there was a "national teach-in" to which President Johnson felt obliged to send two spokesmen.

From this point on, there was never any doubt that the nation's schools would have a say in the political evolution of the war. This made the situation altogether new and different.

THE FIRST ANTIWAR march on Washington, sponsored by SDS, occurred on April 17, 1965. It drew in about twenty-five thousand, Beth and I among them. For that period, this was a vast sea of people. The march definitively put the Vietnam debate on the national agenda.

On the overnight bus ride from Ann Arbor to Washington, sitting with former SDS president Todd Gitlin, a warm, scholarly grad student, Beth and I began our crash course in the history and current situation of the movement and SDS. There were two immediate points of focus.

The first involved SDS's parent organization, the venerable League for Industrial Democracy, whose board of directors included such prominent American lefties as Norman Thomas, Irving Howe, Michael Harrington, and Bayard Rustin. The LID angrily repudiated its student wing's stance on the war and threatened action of some kind against SDS if SDS did not moderate its evident support "for the other side." This represented a serious threat to SDS as an organization.

And second, a mysterious ultraleft group, the Progressive Labor Party, called PL, started growing more interested in SDS despite espousing a crude Marxism that had nothing in the least in common with SDS's freewheeling participatory democracy. PL had been expelled from the American Communist Party in 1962.[2]

PL at first seemed content to stay in the background at SDS meetings, but by the summer of 1965 it had organized a campus-based group it called the Worker-Student Alliance. The WSA espoused a special version of PL's line that only workers were of political importance. The WSA's pitch to students was that if they were really serious about opposing the war, they would leave school, get a job in a plant, and try to organize the workers.

PL wanted to occupy decision-making positions in SDS, but it refused to open its own ranks to SDS people. Later I made a special effort to "organize" a few PLers, guys who seemed to me politically blind and willful in the aggregate, but who individually and in off-hours were fine poker buddies. My effort failed, and I was left with increasing skepticism about PL's real identity and purpose. I started to wonder if PL really meant "police." I could see nothing in the way of any independent PL program. Its whole purpose seemed to be to come to our meetings. Its sole reason for being seemed to be to make trouble for SDS and the student antiwar movement.

SDS's problems with the LID and PL would ultimately interact with SDS's intrinsic weaknesses in a way that proved fatal to us. Even as SDS began to grow at an exhilarating rate, the forces that would destroy it were collecting their resources.

BETH LEFT FOR HOME right after the march, going by way of Cleveland to pick up the kids at her mother's, and I took a few vacation days from Bendix to stay in Washington and meet more SDS people in a three-day National Council meeting. I met black leaders of the Student Nonviolent Coordinating Committee, notably Stokely Carmichael, Julius Lester, and Charlie Cobb, and saw a bit of black Washington that white people didn't normally get to see. Julius and I had a chance to sit down together in an empty room with his fine old Gibson steel-string guitar and sing our songs for each other. He taught me the only blues lick I was ever to learn. "No, no, my friend," he would say with gentle amusement at my four-square approach. "The riff starts *off* the beat." It was almost a rule for life.

I was dazzled by the SDS people I met at the NC meeting. They were sexy, smart, articulate, and well informed. But most amazing to me, these "kids," as they called themselves, actually *listened* to each other. They allowed their opinions to be changed by what they heard each other say. They always treated each other with respect.

SDS officially offered me a job—my first task being to raise my own salary—to be the organizer and director of a newly created unit we called Research, Information, and Publications. My mission was to develop a body of publications that presented our picture of the world to a nation that had pegged us as kooks and malcontents, if not traitors. This was an urgent and frightening mission. It was like writing act one of a two-act play and going straight into performance before a hostile audience and with no time for rewrites or rehearsals or the least idea of what was going to happen in the last act. All you knew was that you were part of a great cast. And that the play you were part of was about blood and death, and that it was real.

I crowded into a car with other SDSers for the overnight drive back to Ann Arbor and arrived just in time to get into a clean white shirt, my gray flannel suit, and my blue badge of clearance and show up at Bendix Monday morning, no more exhausted than if I'd spent the weekend with my Bendix pals on the golf course.

MY FIRST SOLO FLIGHT in the big sky of Manhattan occurred shortly thereafter. The New York chapters of SDS had scheduled an antiwar rally for May in Greenwich Village. Several of their members had heard my rap and asked me to come. So I got to New York in another car loaded with SDSers and climbed atop a sound truck at the southern side of Washington Square to deliver my first open-air antiwar speech. Not counting the sizable contingent of New York's finest who flanked us and a bevy of unsmiling men in business suits, shades, and fedoras, the crowd was a decent size for that moment, somewhere between five and six hundred, mostly students but with enough grown-ups among them to make you think that the horrors of the war were beginning to register on the taxpayers, too.

Grouped on one side, as I could see from the top of the truck, were fifty or so tough-looking young guys who, at some point in my speech, started heckling me loudly. It pissed me off. Not yet knowing the etiquette of these situations (ignore the hecklers), I directed some of my words to them, saying something like, "We're doing what we believe is right. If you believe this war is right, why do you leave it to others to fight it? Why don't you join up and volunteer for Vietnam? Are you cowards?" Inspired by the crowd's enthusiastic response to this, I led us in a little moment of friendly counterheckling: "Cowards, enlist!" we chanted, "Cowards, enlist!" After our speechmaking was done and as the main part of the crowd was marching off to continue the demo at the United Nations, a Japanese reporter from *Asahi Shimbun* kept me back for a brief interview, another first for me.

My Ann Arbor friends Roger Manela and Jerry Badanes had waited for me. As we left the rally area to rejoin the main group, we quickly realized that we were surrounded by a gang of twenty or so of the hecklers, young, crew-cut, stern-faced guys in jeans, light athletic jackets, or sweatshirts. The cops were no longer to be seen. These guys were tired of heckling, it seemed, and needed to let us know in direct physical terms what they thought of us. They hit us all at once, fast and hard, punched us up for a few seconds, and were gone before we could get back to our feet. It's nothing to call a battle scar exactly, but I still have a little click in my jaw from the experience.

As Roger and Jerry and I were helping each other back to our feet and checking for damage, the cops almost magically reappeared. One of them approached us and said, "What happened?"

"You didn't see it?" said Roger.

"We didn't see anything."

"Look," I said, "will you help us find these guys? They can't be far away."

"What do you want to find them for?" said the sergeant. "You gonna press charges?"

"No. All we want is a chance to talk with them."

"What do you mean by talk?"

"I want to know what they thought they were doing and why they did it."

Bless his heart, the cop seemed intrigued. He stepped away and talked briefly with another cop, who gave us a long look.

The two of them came over to us. The second one said, "What's the problem?"

"Problem?" I said. I couldn't believe the cops hadn't seen it all. "Hey, these guys just beat us up. I want to know why they did that. Because I think they've got some wrong ideas."

"You know we could bust you for inciting," the second one said.

"That's your call, officer. All we want to do is talk." The two of them looked at each other a moment, then the second one said, "All right, come on." Jerry and Roger and I crowded into a police car.

We started cruising the neighborhood and very soon found the main group involved in the attack, all of them guys of eighteen or so.

The second cop got out and talked briefly with one of them.

So we three SDSers were soon sitting in a room in the station house with six guys who did not admire us and two cops who also did not admire us, rapping back and forth about the war, dissent, patriotism.

"Ain't you guys Commies?" said a tough kid named Louie, who seemed to be the leader.

"No. I do secret work for the Defense Department," I said, not at all above using it. "That's why I'm against this war, because I know the government's lying about it."

"How do we know *you* ain't lying?"

"You don't. So I'm gonna ask you a question. Are you a Commie?"

"I ain't no damn Commie," he said with a scoffing laugh.

"How do I know you're not lying?"

"Hey. Gimme a break."

"Will you give me a break?" He seemed to study my eyes.

Roger dared a riskier tack. "Do you believe in America?"

"Fuckin' A."

"So you must support civil rights for black people, right?"

Louie scoffed again. "I ain't no friggin' nigger-lover, pal, if that's what you mean."

"So you believe the government's wrong about civil rights?"

Louie saw the trap. "Maybe it ain't. Maybe it is. But you gotta support our troops."

"We support the troops," said Jerry. "That's why we want to get them out of there, bring them home."

"And just let the Commies have it?"

"You sound like the British in 1776, you know what I mean?"

"There wasn't no Commies in those days."

"Right," said Jerry, "but the British owned this country then. New York was one of their colonies. And they wanted to keep on owning it. To them, the Minutemen were just as bad as we are to you guys."

And now we were talking about history, the politics of revolution, the parallels between the Redcoats in America and the Yanks in Vietnam. Nobody won this debate. We certainly didn't make SDSers out of these guys. Maybe they only cooled off because they were in the police station. But I thought they saw that there was a real argument here about what was best for the United States and Vietnam. It was like a little teach-in, with both sides having their say. And I thought that very fact was a victory. By the end of the session, we all shook hands. They still disagreed with us, but yeah, we had a right to say what we believed, we weren't dirty Commies, and they were sorry they'd jumped us.

There was a large crowd of their pals waiting at the door of the station house when we all came out after about an hour. They looked ready to rumble, but Louie called out, "Cool it. These guys are all right." We three SDSers mingled with them and talked about what it meant, and what it didn't mean, to protest the government's policies. We didn't recruit anybody, but the vibes transposed from anger to debate. We could live with that. We shook some hands and went on our way. And despite my sore jaw, I was glad finally that the whole thing had happened. I'd learned something. I'd been baptized by a little fire. I hoped it wouldn't get worse than that.

———————

THE BIG DEBATE that capped the teach-in movement pitted heavy prowar and antiwar pundits against each other in a glitzy chandeliered ballroom in the Willard Hotel in downtown Washington. The prowar hero was to have been the brilliant, sharp-tongued McGeorge Bundy, who bore the shield of special adviser to the president, but he pulled out at the last minute to tend to a new crisis in the Dominican Republic. He was replaced by the liberals' liberal, Arthur Schlesinger Jr., who was later to say he regretted his support for the war. The antiwar side was led by Hans Morgenthau, a reigning foreign-policy academic, who succeeded so well in distancing himself from us protesters as to leave us wondering what side he was really on. So we had a "great debate" in which the prowar star was turning against the war and the antiwar star was afraid to attack it. Was this just how Washington does its thing?

The much better debate was the one in that precinct station in New York.

THE NEXT DAY Columbia's Reserve Officers' Training Corps (ROTC) seniors were to hold an outdoor commencement exercise, and the SDS chapter wanted to put in an appearance. Nothing really heavy, just to see and be seen, hold up a few signs, chant a few slogans. But it turned out to be raining lightly, so the ceremony had been moved inside, and our SDS group of fifty or so hadn't been able to find out where. For several long minutes we huddled idly in the rain, not knowing what to do. But then a student passerby told us the ceremony was going on at that very moment in Low Library, the massive Romanesque building in the center of the campus.

This was a disappointment. We had missed our chance to make a point. But most of us straggled over to Low anyway to see what was up. We were surprised to find the doors closed and locked. Frustrated, cold, and wet, we shivered under the high, narrow portico thinking we'd missed the whole show.

Then we saw, at the far end of the quadrangle, a single Marine in full-dress uniform striding purposefully toward us, resplendent in red, blue, and gold and a white visored hat. A few of us started sending up an antiwar chant, and on he came, the only figure visible in the entire quad. The gloomy drizzle made his colors seem even more brilliant. Soon we were all focused on him, all chanting "End the war in Vietnam now!" There was no plan to this. There was certainly no intention to block the Marine's way. We had no idea what we were going to do.

But the Marine's way of marching toward us conveyed a very clear impression that he certainly knew what *he* was going to do. He was going to go up those steps and into that building, and nobody was going to stop him.

Nor did we try. People in his path moved aside to let him pass. But at the top of the steps, the crowd was too thick. A young woman couldn't get out of his way fast enough. As glorious a figure as any bullfighter in his suit of lights, the Marine reached out with his white-gloved hands, grabbed the woman by the shoulders, and roughly shoved her out of his way. The crowd right around him stood stunned at this show of rude force. He produced a key, unlocked the door, and disappeared inside.

Now with a rush of shared insight, we realized that the ceremony that we thought had been going on inside the building had not yet begun. The celebrants must still be on their way. And in the next second, without the least discussion, we decided that fate had put us there to block their path.

We could in no way have planned this. Had we sat down calmly beforehand to consider the idea of staging a sit-in to block this ceremony, a few nuts might have spoken up for it, but the rest of us would have laughed it off. As it was, we were suddenly fused in a common cause, mainly, I guess, because the guy had been so rough with that woman. The gods of politics had put us there to block the door.

For the next hour, as the celebrants arrived, the steps of Low Library were the scene of constant pandemonium as we sat down and locked arms in front of the door and on the steps.

Squads of police were soon on campus. It was the first time such a thing had happened at Columbia, although apparently the police were under instructions to make no arrests as long as our resistance was passive. The handsome officers in full-dress uniform and medals and their wives in lovely gowns began arriving in limousines at the campus gate, no doubt enjoying their long, brisk walk toward us across the Quad, the officers to stomp and the wives to step daintily over masses of writhing demonstrators surrounded by New York's finest. To be sure, there was a kind of joy in it, and doubtless on both sides. The comradeship was certainly intense on our side, but there was also a common feeling that we didn't know what we were doing anymore.

Soon the military folks were all inside. A few others and I took brief turns on the bullhorn. Then the drizzle turned to rain and we called it a day.

That evening I got into another movement car and wheeled away on the overnight drive to Ann Arbor. I was back to Sunnyside in time for a quick shower and a hot black cup. My gray-flannel uniform was fresh from the cleaners. With a clean white button-down shirt, a bright red tie, and my blue badge, I was another man, as well furnished as those Marines. I hopped into my Alfa and made it to Bendix on time, a little tired and with a sore jaw but functional enough to get the Jungle Canopy progress report to the printer on time. Nobody asked if I'd had a pleasant weekend.

Beth ardently agreed with what we took to be SDS's basic political ideas in the spring of 1965. I was less convinced. I thought people were kidding themselves about what it would take to stop the war. But Beth thought we had to join up. We had to change our lives.

"Somewhere, sometime," said Beth, "someone has to stand up against all these lies. With your job you know this stuff from the inside, Carl. Whether you want to call it destiny or some kind of dumb joke, you're in a position to tell the truth about it all and be believed. And here are these SDS people standing up. How could we not join them?"

Beth's question made me think more about my own position. Yes, I believed SDSers were right to focus on Vietnam. And I thought they were right to claim that the way the war was growing showed that there was something deeply wrong with how we were being governed. There was indeed a military-industrial complex, as President Eisenhower had warned in his farewell address, and I worked for it. And I knew flipping the switch from Republican to Democrat would not stop the war.

I also agreed with SDSers on the need for an immense effort by the true, "small d" democrats among us.

But I parted company from Beth and the SDSers I had met in one important respect: I believed that America's "small r" republicans would also have to get engaged if the antiwar cause were to have the least chance of succeeding.

That made me a centrist rather than a typical New Leftist. I was a democrat in believing that only the people can make the laws, and I was a republican in believing that only the Constitution can properly rule. But I was also a radical in believing that if either part of this equation were broken, then some kind of exceptional protest was necessary, something outside the system.

I gladly followed the Left in outrage that the government itself was rampantly violating the law, as in the campaign in Vietnam or the systematic denial of the civil rights of blacks. I believed that you had to do all you could to jam the gears of the machine to ferret out the beast that had seized control of it. You had to march through the streets of Selma. You had to sit down on the steps of Low Library.

But you didn't do this because you rejected the Constitution. On the contrary, you did it because you believed the Constitution was what made us tick as a people.

In what became my basic stump speech against the war, I always said something like "I am not against the American Constitution. Rather, I am against those powerful enough to violate it whenever it suits them. I am a republican democrat and at the same time, yes, a democratic republican. Or in brief, I am a radical centrist. This is not an oxymoronic contradiction in terms. Democracy without the rule of law is anarchy, just as republicanism without democracy is tyranny."

In a few years, such ideas would get me in trouble with the people I was about to bond with. But these ideas were strong enough and cogent enough for me to recognize the validity of the path Beth wanted us to take. And so it was that we sold our house on all-white, middle-class Sunnyside Street, put some money in the bank, rented an apartment in a poor, racially mixed part of town, and started trying to explain to our family and friends what we thought we were doing.

JUNE 5, 1965, was my last day at Bendix. Farewell to the blue badge.

Three days later, Beth and I left Aron, Shay, and Caleb with a friend and drove off to the SDS convention at Camp Kewadin in upstate Michigan.

SDS did three things at this convention that I remember keenly.

First, it considered a proposal that its author, the outgoing national secretary, Clark Kissinger, called "the Kamikaze Plan." Its basic idea was that SDS should find a splashy way to violate the National Security Act, such as by publicly advising servicemen to desert. When we got attacked for it, our defense would be that the statute could not be invoked because Congress had not declared war. The larger point of this proposal was that Congress was evading its responsibility in allowing LBJ to fob the war off as a "police action."

The Kamikaze Plan was foolish and quickly rejected, but this convention was heavily covered by the national media, so it was widely reported. The perversity of the Kamikaze Plan seemed to capture the media's imagination.

Second, SDS dropped the anti-Communist clause from its constitution. This was not because of any sympathy for the Communist Party, which, on the contrary, was seen throughout SDS as a toothless relic. The motivation, rather, was that SDS was libertarian about ideas and therefore opposed to Red-baiting. This subtlety, however, did not play well on the evening news. What got reported was that we no longer opposed the international Communist conspiracy. Some reports implied that we might even be a part of it.

The third crazy thing the convention did, memorable at least to me, was to elect me president.

This happened after several people introduced a proposal to eliminate the offices of president and vice president. Such offices, they said, were inherently elitist. Among several others, I spoke up against this proposal. I argued that our position in the vanguard of the emerging antiwar movement was likely to draw increasing media attention and that we could best cope with this through elected representatives who would be accountable to SDS for what they said on its behalf.

The amendment failed. We would keep our officers. So we went on to the nominating process. A dozen or so delegates were nominated. Roger nominated me.

We nominees were then asked to say whether we accepted or declined. By some awful accident it fell to me to speak first. I said I was humbled by the nomination and that I felt immodest in accepting it because I'd so recently become a member. On the other hand, in view of what I'd had to say about the office itself, I thought it would be best if *all* the nominees answered the call. This would give the group the widest array of choices.

I thought I'd made a good case and that all the nominees would follow my example, but out of the dozen who were nominated, only five accepted. After two rounds of balloting, I was the new president of SDS.

This shot me into an orbit that I was never able to get out of.

And most immediately, it put me in the position of having to answer for the Kamikaze Plan and deletion of the anti-Communist clause from our constitution. It didn't matter that we had not even considered the Kamikaze Plan or that we had deleted the anti-Communist clause on purely libertarian grounds. Merely talking about breaking the National Security Act in the same breath as deciding not to be anti-Communist anymore was enough to get the bull's attention. These things led the news stories about our convention.

The first to wonder about all this would have to be my old colleagues at Bendix. Was I going to betray military secrets? Was that why I'd been elected president on my first day as a member?

So as soon as I got back from Camp Kewadin, I put in a call to Tony, the personnel director. I had not been wrong. The Bendix folks had read about the SDS doings in the *Ann Arbor Daily News* and needed no filling in on the basics.

Tony asked me to meet him at the Pretzel Bell, the place where I'd had that strange session not long before with the man from Trojan. Tony and I had stayed a bit on each other's bad side since crossing about the flag on the day JFK was killed. He brought along the company's number-two officer, executive engineer Jim McDonald, a tall, fiftyish, gray-haired, no-nonsense slab of a man. This told me they were seriously concerned about the recent changes in my life, and not happily. There were no pleasantries. They sat across from me in a booth. We ordered coffee and got down to business.

"Are you going to get us in trouble?" said Mac.

"No. But I knew you'd wonder about all this," I said. "That's why I called. I've been trying to think of a way to reassure you."

"Make it good," said Tony.

"No, make it *very* good," Mac said.

"Look, my friends," I said, "remember that I swore an oath not to reveal government secrets. I would get in big legal trouble if I violated that oath. And I think you know I'm an honest man. After all, the government did clear me."

Mac said, "We wouldn't want the government to wonder if it had made a mistake."

"Yet here you are," said Tony, "hooking up with an outfit that's talking about violating the National Security Act, right?"

"We're not going to do that."

"And this same outfit makes you its president when you just walked in the door from a secret job in the defense business. Excuse me?"

Said Mac, "So what are we missing here, Carl?"

"I can see your problem," I said. "In your place, I would wonder, too. Like I said, that's why I called you the first thing. I wanted to explain it."

"So explain," said Tony.

"Okay. About violating the National Security Act. First, that's not going to happen. The press made a big deal out of it because it made a grabby headline, but it was never even formally proposed. The only reason it came up at all is that SDS is trying to find a way to generate a national debate about Vietnam, to get people to start thinking about it."

"Meaning what?" said Tony.

"As I understand it, the National Security Act can only be invoked in the case of a legally declared war, and as you guys know as well as anybody, that's not the case with Vietnam. Okay? The Constitution says that only the Congress can declare a war, and the Congress isn't even close to doing that."

Tony was shaking his head. "Sounds sort of pinko to me."

"The Constitution is sort of pinko?" I said.

"Forget the Constitution," said Mac. "One day you're working in the defense industry with a secret clearance. The next day you've joined up with an outfit that's talking about violating the National Security Act. The day after that, this outfit makes you its president. What the hell's going on, Carl?"

"For one thing, Mac," I said, "SDS people and I have been talking for a half year. We know each other pretty well. This didn't happen overnight."

"This is not reassuring," said Tony.

"For another thing," I said, "a lot of SDSers are new members. It's a fairly new organization, and it's growing faster than it can keep up with. And as for SDS making me its president, I think this was probably because SDS people see me as the kind of middle-class, middle-American professional they want to reach out to. But whatever the reason, there is no plot afoot here. Please don't be afraid that what I'm doing poses the least threat to Bendix or to national security."

Mac and Tony still stared at me. They weren't buying it.

Finally Mac said, "Tell me this. Would a man like me want to join this SDS?"

"I don't think they have a golf league, Mac."

"I'm asking you a serious question, Carl."

"Mac, if a person like me can join SDS, then so can people like you and Tony. Okay?" I was ready to go on with something pious about democracy in action, but Tony cut me off.

"Look," he said. "Point-blank. Do you mean to disclose national secrets that you learned in your job at Bendix?"

"Point-blank right back at you, Tony. No. Absolutely not. I would never even consider it." They did not seem reassured. "Tony. Mac. I'm not the only guy who ever left a job in the defense sector."

Mac snapped, "But you may be among the few, Carl, who ever left a job in the defense sector to become the head of a radical antiwar group."

"My friends," I said, "what more can I say? I love this country. I'm a patriotic man. I'm proud of having worked for Bendix. I have no intention of violating my oath of secrecy."

They looked deeply unconvinced.

I said, "Look, I think you should call the FBI and the navy security people right away and make sure they're informed. All I can tell you is that I've sworn a solemn oath to keep the government's secrets. I have no intention of violating this oath."

We stared at each other. They still were far from satisfied, but what more was there to say?

Mac looked at Tony and said, "Let's get out of here." Tony tossed a few bucks for the coffee, my last benefit.

Also intensely curious about SDS's flirtation with the Kamikaze Plan and its anti-Red-baiting amendment were the elders of our parent body, the League for Industrial Democracy. The LID had been founded half a century before by Jack London and Upton Sinclair, two of America's great native radicals. The LID directors had sent a message to Helen Garvy at the SDS national office, inviting us in language not to be mis-construed to come right away to New York for a story conference. We met in the LID's downtown office. Beside me on the SDS side were Paul Booth, our new national secretary, and Todd Gitlin, a past president. On the LID side were Bayard Rustin, a mild-mannered black social critic; the aged and frail Norman Thomas; and Irving Howe, a great social critic and essayist whose writing I particularly admired.

Howe led the LID charge, and he made no effort to conceal his fury. The veins bulged in his temples, and his powerful arms pounded the table as he attacked us not merely for the childishness of the Kamikaze Plan and the senseless bravado of striking the anti-Communist clause, but even more passionately for our decision to oppose the Vietnam War.

"We of the democratic left," Howe thundered, "are constantly chal-lenged to prove our loyalty to this country. Yet here you are, in a time of war, seeming to support the other side!"

"How else would you oppose the war?" said Paul mildly, trying not to cringe before this blast.

"You must criticize both sides equally!"

"Irving, how do you criticize both sides equally for saturation bomb-ing of civilian targets?" said Todd.

Howe swept the table with his arm, as though ridding it of our naive words. "The League for Industrial Democracy has fought for decades," he said in full throat, "to establish the legitimacy of radical critique on the

American democratic left. Now here's our student wing putting all of this work in jeopardy in one thoughtless act! Even our tax status now looks uncertain! You do not begin to grasp the damage that you have done!"

Rustin supported Howe on this, though he seemed more melancholy than angry when he said, "In SDS, we are staring our own failures in the face."

Only Thomas showed support for us. Remaining silent for most of the session, he at last cleared his throat, at which Howe broke off his harangue and along with Rustin turned to him in deference.

"For all their mistakes," Thomas said in a weak, whispery voice, "these young people are at least trying to create an opposition to the Vietnam War, and for this they deserve our credit and respect."

The LID did finally come to oppose the war, but the split with SDS could not be stopped. It was formalized that October. We lost our tax-exempt status, a modest financial subsidy and a thin veneer of legitimacy.

BETH AND I and our children hurriedly remade our lives out of cheaper stuff. We moved into a cramped apartment in the student ghetto. Some of the teach-in people helped us pay the rent and sometimes gave us bags of groceries. It was not an emotionally satisfying experience.

We had barely finished moving, were still asking ourselves what the hell we were doing, when I got a call from Jeff Segal at SDS's national office in Chicago.

Jeff said, "A guy from the national teach-in committee just called. They're wondering if your passport's in order."

"My passport? Who's got a passport?"

"Can you get one?"

"I guess so. Why?"

"Can you be ready to travel as soon as you get one?"

"Travel where?"

"South Vietnam."

4 | The Bourgeois Gentlemen of Vietnam
Saigon and Hue, 1965

"**THE NATIONAL** teach-in committee," said Jeff, "has decided to send a small fact-finding team to South Vietnam. They want you to be part of it. We've polled the National Council and no one objects. We're making all the arrangements from here."

"Wait. Why me?"

"You're going to be talking about the war a lot, so it would be good for you to be able to say you've been to Vietnam. You disagree?"

"Well, no, but can't I have a little time to think about it?"

"Sure. Time's up," said Jeff. "You'll leave as soon as you get your papers. You'll stop for about a week in Paris on the way over and another week in Tokyo on the way back, so you can establish contact with French and Japanese antiwar groups. We think these groups are going to be very important. You'll be in South Vietnam for a couple weeks. You'll be based in downtown Saigon at a joint called the Hotel Metropole on Tu Do Street. You'll be taking day trips to the surrounding countryside, and maybe you'll get up to Hue. That's the old Imperial City just south of the demilitarized zone. It's supposedly a beautiful place. You'll enjoy it. In Saigon, you'll hook up with two Southeast Asia scholars, Bob Browne from Fairleigh Dickinson University and Jonathan Mirsky from Rutgers. They're both fluent in several dialects of Vietnamese, and they know a lot of Vietnamese people. They'll see that you get introduced in the right places. Questions?"

"Jeff, wait. I haven't said I'll do it yet."

"Well, yeah, but, you know, you will, so why screw around? The national teach-in group is going to handle your tickets. You can pick them up at the airport. I'll call with your flight data tomorrow."

A little pissed off by these imperious orders from high command, I was also excited to be put on such a trip. And I had no doubts about its political wisdom. The teach-in movement was being criticized for a lack of direct experience of Vietnam. The main purposes of this little expedition were to make it possible to say that we, too, had been there and that we were in touch with others around the world who share our concerns.

THE YEAR 1965 had been busy with developments in the war, far busier than any of us outside the castle walls could have known. Students of the war's history will know the following, but for those whose memory is shaky, and because the opposition movement can only be appreciated in the context of the war itself, the following time line will give a sense of the curve we all were riding.

January 1965: Brothers William and McGeorge Bundy, both foreign-policy advisers to LBJ, told Secretary of State Dean Rusk that *"some stronger action"* in the war was needed, although they weren't sure what it should be. The idea of supplementing the twenty-one thousand American "advisers" then serving in Vietnam, they told Johnson, "has a great appeal to many of us."[1]

February 7: Viet Cong guerrillas attacked two American installations in South Vietnam, a helicopter base at Pleiku and a nearby command center. This was the first time the VC had mounted direct assaults on American positions. In reprisal, Johnson ordered the first air raids against North Vietnam. Forty-nine navy jets hit a training base north of the demilitarized zone at the seventeenth parallel.[2]

February 8: McGeorge Bundy returned to Washington from a fact-finding mission to Saigon to tell Johnson, "The prospect in Vietnam is grim. The energy and persistence of the Viet Cong are astonishing. They can appear anywhere, and at almost any time. They have accepted extraordinary losses and they come back for more." Bundy's conclusion was that "at its very best, the struggle in Vietnam will be long."[3]

February 11: Three hundred members of Women Strike for Peace picketed the White House against the war.

February 13: Johnson ordered Operation Rolling Thunder, sustained bombing of North Vietnam. He justified this at the time as a further response to the VC raid on the base at Pleiku, but his national security adviser, McGeorge Bundy, later said, "Pleikus are like streetcars."[4]

February 14: *The New York Times* published a poll showing that 83 percent of Americans supported the U.S. bombing of North Vietnam.[5]

February 19: Fourteen antiwar activists were arrested for blocking entrances at the U.S. mission to the United Nations in protest of Johnson's new Vietnam policy.

February 20: Four hundred SDSers and others demonstrated in Washington against the war, and hundreds of others in at least nine other cities. Antiwar ads appeared in major newspapers. The White House got more than a thousand wires against the bombing. Democratic senators Frank Church of Idaho, Eugene McCarthy of Minnesota, Gaylord Nelson of Wisconsin, Wayne Morse of Oregon, and Ernest Gruening of Alaska publicly challenged the recent escalation.[6]

February 21: Black nationalist Malcolm X was assassinated while speaking at the Audubon Ballroom in Harlem, apparently by a rival Muslim group. He had just come out against the war.

February 24: Operation Rolling Thunder was followed by sustained bombing of North Vietnam. The army chief of operations, Brigadier General William DePuy, told the press, "We are going to stomp them to death."[7]

February 26: Johnson granted the request of General William Westmoreland, commander of U.S. forces in Vietnam, for thirty-five hundred Marines to protect the U.S. complex at Danang. It was the first appearance of U.S. combat troops.[8]

February 27: The White House released a white paper, "Aggression from the North: The Record of North Vietnam's Campaign to Conquer South Vietnam." *The Washington Post* hailed the administration's "incontrovertible" argument, but adviser William Bundy later conceded that the paper was "a disaster."[9]

March 15: Rev. Dr. Martin Luther King Jr. led a Salem-to-Montgomery march against racial segregation. Former SDS president Todd Gitlin later hailed this as "the high-water mark of integrationism."[10]

March 15: *The New York Times* began a series on activist college students. Its treatment of SDS was highly favorable.

March 16: Mounted police wielding cattle prods attacked civil-rights marchers in Montgomery.

March 21: The King civil-rights march reached Montgomery under the protection of the National Guard. LBJ spoke in support of the marchers. "We shall overcome," he said. He promised to push the Voting Rights Act through.[11]

March 24: The first teach-in on the war drew more than three thousand students at the University of Michigan. The hall was cleared twice because of bomb threats. Each time the crowd reassembled, it was larger than before.

March 25: Civil-rights marcher Viola Liuzo, a white woman, was murdered in Lowndes County, Alabama.

March 26: Alice Herz of Detroit, an eighty-two-year-old Quaker and a member of Women Strike for Peace, immolated herself in protest of the war.[12]

April 1: Johnson changed the mission of U.S. forces in Vietnam to include offensive ground operations, another big step toward "the wider war" that he kept saying he did not seek.[13]

April: To review American options in the war, Johnson convened the first meetings of the group he called his "Wise Men." The roster included Dean Acheson, George Ball, McGeorge Bundy, Arthur Dean, C. Douglas Dillon, Arthur Goldberg, Henry Cabot Lodge, Robert Murphy, and Cyrus Vance as well as army generals Omar Bradley, Matthew Ridgway, and Maxwell Taylor. Foolishly, he invited no one from SDS.

Of this group, only Ball expressed doubts about the war. The rest of the Wise Men advised Johnson that he was on "the right track" to victory and that he only needed to "stick it out" to prevail.[14]

April 7: Johnson told a Johns Hopkins University audience that he was prepared to enter into "unconditional discussions" with North Vietnam. White House press secretary George Reedy later acknowledged that this speech was "a response to the teach-ins."[15]

April 17: The SDS march on Washington, the first big antiwar demonstration, drew fifteen thousand to twenty-five thousand, Beth and I among them, our first demo. The event put SDS on the media map. Even when it was negative, the publicity helped us recruit new members and raise funds, propelling us into a period of growth too rapid to be orderly.

April 18: The National Council, SDS's governing body, met the day after the march, on the campus of Georgetown University. Most NC delegates were still skeptical about a prominent antiwar role for SDS, arguing that we were simply too late on the scene and too small to affect the course of the war. Our best hope, they said, lay in community organizing around local issues.

April 28: The United States invaded the Dominican Republic with twenty-two thousand Marines, ostensibly to protect Dominicans from Communists but more probably to protect the military junta that the United States had installed, a corrupt and undisciplined group that seemed incapable of establishing order in its own ranks, much less in the country. The administration's white paper on the Dominican Republic occupation was authored by Daniel Ellsberg, General Edwin Lansdale's chief assistant. Ellsberg later told an interviewer, "We were a hundred percent lying about what we were doing in the Dominican Republic."[16] Six years later, Ellsberg made public the "Pentagon Papers," boxes of secret military documents on the Vietnam War, thus exposing the lies that lay at the heart of the war.

April 28: The U.S. First Ranger Company was mauled at the Battle of Bau Trai. Two days later, Colonel John Paul Vann wrote to a friend, "regrettably, we are going to lose this war."[17]

May 7: Johnson announced suspension of Operation Rolling Thunder, the bombing of North Vietnam, for five days. When depleted ammo dumps were restocked, bombing was resumed.[18] Secretary of Defense Robert S. McNamara later reported in his 1995 memoir that Operation

Rolling Thunder dropped more bomb tonnage on North Vietnam than had been dropped on all of Europe in World War II.[19]

May 15–16: The national teach-in on the war was held in Washington, D.C. Media coverage was wide, serious, and generally favorable, though this sympathy was soon to die.

July 7: A Wednesday evening, I arrived in Saigon.

THE AIRPORT AT Ton Son Nhut near Saigon was all astir because Secretary of Defense McNamara had left shortly before I arrived on an Air France flight from Paris. From his 1995 memoir, *In Retrospect,* we know that McNamara had come to share the antiwar movement's doubts about the war. "Surprising as it may seem to some," he writes, "I felt great sympathy for the protesters' concerns."[20] Unfortunately, he kept his sympathy to himself.

I was in South Vietnam about two weeks in the middle of July, most often in Saigon at the Hotel Metropole, but several days in Hue, just south of the demilitarized zone, sometimes alone and sometimes with Bob Browne and Jonathan Mirsky, the other two members of the teach-in delegation. Browne was an academic economist who had recently worked in South Vietnam as a U.S. aid official and was married to a well-educated, upper-class Vietnamese woman, Han, who was often with us. Mirsky was a highly regarded China scholar.

One sweltering evening at a luxurious villa on the outskirts of the city, Mirsky, Browne, and I met with a group of eight Vietnamese whom I came to think of as the bourgeois gentlemen of Vietnam.

They were leading members of a group of about 150 intellectuals and political activists known generally around Saigon as the "Notables." Many of them had been arrested that February for having dared to call upon the governments in Hanoi and Saigon to negotiate a peace agreement. There was something formal, even solemn about our meeting. I sensed that Mirsky, Browne, and I had been the subjects of a difficult prior discussion: Was their risk, if we were someone's secret agents, greater or less than their opportunity if we were really what we said we were? I felt that they had prepared for us, that they had arranged themselves.

The same was true of Browne, Mirsky, and me. We had to assume that at least a few of the Notables were connected to the Viet Cong or Hanoi and another few to the CIA, and maybe one or two to both. Such likelihoods were just part of the game in the Saigon of that era, something you couldn't escape. We told ourselves to keep our wits about us and try not to do anything too stupid.

That evening we sat with a former minister of defense; a top Saigon lawyer who was a veteran of both the revolutionary Viet Minh and General "Big" Minh's Council of Notables; two professors; a publisher; a priest; a business statistician; and a former minister of the economy, our host, whom a political opponent had characterized as "the most moral man in Saigon." He was also quite affluent; had a fine, richly furnished house; and wore clear polish on his nails, gold cuff links, and a silk tie. His table was set with fine linen and silver. His servants offered us premium brandy after a superb Vietnamese meal. All of these notables spoke English, the host with special fluency. They went around the table to tell us who they were. Some were from the North, some from the South. Four of them were Catholics, three were Buddhists, and one, a philosophy professor, said he was a Confucian, explaining that a Westerner might call him a humanist. In common they were used to power, privilege, and security, and perhaps at that moment they were beyond all three. They consciously identified with the French nobles of the eighteenth century who sided with the revolution. "They were fully aware," said the Confucian with a wry smile, "that their own heads might well be among the first to roll whether the revolution failed or succeeded."

Any resolution of Vietnam's civil war faced them with personal disaster, from exile to banishment to imprisonment to death. They were safest when the situation was most agitated and unresolved. Yet they begged for peace.

"The war must be ended at any cost," said our host after dinner, an eloquent man whose face seemed tight with anguish or anxiety. "Those who draw historical diagrams," he said, "in well-guarded mansions and speak of the unfortunate necessity of war, these are men who have not looked at war face to face." He showed us glossy photographs of civilian napalm victims, of children whose phosphor-pellet wounds were beyond the ken of the available medical care. "This is all one may say of this war," he said quietly. "Nothing else." He claimed they all feared the Communists. A Communist victory, he said, would be a personal defeat for each of them. "But what we fear is not what the people fear. For the people, all that communism means is a change. For them, any change at all would be an improvement."

The Confucian extended our host's point. "Even with peace," he said, "the lives of the people will remain wretched. Even with peace, a Vietnamese peasant can expect to live forty years. Nothing the VC can do to the people will make their lives worse than they already are. This might be true of the government, too, but the government wants to do nothing for the people. Now suddenly there are a few provinces where the government builds schools and hospitals, but there are no teachers or doctors to staff them—only soldiers. The government builds these shells to prove that it loves the people. Why not before, when it was still not too late? Now the government is all for helping the people, and everyone in Saigon claims to be a socialist. But there is, of course, the excuse of the war. Win the war, the government says, then help the people. But the people can see through this. The government helps them only because it needs their support to win the war. For six years, there was no war. The people got nothing from Diem but promises that were made only in order to be broken."

Showing some anger, our host broke in to say, "Why was this permitted?" He seemed to address his question more to his group than to ours. "We had so much American money! We might have done so much! Instead, half the money was deposited in secret personal accounts in Swiss banks, and with the other half we bought guns and made an army because we wanted to frighten the people out of sympathizing with the revolutionaries. This was a colossal strategic error, my friends. The people always knew where the money that was meant for them was going."

Browne asked if he might be somewhat exaggerating the political sophistication of "the people."

The lawyer answered. "Only think of what you know. Off and on for thirty years, mostly on, the peasant of Vietnam has been at war and has seen foreign troops everywhere, every day. First the French, then the Japanese, then the British. In the North, there were the Kuomintang Chinese. Then the French came again. And now the Americans are here. Any war, and especially this kind, a war against guerrilla forces, politically speaking, is a highly educational experience. Reading? No. Arithmetic? Just enough to count liters of rice. But the politics of war? Yes. From his childhood to his grave, the peasant of today's Vietnam is schooled in the politics of war. It is not like being an American farmer."

Our host broke in to argue that this was no longer relevant. "The people want only peace," he said. "If the people were allowed to choose between war and the Front, seventy percent would choose the VC. At least."

But I thought that was a bit misleading. By the logic of his argument, the people would prefer anything to war, even the existing government.

I said, "But what if the choice were between war and a peace under a government controlled by the United States? Would seventy percent still prefer peace?"

The question seemed to divide them, and they spoke among themselves in Vietnamese. It was as if they had disappeared from view for a moment. Then they resurfaced, most of them nodding. Our host said that we would perhaps find the answer to that somewhat difficult, though it was substantially what Mirsky and I heard a few days later from another gentleman of Vietnam, a vibrant young journalist of no apparent faction who called himself, as I heard it, Cao Giao. Our meeting with him had been set up by the Confucian.

MIRSKY AND I had sat down to wait for Cao Giao, as arranged by our go-between, under an awning at a sidewalk café on the clamorous, bustling Rue Catinat in the middle of Saigon, the afternoon heat sweltering, the sidewalk crowded with hurrying people, the street jammed with buses, small French cars, and a multitude of motorbikes doing their best to make the air noxious. It seemed that every Vietnamese in town was going somewhere else.

Cao Giao materialized from the street crowd just a few minutes after Mirsky and I had gotten our tea. He seemed cool and dry in a short-sleeved light-blue dress shirt with a button-down collar and a ballpoint pen in the pocket.

Cao's energy level matched that of the traffic. He had a small but well-fed compact frame with broad shoulders; black, well-combed hair; high cheekbones; and bright, smiling, inquisitive eyes. I guessed him to be in his middle thirties. He spoke quickly in fluent English. His small hands flew continually as he spoke. At the least sign of an interruption, he would stop at once, lay his head to one side, and say, "Yes? Yes? You fail to understand?"

Cao Giao said he had left the Viet Minh after 1954, the year of the Geneva Accords that were to have brought peace to Vietnam. Then for two years he was a leader of the Duy Dan southern socialist party. Then Diem jailed him for a while. But by 1959 Cao was in Diem's service as a trainer of the guerrillas whom Diem was sending into North Vietnam. When Diem fell in 1963, Cao Giao became the editor of an opposition paper whose name he had to change constantly to evade the censor.

He got right down to business.

"This government," he said with a smile and a shrug, "is a mere impostor. Who doubts this? Who does not know it? You Americans like to say the Vietnam problem is complex. But this is only an excuse to not face the truth. The truth is that the Vietnam problem is not complex at all. It is only impossible. Do you see? If it was complex, you could try to solve it. But it is simple because it is impossible. Because it is simple it cannot be solved." He laughed. I nodded soberly while trying to get his words onto paper and wondering if Cao had some kind of Oriental thing for riddles.

"Vietnam needs two simple things," he said. "It needs to be independent, one. And two, it needs to be rich again, as in the old kingdom. These needs stand together and cannot be separated, but they cannot both be satisfied at the same time. Any regime that makes us free will also make us poor. Any regime that makes us rich will also make us slaves. Do you not see? This is very simple. An honest Vietnamese government that embraces the Americans might develop Vietnam, but it cannot make Vietnam independent. A government that frees itself from the Americans can make Vietnam independent, but it cannot develop it."

He sat back and sipped his tea, looking at us with a little smile. Buses roared and motorbikes buzzed on the street. I wondered what he meant to tell us with all this.

"Where does this leave you?" I said.

He shrugged and smiled. "Do our officials struggle with this dilemma?" he said. "No. Their only struggle is to deposit as much American cash as they get their hands on in the banks of Paris. Do you think this theft is disguised? It is part of the office routine!"

Cao paused a moment to see that we were getting it, then dropped his grin, and for some reason his English for a moment, and leaned toward us. *Je connais les Rouges très bien,* he said with a very un-Vietnamese glare. "The Viet Minh will make us a drab people. Communists do not tolerate the bizarre. They mistrust the artist, the critic, the lonely spirit. See what a gray city they have made of Hanoi!"

"Great city?" I said.

"Gray!" he said. "*Une ville gris!* But! They promise both independence and development. And they can easily deceive the people because they say what the people want to hear. This is why they grow. We do not give the Viet Cong the opportunity to expose themselves as makers of false promises. We provide them with excuses for their failures. We justify the tyranny they would impose in any case."

Cao paused again, stopping his hands and staring at us with his sharp brown eyes.

Mirsky said, "So we have to ask again, Cao, what do you conclude from this analysis? You seem to be dooming yourself to solitude."

Cao broke a smile as though he liked the idea. He was immediately in motion again. "This is the reality we face," he said. "The Viet Cong are winning the war. Why? Because they are winning the trust of ordinary Vietnamese people. This is disgraceful for us. It is tragic for Vietnam. But the Viet Cong started small and are growing large. The government started large and is growing small. Why does this happen? This happens because the government has nothing to say to the people. Now we ask the people to fight for what this Nguyen Cao Ky has the insolence to call 'freedom.' Nonsense! What freedom did he ever show them? And what freedom do the peasants want when their children die from hunger and sickness even when there is no fighting? We must stop pretending to be happy for this empty American freedom. We must rise instead to attack the Viet Cong as traitors to the nationalist revolution. We must help the people become healthy again. Then maybe the people will come with us. Do you see?"

I nodded slightly, not at all sure that I did see, and glanced at Mirsky, who was nodding slightly, too. I bent to my diary and jotted some more notes.

Cao leaned back and resumed in a cooler voice. "Allow me to tell you another truth, a truth of equal simplicity and importance. Carl, I understand that you are a writer. You must write this. The problems of Vietnam must not be seen through Cold War eyes. Do you understand? We do not want to be eaten for dinner by Comrade Mao. But we cannot stand like sentries on America's side. That would betray Asia as well as ourselves. You must learn this. What is happening to us in South Vietnam feels like invasion and conquest. You tell yourselves that you are our liberators. But the Vietnamese are not fools. Must we choose between being conquered by Ho Chi Minh and being conquered by Johnson? Tell me. Which one is a countryman?

"And there is something else you Americans must understand," he said, no longer pausing to make sure he was getting through. "We Vietnamese detest foreign meddlers, but worse yet in our eyes are the Vietnamese who collaborate with foreign meddlers. This was true when the French were here. It remains true now that you Americans are here. You tell us that you are different. But for us Vietnamese, the difference is hard to see. Both are white. Both are tall. Both carry big guns. Both pretend to know what they are doing here."

Despite his clarity from sentence to sentence, Cao Giao was confusing me. I broke in to say, "Does this mean you favor an American withdrawal? Are you saying the United States should just get out of Vietnam? Are the Viet Cong right?"

"No," he said, showing no hesitancy. "If you withdraw your soldiers, our soldiers will throw down their weapons where the Viet Cong will find them. The Viet Cong will march into Saigon. You must protect and care for the ones you have hurt. You must help repair the damage you have done. But you must let us find our own path to a new government. Any government you try to make will only make our lives worse than your army has already made them."

But what could that mean? How could the United States disengage politically while remaining militarily involved and continuing to supply economic aid?

Cao's lucidity faltered. He flicked his hands this way and that, then he flared. "But this is your problem," he said, showing a touch of anger. "Why? Because you have made it your problem. We Vietnamese did not make the decisions that brought you here. We Vietnamese did not divide Vietnam in half and make us go to war against each other. But for your own sake as well as ours, if you understand nothing else, you must understand this." He opened his fingers and looked at us piercingly, speaking one word at a time. "Any Vietnamese solution to Vietnam's problems is better than any American solution. If America refuses to see this, many lives will be lost for nothing. I cannot say that I know America well. But I think if you ignore this simple fact, you will lose something in your heart. You will become something that I think you do not want to be."

Cao Ciao abruptly stood up. "We wish you the best fortune," he said. "Many lives depend on you." He bowed slightly and quickly disappeared into the traffic.

I wiped my brow and said to Mirsky, "Jonathan, who is this guy?"

He shook his head and smiled. "You've got me, my friend. But I think I need some lemonade."

Mirsky might make do with lemonade, but for me, it was time for some serious air-conditioning. I hurried back to the hotel to take a cold shower, write up my notes, and get down to wondering if I had the least idea what was happening.

AS WITH CAO GIAO, the bourgeois gentlemen's peace plan rested on twin beliefs, both of which were borne out by the subsequent course of events.

One was that both the Saigon government and the Hanoi-VC insurgency, even though each preferred outright military victory, had to recognize, as our host had put it, that "neither side is strong enough to win or weak enough to lose."

The other was that either side's "continued pursuit of victory can only result in the destruction of Vietnam." Vietnam, he said, "is a small country cowering on the frontier of the Cold War. It can survive only if it attains equilibrium vis-à-vis the two contending giants."

The group presented their seven basic points as though they had done so many times before.

First, a month-long cease-fire agreement should be signed by Saigon, Hanoi, and the VC. Its central purpose would be to test the good faith of all parties. The agreement would not demand the breakup of the VC, the departure of North Vietnamese guerrilla units, or the withdrawal of U.S. personnel and equipment, but it would suspend arms shipments and troop movements on both sides.

Second, this agreement would be guaranteed by the signatures of the generals who were actually directing the war, not by politicians. Thus it would involve no political or legal recognition, neither of Hanoi and the Viet Cong by Saigon nor vice versa. This was a subtle but important point. It meant that the VC would be encountered directly by Saigon, not through Hanoi, and that it would thereby have the right to speak for itself. At the same time, there would be no implication that Saigon recognized the VC's claim to independent status.

Third, the cease-fire would be controlled during this one-month period by a mixed commission of government and VC officers. The politics of this method continued the thrust of point two, that is, to be generous as to realities but tight as to symbols.

Fourth, the inevitable peace conference would follow the cease-fire by a month and would be held under the supervision of a strong international control commission. This commission's basic task would be the rapid formation of a strictly provisional, custodial government for the South. It would be made up of delegates from Hanoi, the VC, Saigon, and the United States. This commission would plan and oversee general elections to be held within four to five months of declaration of a truce. "Sooner would probably be too soon," said our host, "but later would almost certainly be too late."

Fifth, the purpose of the first election would be to choose a national assembly, either directly or through an electoral college. This assembly's primary task would be to draft a constitution that, among other things, would establish a method for electing a president and an assembly. A general election would then be held and the government established. This plan, one of the professors pointed out, followed in compressed form the sequence of events by which the government of the United States itself had been established after its own national revolution: first a declaration of independence, then a constitution.

Sixth, the group believed that Saigon should immediately begin forming "worthy cadres" who would begin working with the people at the onset of the month-long settlement period. These cadres, they said, should be prepared with "an ideology" that transcended Vietnam's political divisions between Buddhists and Catholics, country people and city people, traditionalists and modernists. The program must be basically socialist in that it would establish the government rather than the wealthy as the primary organizer of the economy, and in that it would be detailed by the people themselves, who alone can determine national needs.

Seventh and finally, the group recognized that it would be unwise and unrealistic to demand that the United States disappear overnight. But the United States' interest in Vietnamese neutrality—independence from both the Soviet Union and Red China—would show it the prudence of supporting a socialist program first in the South and then, after reunification ("someday"), throughout Vietnam. And since no state can demand moral heroism of another, the Vietnamese must not trifle with American insecurity. They must allow a provisional American military presence. Thus, the group argued, Danang should remain an American base, a strategic position, but one from which there would be minimal interference in Vietnam's internal affairs.

What the group claimed for this plan was that it removed the two major obstacles to negotiations as they were seen at that time: first, that the United States did not want to lend credibility to the VC by admitting it to formal negotiations, and second, that the VC did not want to accept a continuing American voice in Vietnamese affairs. If the United States could accept the VC to the extent of allowing it a place in a provisional government, then the VC could accept a genuine American interest in the outcome. If the United States could live with a program of genuine social reform truly aimed at bettering the quality of Vietnamese life and accepting in principle the idea of Vietnamese independence, then the VC could live with a continuing American presence. Okay? Deal?

The certainty with which the bourgeois gentlemen claimed to know what the VC would or would not accept made Mirsky, Browne, and me wonder if they were actually speaking for it, but we had no way to know. We had no idea whether anyone in Saigon or Hanoi or Washington or Moscow or Peking would see the least virtue in this group's proposal, or whether anyone outside Saigon had even heard of it, or if they had, whether they had given it a second thought.

The ghastly fact to contemplate decades later is that, in its salient points, this is almost exactly the peace plan that was adopted in 1975, ten years after that meeting and as many as three million lives later. The big difference, of course, is that the United States pulled out completely.

Shortly after I left Vietnam, Air Marshal Nguyen Cao Ky, head of the military junta that had seized power on June 11, 1965, against a backdrop of Buddhist monks publicly immolating themselves, proclaimed "neutralism" a capital crime against the state. This meant that the sort of action the bourgeois gentlemen and Cao Giao had taken in meeting with us antiwar Americans could put them in jail, if not before a firing squad, for what Air Marshal Ky was pleased to call treason.

If Ky thus moved to seal their fate, he sealed his own as well as that of the tragicomic Saigon regimes that were to follow. From almost everyone we talked with in Saigon and Hue, whether right, left, or not saying, we got the impression of a wide consensus that the VC had never represented a desirable solution for South Vietnam, but that neither had the permanent partition of Vietnam behind a Communist wall in the North sponsored by the USSR and an anti-Communist wall in the South sponsored by the United States. In November 1963, with the mutiny of Saigon generals against Ngo Dinh Diem, who was assassinated, there had been a moment of hope that at least the situation could be stabilized, that the process leading to peace talks could begin.

But as coup upon countercoup condemned that hope, the wait-and-see loyalty of the middle and upper classes of South Vietnam was forced into a curiously apolitical neutralism in which it was possible only to speak of the desirability of peace over war. And coup still followed coup, each violent and peremptory change bringing with it a deeper penetration into the southern government by increasingly exasperated Americans.

For proud South Vietnamese, Ky and those who followed became national humiliations. The politically important intelligentsia began to drift from loyalty to neutralism, from critically supporting Saigon and the United States' mission to an increasingly agonized quietism and despair.

What did we Americans want? Some wanted two Vietnams and some kind of truce between them. Others preferred a war with China or the Soviet Union, believing that such a war was inevitable and that it would be best to get it over with. Some were trying to build schools and hospitals. Others were defoliating the jungle and carpet-bombing villages.

As James Reston of *The New York Times* was moved to wonder at about this time, would we unquiet Americans end by "trying to win the war by methods that cost us the sympathy of the people"?

BESIDES LISTENING to a lot of Vietnamese, learning about the war also meant watching from a rooftop patio in the outskirts of Saigon one night as a squadron of B-52s, flying so high they could just barely be heard, assaulted suspected VC positions around Tan Son Nhut Airport, about a mile away. Browne, Mirsky, and I at first tried to continue our meeting with the Buddhist activists who had come to meet us, but the sustained thunder of the bombing finally became so loud that we could not talk without shouting, so we all just turned to watch the bombing, each of us in his own silence, as the earth trembled and the clouds were lit up from below. The raid at last ended and we returned to our now desperate-seeming talk of brotherhood and international understanding.

In Saigon as well as Hue, we met with many prowar as well as antiwar Vietnamese. The political-affairs officer at the U.S. embassy warned us that certain Vietnamese rightists were aware of our group's presence and unhappy about it. This was perhaps a polite way to tell us that the U.S. embassy itself was unhappy. In any case, it was a subaltern of South Vietnamese premier Nguyen Cao Ky who became our most abundant source of antiwar anecdotes. He told us of "friendly" villages bombed by mistake, of U.S. aid money finding its way to private Vietnamese accounts in European banks, of high Saigon officials who were actually VC sympathizers. The laughter never left his voice.

I spent a few days in Hue, a lovely university city on the River of Many Perfumes, the green mountains of Laos rising abruptly to the west and the misty islands of the Gulf of Tonkin to the east, not many miles below the seventeenth parallel, the dividing line between North and South Vietnam that had been drawn by the 1954 Geneva conference.

Hue was reckoned a VC citadel by Joe O'Neal, the chief of the city's U.S. consulate, and he seemed not to mind who heard him say so. Nor did he seem to care.

O'Neal held court every night in a rooftop bar in the student quarter and loudly declared to all who would listen to him that the only reasonable thing for the United States to do was to get out of this war.

"Yes," he said, "as smoothly as possible and with all deliberate speed, but above all, get out."

"Even if it means a Communist victory?" I asked, amazed to hear such views openly expressed by an American official.

"The Communist victory has already taken place," said O'Neal. "Every other member of the Saigon government is tied into the Viet

Cong one way or another. Half of our aid ends up in Hanoi, and most of the rest in a Swiss bank. Screw it. We tried our best. Let's pack up and go home."

What did it mean that an important American official was publicly proclaiming such ideas? This question became all the more intriguing when German members of the University of Hue's medical faculty informed us that O'Neal was widely seen by the locals as the CIA's chief of station.

Maybe so. Maybe not.

Either way what the hell was going on?

One day Bob Browne and I took a cyclo trip outside metropolitan Hue. We were headed to the Gia Lam pagoda, about five miles outside the city, where we were going to meet with Browne's close academic friend Thich Nhat Han, an influential Buddhist prelate.

Trying to handle everything by the book, we informed the local U.S. officials that we intended to take this excursion. Some of them asked us to reconsider. We would be in VC territory and beyond our government's power to protect us. But O'Neal doubted that we would have a problem, since we had been personally invited by Thich Nhat Hanh.

We did not get to see Nhat Hanh. Sometime that year, and it may have been at the time of our visit, he embarked on a worldwide mission for peace, meeting with, among others, Dr. Martin Luther King Jr.; Pope Paul VI; and Secretary of Defense Robert McNamara, to whom he appealed for the United States to stop the bombing.

Instead, we got divided up and passed around separately among a number of other English- or French-speaking Vietnamese, who tried to explain to us the meaning of the suicides-by-fire of several monks that had begun two years before. They emphasized the Buddhist concept of *nghia,* the sense of a right and lawful order to the universe connecting the individual, the society, the world, and the cosmos. It was this concept, they told us, that underlay the priests' suicides: In a world in which nghia had been disrupted by tyranny, corruption, and war, the priests had felt obliged by the terms of their faith to adopt public suicide as the only meaningful human act.

Then they showed us the sights for several hours, including the ruins of the ancient palace, put us back in our cyclos, and bade us farewell.

As we were halfway back to Hue in the late afternoon of a hot, muggy day, out of the jungle stepped a young Vietnamese man in a starched white shirt, with a bicycle under his arm.

"Hello, Americans!" he said cheerfully. "Do you need a guide?"

This was Phan Hoang Quy, who seemed to know all about me and Browne. Browne was headed off on some other errands, and without him I would know even less what I was doing than I already did. So, yes, I did need a guide. Quy appointed himself to that position and said right away that I needed to go see the old Imperial City, which was to be destroyed in the Tet Offensive of 1968. We talked of cabbages and kings, Vietnam-style.

Quy also arranged a meeting with four young men, all "peace activists" at the University of Hue. We met for perhaps an hour on a hot, bright afternoon in an anteroom of the university cathedral. They all wore clean white shirts with starched collars. This seemed the standard uniform for middle-class Vietnamese. They seemed tense. The one with the best English, named Kai Son, did almost all the talking, often interrupting our dialogue to speak with the others in Vietnamese.

"The war is terrible for Vietnam," said Kai. "We do not like the Communists, but we must have peace. The Viet Cong do bad things, but they are our fellow Vietnamese. North and South Vietnam are one. We must stop killing each other. America is a beautiful country and can help us in many ways, but not by bombing us."

Kai asked many questions about the American antiwar movement. How numerous were we? How were we organized? What were our plans? Did we have support in the media? How long will the government continue to tolerate our demonstrations? Will ordinary Americans ever join our cause?

The hour passed quickly. They all shook my hand and bowed slightly. "Please continue to struggle to stop the war," said Kai. I told them that we would certainly do all we could but kept to myself a growing fear that all we could do would not be nearly enough.

As I watched them pedal off together, their white shirts gleaming in the summer sun, I couldn't help but wonder which of them was VC, which one was CIA, which one would soon be killed.

A little later, Quy and I said good-bye on the bank of the River of Many Perfumes. He said again that I was right to oppose the war. He said we should keep in touch and that he would visit me in Michigan when the war was over. He was eager to see New York City and the Great Lakes. I wrote him several letters but never got an answer.

I SPENT A WEEK with a fledgling but lively Japanese antiwar movement in Tokyo, a guest of Zingakuren, a non-Communist peace group. A few of my hosts would take me to a meeting hall. I would say the first line of a short statement, something like "I am honored to bring greetings from the American antiwar movement," then back away from the mike while one of my chaperones read the rest of my statement in Japanese. After handshakes and little bows, I would be taken to a car to go somewhere else and do the same thing.

But one day I was a surprise guest on Japan's nationally televised teach-in. I spoke my line and backed away. Then pow!—I was slugged from behind, my glasses went flying, and I was on the floor in the grips of two very beefy Japanese who evidently disapproved of my views, all in full glare of the TV lights. Guards quickly wrestled my foes away, and my specs and I were hardly the worse for it, though I had a good bruise to go with the one Louie had given me. It seemed worth it, though, when many people in the streets the next day smiled and gave me the peace sign.

I broke off my trip when news came that a bad riot had erupted in Watts, an L.A. suburb made famous by Simon Rodia's Watts Towers. I was worried that my new friends might have been hurt or arrested in the rioting.

It was late in August when I landed in San Francisco having, as my first act as SDS president, circumnavigated the globe. I got a big briefing on the Watts scene from the local SDS people and gave my first report on what I had seen and learned in Vietnam, in a speech from the steps of Sproul Hall Plaza, a place made famous by the Free Speech Movement of 1964.

Next I was sent to Oakland to tour parts of the black ghetto that were politically sympathetic with what was already being called "the Watts rebellion." I was put on TV to say that SDS supported the black community's increasingly militant demand for equality in America. An FBI report that I came by later through a suit under the Freedom of Information Act quoted me as saying that "as long as the United States refuses to acknowledge its responsibilities toward blacks, what has happened in Watts is on the agenda for every other big city in this country."

It was good, though I wouldn't say comforting, to know that the FBI was getting it.

Soon I was down the coast to UCLA, where I met some young Republicans who were easily just as angry about the war as anyone I had yet met in SDS.

"Why should a true conservative be in favor of this war?" said one. "The state exerts no power over the individual greater than the power to put a guy in a soldier suit and make him march off to shoot at somebody he doesn't even know. To hell with that!"

The SDS regional office for the L.A. area was run by a quiet, thoughtful, crew-cut, working-class guy named Mike Davis, who went on to write a celebrated history of Los Angeles and have a tenured faculty position at U.C. Irvine. In '65, Mike was close to Watts-area black activists. Through his guidance, the SDS chapter set up meetings between black activists and a white guy from Hollywood in which the activists tried to explain the anger that had exploded. I recall the activists saying things like "Can you imagine what it's like to be taught that you're free and equal and then made to live in squalor under the glare of cops that hate you?" The Hollywood guy took notes.

In an eerie reprise of the night of the airport bombing in Saigon, Mike and I and half a dozen or so SDSers collected on the third-story porch outside the SDS office to gaze in fear and wonder at the smoldering embers of Watts. With glasses, we could make out that Rodia's Towers were still standing.

While we were taking in this view, some angry fraternity guys from USC were trying to set our own place on fire. Mike and I smelled the smoke, and we confronted the would-be arsonists in time to save a fire alarm.

"God!" Mike yelled, stamping out the papers burning at the foot of our door. "What the hell are you guys trying to prove?!"

"This is for America!" one of them yelled.

"Love it or leave it!" yelled another.

We had no uncomplicated answers. How to tell them about the antiwar conservatives of L.A., or the guys in New York who had begun by attacking us and ended by talking with us? We were glad enough that they just left the building and Mike and me still standing.

From L.A. I jumped off—was pushed off—into a national tour of antiwar groups that had been forming during that summer all over the country.

Now that I had stopped trying to be an actor, I found myself on some of the world's great stages, from New York to Paris to Saigon to Tokyo, speaking my own lines in behalf of a cause I believed in to enthusiastic crowds, connected to a movement of bright, passionate people, a movement that was now carrying me and my family along with it as part of an international phenomenon that no one, neither its defenders nor its attackers, knew how to explain or predict.

I got back to Ann Arbor just in time to get sick for a month (pneumonia is a great way to hide from life) before my term as SDS president began in earnest.

The stronger SDS got, of course, the more viciously the war raged on. On July 28, 1965, Johnson approved the army's request for 125,000 more troops and announced that the military draft was to be doubled. Through the invaluable research of Naval War College historian David Kaiser,[21] we now know for a fact what many of us in the opposition suspected at the time, namely, that the joint chiefs of staff were aggressively campaigning for escalation. Some of them were even eager to use nuclear weapons! And we know that Johnson was going nuts, though it would be decades before presidential adviser Richard Goodwin reported that Johnson told a group of reporters in 1965 that "the Communists control the three major networks and the forty major outlets to communication," that "Walter Lippmann is a Communist and so is Teddy White. And they're not the only ones." His paranoia rivaled Captain Queeg's.

The whole prowar side seems to have shared in this madness, clinging against all evidence to its delusion that there was a military "solution" to the "problem" of Vietnam, constantly claiming that U.S. forces had at last "turned the corner" and could now see "light at the end of the tunnel," that each new escalation, Scout's honor, would be the last.

What was different about 1965 was that the middle class, led by the academic community, was starting to pay attention. The teach-in, the means invented for putting a clear picture of the war in people's minds, was beginning to generate an informed community. The teach-in was the nation's crash course on Vietnam.

August 3: The first Vietnamese peasant homes were torched by U.S. troops, who said they believed them to be the homes of VC sympathizers. If that village had not been a VC stronghold before, it certainly was there after.

August 5–11: Back to Japan to represent SDS at Hiroshima-Nagasaki Day commemorations. I was under the wing of one of Japan's premier young poets, the burly Makota Oda, who had spent time in the States on a Fulbright. I learned from a State Department document released to me through a Freedom of Information Act request in 2005 that the State Department had somehow arranged for Oda to be my host. This was to ensure that I wouldn't fall into the hands of Japanese Communists, who had a competitive antinuke group.

One evening over saki, Oda assured me that the American antiwar movement was too weak and too late to make a difference. Our protest, said Oda, was an empty gesture.

"Suppose it is," I said. "What would you have us do?"

He stared at me—affectionately, I thought. He had taken me to a kabuki performance that evening, so exquisite in song and gesture that I came out thinking I could almost understand Japan. Now we were in his apartment surrounded by dozens of statuettes of Buddha and pots of bonsai.

In answer to my question, he refilled my cup of warm saki, then gazed into the air. Either reciting or improvising a haiku, he said softly:

> *A porcelain vase*
> *Will be at its loveliest*
> *Filled with emptiness.*

In mid-August, a coalition of antipoverty and civil-rights groups, the Assembly of Unrepresented People, convened in Washington. I represented SDS there. I met Jerry Rubin, leader of Berkeley's energetic Vietnam Day Committee, a short, dark, intense man in his late twenties and a fireball at the rostrum. I was surprised to hear him call himself a Trotskyist. I had blithely taken Trotsky to be a relic of mere archaeological interest to sixties heads.

Well, I was still learning.

THE FALL 1965 issue of the political magazine *Dissent* carried an essay of mine under the title "The Teach-ins: A Student Response," laying out the politics of the New Left as I saw it.

> The teach-in movement must change the American campus from an assembly line for managers and technicians into the seat of a new American learning, a resilient and self-conscious scholarship turned inwards upon our institutions, outwards upon their impact on the world, and broadcast everywhere.

Behind this somewhat orotund rhetoric was my belief, bred in the teach-in movement, that schools had become an important political arena and that teachers and students could exercise real power through them. This idea still seems solid to me. But in about three years, it would ensnare me in a losing argument within SDS itself.

ON OCTOBER 5, at Hope College in Holland, Michigan, I debated the war with my old candidate Congressman Wes Vivian, whose need for a Vietnam position paper had prompted all these changes in my life more than a year before. Vivian still favored American intervention to "save" South Vietnam. He was moving slowly toward full opposition to the war, but at this point he was only willing to concede that it was the poor among us who bore the brunt of the effort and that there was something shameful and dangerous in this.

October 15–16 were the antiwar movement's first "International Days of Protest." Large crowds gathered in the major cities of Western Europe and Japan. There were demonstrations in sixty U.S. cities. Thirty thousand people marched in New York. In Berkeley, fifteen thousand tried to march on the Oakland Army Depot but were stopped at the Berkeley-Oakland city line by the Oakland police, who seemed eager to use tough-cop tactics to keep the crowd contained. To show how badly the tough cops scared them, SDS males started burning their draft cards.

5 | # Build, Not Burn!

Washington, D.C., 1965

SDS FELT THE heavier guns of the prowar media for the first time in October 1965 when a volley of public attacks came down all over us. Suddenly our numerous failures were under fire from *Time, Newsweek, The New York Times,* and the major networks. More menacing than mass-media disdain was a new interest in putting SDS on trial. We were well accustomed by this time to being Red-baited by amateurs, but it felt different to be accused of statutory treason in the well of the U.S. Congress. I began to hear that SDS officers might be liable to arrest and prosecution under the Espionage Act, the National Security Act, and the Logan Act.

The Espionage Act was held to apply, if the nation was indeed at war, because we had publicly threatened to break it. Our threat was empty because we didn't really know how to carry it out, but our purpose was to put the war itself on trial. We thought there were serious legal flaws in the policy of escalation. We wanted to find a court in which to state our argument that U.S. military action in Vietnam was illegal.

The National Security Act was sometimes invoked against us because the law requires private citizens who represent foreign nations to register with the government, and some of our critics accused us of representing North Vietnam.

The Logan Act, the law most often invoked against us, prohibits private citizens from involving themselves in the foreign-policy process, which some felt a few SDSers had done in talking with North Vietnamese officials in Europe.

None of this happened. Neither SDS nor its officers were at this point charged with any crime. But even if the idea had been merely to intimidate us, it was a flop. The main effect of these attacks was to put SDS on the media map.

The volley of attacks clearly called for a response. So the twenty or so members of SDS's National Interim Committee consulted with the much larger leadership group, the National Council, and the NC members consulted with our chapters across the country on the question of what was to be done. There was a strong consensus that the moment called for something in the way of a counterattack through the mass media, and that it should take the form of a statement to tell the world who we really were and what we were really trying to do.

So our national secretary, Paul Booth, announced a press conference in Washington and called me to come help out. Booth knew that we had become hot copy. He rented the Grand Ballroom of the National Press Club, a huge, majestic place. Every chair was taken, and people were standing along the walls.

The theme of our response was announced in the title of our hastily written statement, "Build, Not Burn!" This statement made three basic points.

First, it explained that we opponents of the war were members in good standing of the great American family, exercising our most basic rights. We were your kids, your brothers and sisters, your cousins and friends, your fellow students, your teachers, some of us your mothers and fathers, your neighbors, your fellow citizens, your peers. And we were saying that our goal was to build America and stop burning down Vietnam.

"We say this," I said to the gathered press, "because if anyone in the current situation has a right to complain about pathologies of patriotism and failures of basic respect for the law, it is we dissenters who have it, or, as it pleases some of you to call us, we 'alienated youth' and 'malcontents.'

"This is why we are here to ask: In the name of the United States Constitution and a basic respect for the laws of the land, why have the Congress and the pliant media allowed President Johnson, with so little discussion, to wrap the flag around the Vietnam War and fight it without a declaration of war?

"And why would the president want to do this if he were honestly convinced that this war really did serve the interests of the American and the Vietnamese people?"

In the initially hostile Q-and-A that followed our statement, a reporter from one of the prowar newsmagazines belligerently asked Booth to say "at long last" if he was or was not a Communist. Booth just chuckled and said, "I'm not gonna answer a question like that."

"Could you tell us why not?" someone shouted.

"Because it's wrong to assume that if you oppose the Vietnam War, you're a Communist. We're here to talk about an illegal war."

"What about you, Mr. Oglesby?" the questioner said. "Are you a Communist?"

Where Booth had responded with wry disdain, I took a different tack. "I'm not as principled as Booth," I said, "so I don't mind answering for myself if you'll give me a chance to say why I think Booth refused."

"All right, go ahead."

"I'm not a member of the Communist Party now, I never have been, and I've never in the least wanted to be. Before I joined SDS a few months ago, I had worked in the defense industry and held a secret clearance for eight years. How many of you people are cleared for secret? And no, I'm not going to tell you what military secrets I know, so don't ask. I will tell you, however, that you don't have to know military secrets to know that this administration's Vietnam policy is foolish and illegal. You can read all about it in your own newspapers. As for why my friend Booth wouldn't answer your question, I think it's because he objects to the unspoken assumption behind it, namely that if people oppose the war they must be traitors."

Booth stepped up to his mike to say, "Yes, this is called Red-baiting, and most people who try to think straight won't stoop to it. Listen, you guys, the concerns about the Vietnam War that SDS is trying to raise are many and real. They're not Red propaganda, and they're not the illusions of a few idealistic, alienated college kids. Sooner or later, you guys are going to have to face them."

"And what questions are these?" the reporter said.

"All right, is this growing war really a police action, or is that Johnson's way to get around the fact that only the Congress has the constitutional authority to declare war?"

"I am not here as an authority on the Constitution, Mr. Booth."

"Authority? Hey, we're talking Government 101, my friend. But if you can't handle that one, what about the use of napalm against civilian targets? What about carpet bombing? What about using poison aerosols to defoliate the rain forest?"

"I'm a reporter, Mr. Booth. I'm not paid to have views on such things. I'm paid to ask tough questions and get answers."

"All right, what happens when you punch your time clock and go home for the night? Do you have views on such things then? Surely you know it is a war crime to attack civilian targets."

"I'm not a military expert."

"What would a military expert know about poisoning the jungle or bombing a village that an ordinary person can't get?"

"If that's happening, I assume there's a good military reason for doing it."

"Why do you assume that?"

"I trust our military people to know what they're doing."

"Oh, trust," said Booth with a grin. "I thought you were paid to ask tough questions."

Another reporter stood up. "Charlie, let me take that. I was in the army, and I can tell you there are use doctrines for all our weapons."

"What's the use doctrine for defoliants?" said Booth.

"VC guerrillas often hide their trails in the jungle, so we use these chemicals to expose them."

"Don't they just make other trails?"

"Actually, that is a problem," the army vet said. "Then we have to defoliate a wider area."

"And on and on?" said Booth.

"It can be extensive, yes."

"Sounds like we're talking about a lot of poison. What, maybe several hundred pounds?"

"Frankly, for the required area, it can be in the tons."

"Tons! How do you keep it out of the food?"

"I know our people do their best, Mr. Booth."

Another reporter said, "Hank, to your best knowledge, where has this been going on primarily?" Another piped up, "How do we protect the friendly Vietnamese?" Another said. "And our own guys?"

The reporters were soon talking about defoliation among themselves. By the time our two hours were up and we had to leave, the press conference had become a seminar. Many reporters walked away from it, but many stayed. And as their dialogue continued, as much among themselves as with Paul and me, it became clear that several of them were troubled by the Fifth Estate's record in reporting the war.

And Booth was not above rubbing it in. "Look what happened to *The New York Times*'s ace reporter David Halberstam," he said, "when Halberstam started reporting unpleasant truths about the war." Booth stabbed the air with the stub of a yellow pencil and said, "He was reassigned to Bulgaria!" He looked around the room with a glint in his eye. "Bulgaria! And from all his colleagues in the media who care so much about the truth, what did we hear about it?" There was a ringing silence in the room. "Not one single peep," said Booth quietly. He let the words hang. He knew he had drawn blood.

When the moment had been properly milked, Booth returned to the main theme of our statement. "SDS people are not trying to avoid service to this country. But we fail to see the patriotism in fighting an undeclared war against people who pose not the least threat to our national security. SDS is saying no to that. It's immoral and it violates the Constitution. SDS wants to build, not burn!"

I threw in a riff on Booth's theme: "You could even say that we want to help build a Great Society! A slogan of ours just a year ago, some of you may remember, was 'Part of the way with LBJ.' Put the money being spent on the Vietnam War into programs for helping Third World people get a grip on life, and you won't have to worry about 'the Communist menace' ever again."

Thus did Booth and I come right to the edge of proposing before the national media, in the name of an SDS that had not in the least considered such a thing, a national program of alternative service. That would get Booth and me in trouble at home. But I still think it was right. It let us take the offensive from a position of strength. We turned the press conference into a teach-in on the war. Booth and I handled ourselves with reasonable poise, and what do you know—the coverage came out largely sympathetic.

From the standpoint of the outer world, we had carried the day, largely reversed the media assault upon us, and won some new friends. We had shown some media people that you didn't have to be a traitor to see that the Vietnam War sucked. Even a journalist could see that.

THE DAY AFTER the press conference, we found that we had some allies in the administration itself when top officers of the Peace Corps invited Booth and me to tour their premises and speak to their staff. While we were there, moreover, one of them asked us to review the Peace Corps' training program to see if we could suggest ways to spike it up. He invited me to speak at Peace Corps training centers in Oklahoma and Puerto Rico, an invitation I eagerly accepted.

Among the trainees at the Puerto Rican Peace Corps camp high in a mountain rain forest, I was startled to run into open support for the Vietnamese revolutionaries. These were kids who remembered what they had learned in American History 101. They knew what King George III's minions had said about Thomas Paine, Samuel Adams, George Washington, Thomas Jefferson, and the other troublemakers of 1776. They knew that large numbers of French troops had fought in support of the American cause and had actually outnumbered Americans at the Battle of Yorktown by five to one. Thus the administration's argument that North Vietnamese support for the VC invalidated the VC claim to be an indigenous force did not cut ice with them. They could recognize an anticolonial cause when they saw it.

When I asked at the end of one session how many supported the basic aims of the VC—independence from foreign occupation, reunification of Vietnam, North and South—only the camp superintendent, Warren Wiggins, did not raise his hand.

I was afraid at first that I had offended him. But the next day, as I was preparing to pull out, Wiggins asked me if SDS would consider taking over the Peace Corps training program, reorganizing it and putting some of our people in key administrative positions.

"You mean it?" I said, astonished. This went far beyond reviewing a few manuals.

"I think the Peace Corps needs the kind of juice that SDS people could bring to it."

"That's wonderful of you to say, Warren. But wouldn't it get you in trouble in Washington?"

"Maybe it would be all to the good if it did."

I thought it was a fantastic proposal and told the NC about it as soon as I got back, strongly urging that we take Wiggins up on it. My impression was that the Peace Corps at this point was a small bastion of New Frontier activists inside official Washington, and that Wiggins was willing to flaunt an open relationship with SDS as an up-yours to the prowar crowd. But the NC, damn it, thought such a deal went much too far toward making SDS part of the evil empire and turned it down flatly, although several dozen SDSers actually did go to the camp in Puerto Rico on their own.

So taken all in all, the October attack on us and our "Build, Not Burn!" counterattack, turned out beautifully for us, and SDS prospered. We raised some badly needed money, made some new friends, and our membership burst into orbit. New chapters started reporting in too rapidly for the national office to keep up with the paperwork. Just opening the daily mail became a full-time job. To cut through the accreditation problem, we began saying, "If you feel that you're a member of SDS, then you're a member of SDS."

We might have worried a little more about that, but we didn't have the infrastructure to do much about it. So we just let it roll. As of our antiwar march on Washington in April 1965, our membership had stood at about twenty-five hundred. By the end of the year it was more than ten thousand and spiraling upward. There was hardly a campus in the country where we did not have a presence.

AFTER THE OCTOBER press conference, I met in New York with Sandy Gottlieb, director of the Committee for a Sane Nuclear Policy, referred to as SANE and regarded as the leadership group of the American antinuke movement tracing back its connection with Britain's Aldermaston mass marches in the 1950s.

SDS's relationship with SANE was touchy. SANE seemed to feel that its leadership role in the peace movement had been called into question by the success of the SDS antiwar march in April. To reassert its leadership as well as to create a protest event for grown-ups, SANE was now calling for another march on Washington, this one to be held in November.

This way of marching on Washington every other season would become a basic tactic of the movement, but as of the fall of 1965 it was already somewhat suspect. A mass march was expensive, hard to organize, and easily dismissed by the mainstream media as a mere gathering of kooky idealists.

After April, SDS had already had enough of marches on Washington and didn't want to start organizing for another one. But if the SANE march in November were to draw fewer people than had the SDS march in April, the big media and the politicians would conclude that the movement had crested and could be dismissed as a passing phenomenon of the fringe.

So despite itself, SANE had to appeal to SDS to support and organize for the march, thus in effect conceding that leadership of the all-important student part of the antiwar movement now rested with SDS. And equally despite itself, SDS had to climb aboard because we couldn't let the SANE march fail. We had become part of something larger than ourselves. This was something we wanted, of course, yet at the same time dreaded because it seemed to take our identity out of our own hands.

The SANE-vs.-SDS leadership dispute was argued out around slogans. The group organizing an event such as this march has a right to say what slogans will be adopted. Gottlieb was worried that SDS intended to adopt slogans supportive of the VC. He found this all wrong on sheer practical political grounds. He thought we should take a strictly neutral, pacifist position on the war and criticize both sides equally. That was not only SANE's mantra but also that of SDS's fidgety and estranged parent group, the LID.

For its part, SDS thought the American violence far less defensible. We saw the VC as fighting for their national independence against a colossal and routinely brutal occupying force. For both sides to be equally guilty, the VC would have to have a few regiments operating out of Central Park. Not until U.S. troops' March 16, 1968, massacre of at least 237 Vietnamese civilians at the village of Son My and 347 at the nearby hamlet of My Lai did the American conscience—and SANE's—begin to awaken to the one-sided brutality of the war.[1] After Son My and My Lai, the idea that both sides were equally to blame began to lose its varnish even for the mainstream media.

But Gottlieb was relieved to hear from us that we needed just two things to support the November march. First, SANE would have to give me a spot on the program, allowing me to speak as the SDS president. And second, SANE would have to include the SDS slogan "Vietnam for the Vietnamese." Gottlieb readily agreed to these two conditions, whereupon SDS became once again a marcher on Washington against the war.

The bottom line was that neither side got what it wanted or wanted what it got. We SDSers didn't want to march on Washington again but felt compelled to do so. SANE didn't want us there but couldn't make the numbers it needed without us.

It seemed inane, this process of negotiating minute differentials in the balance of protest power when that power was so small compared to what we both faced. But inane or not, it led to my needing to give as strong a speech against the war as I could.

It was a moment that all-seeing fate had been preparing me for on the high-school weekends I had given over to what were called "original oratory" contests. I'd won the Ohio state championship in Columbus and then gone with my speech coach on an exhilarating overnight ride to the national competition at the University of Denver, where I had also won.

My speech had been "Peace or Freedom?" In a perfect prep to my subsequent role as a fiery radical orator, I argued that we should A-bomb the Soviets right now while all the nukes were still on our side. That was 1953. I was eighteen. By 1965 I was thirty. My politics had changed. What can I say?

I BEGAN DRAFTING the speech in Ann Arbor about three weeks before the march. Over the next week or so, as the pages began piling up, Beth chipped in with an always perceptive first read. I had the help of one of SDS's founders, Al Haber, who dropped by every few days with his wife, Barbara, to see how it was coming. I also got a lot of assistance from Todd Gitlin and his wife, Nanci, with whom I had many long talks about the war and SDS's efforts to build the movement against it.

The evening before the rally in Washington, at an all-night session at the Institute for Policy Studies, the draft was read aloud to a self-selected roomful of about thirty SDSers by SDS veteran Robb Burlage, a gentle, lanky, blond man with a soft drawl and a sharp mind. Burlage did such a good job that I remember thinking he ought to be the one to read it at the rally.

After maybe an hour or two of intense discussion, a smaller group adjourned to the Georgetown apartment of journalist Andy Kopkind to spend the night on tweaks, on into the next day, fondling its phrases like doting poets.

SANE had scheduled me at the very end of a program that also included Norman Thomas, Coretta King, Dr. Benjamin Spock, and California representative George E. Brown, the first congressman to speak against the war from the well of the House. Gottlieb told me later that I was put late in the program to hold the SDS crowd. An alternative theory saw it as a way to keep the insane things the SANE people were afraid I would say off the evening news.

The sun was sinking behind the Washington Monument when I

finally got my turn and tottered sleepily to the rostrum, a sheaf of ill-matched papers covered with arrows to inserts in my hand.

Many had already left, but it was still quite a sight to look out on. Estimating the size of crowds at such rallies is guesswork at best and politically sensitive besides. The sponsors and their friends see many where the other side sees few. The SANE estimate was fifty thousand. The Washington police said there were twenty thousand to thirty-five thousand. Even at the lower number, it's a lot of people to be looking your way and waiting for something.

There was nothing to do but read:

Seven months ago, at the April march on Washington, Paul Potter, then president of SDS, stood in approximately this spot and said that we must name the system that created and sustains the war in Vietnam—name it, describe it, analyze it, understand it, and change it.

The sound of one's voice blasting out through such gigantic amplifiers can never be anticipated, nor what it feels like as people begin to pay attention and you realize that you are saying things they've been wanting to hear.

The speech set out what SDS was saying about the war: that responsibility for it lay as much with the liberal establishment as with conservative militarists. Indeed, it was the lame state of American liberalism that the speech focused on:

The original commitment in Vietnam was made by President Truman, a mainstream liberal. It was seconded by President Eisenhower, a moderate liberal. It was intensified by President Kennedy, a flaming liberal. Think of the men who now engineer that war—those who study the maps, give the commands, push the buttons, and tally the dead: Bundy, McNamara, Rusk, Lodge, Goldberg, the president himself.

They are not moral monsters.

They are all honorable men.

They are all liberals.

But the speech also reached out to liberals, arguing that the war contradicted their own core national values:

Will you let your dreams be used? Will you be grudging apologists for the corporate state? Or will you help try to change it—not in the name of this or that blueprint or ism, but in the name of simple human decency and democracy and the vision that wise and brave men saw in the time of our own Revolution?

Then, in case I had failed to get the point across:

We radicals know the same history that you liberals know, and we can understand your occasional cynicism, exasperation, and even distrust. But we ask you to put these aside and help us risk a leap. Help us find enough time for the enormous work that needs doing here. Help us build. Help us shape the future in the name of plain human hope.

At the end of the speech I was something like a rock star. Gottlieb called me back to center stage and raised my hand in a sign of solidarity. SANE and SDS, the old liberals and the new radicals, were going to fight against the war together and not waste energy, as each had begun to do, fighting with each other.

The speech was subsequently printed by SDS without a title but often reprinted as "Let Us Shape the Future." In other printed versions, the word "shape" is rendered as "shake." "Shape" seems more like me, moderate that I am, "shake" more like SDS.

PART 2 | Soaring

6 | Build Not! Burn!
Champaign-Urbana, 1965

THE MEDIA RESPONSE to the "Build, Not Burn!" press conference that Paul Booth and I gave in Washington in October 1965 was by no means universally positive. *Time* of October 29, 1965, included a sneering cover piece on us titled, "The Vietniks: Self-Defeating Dissent," an article worth looking at again because it so well illustrates the prowar mind-set at this moment in the national debate. Said *Time*:

> The Vietniks are not going to be able to talk the U.S. out of Vietnam. They made their best try last spring, with a tide of so-called teach-ins, at a time when the approaching monsoon season in Vietnam was supposed to guarantee Communist victories; rather than submitting to defeat-by-weather, President Johnson simply stepped up the U.S. effort. For a while, the Vietnik decibel count dropped, only to soar up again when it became evident that the course of the war in Vietnam had turned and that, assuming only the will to stick it out, the U.S. and its South Vietnam ally were on the way to winning. This being the case, it seems just a bit improbable that President Johnson and his national constituency will suddenly succumb to the revived outcry of a thumbnail minority.

Time also quoted me at some length in the piece, doubtless confident that this would show how foolish we "Vietniks" were:

The Johnson administration, [Oglesby] says, "is all wet in its theories about the war in Vietnam. We don't think you can explain the South Vietnamese insurrection in terms of North Vietnamese support for it any more than you can explain the American Revolution in terms of its support from the French. And if Chinese belligerence is made a point of doctrine, if we really believe there is no hope for us with China, then let's go ahead and drop the bombs on Peking. But if we believe that a world in which these two powers get along is better than a world in which they fight, then we ought to exercise our imagination to find ways of repairing the bad relations that now exist between them."

These decades later, I'll stand by that. In fact, China was later to cite the antiwar movement as a reason for reopening contacts with the United States.[1] Much later down the road, as Bush *fils* was embracing Beijing as "a partner in diplomacy,"[2] I couldn't help but wonder if *Time* would be equally willing to stand by what it had said about China—and SDS—in 1965.

Truth to tell, it didn't hurt SDS at all to be assailed by the likes of *Time*. On the contrary, in view of *Time*'s imbecilic chauvinism, this was a badge of honor. It gave us a presence on the stage.

More painful by far were the misgivings expressed within SDS. An anonymous paper attacking Booth and me for our "Build, Not Burn!" performance at the National Press Club as well as my little dalliance with the Peace Corps was circulated under the title "Build Not! Burn!" The argument of this screed was that the "correct" answer to the continuing escalation of the war was not, as one of our slogans put it, to "bring the troops home," but rather to "bring the war home."

"Building is for carpenters!" we were told.

"This is no time to be timid!"

"How dare you play games with the Peace Corps!"

I thought the moderates among us had pretty good answers to such macho posturing:

First, SDS itself should not become the issue. And if there were simply no way to avoid it, all we needed to adduce was the "Port Huron

Statement," our commitment to participatory democracy, and our powerful mantra "People should be involved in making the decisions that affect their lives."

Second, collaterally, we should always keep the focus on what we were saying: the war is bad, racism is bad, poverty is bad, elitism is bad. We had arisen to take on anyone who disagreed with these simple postulates.

And third, there was no point in going farther to the left than we had to go to state our basic case. Some of us, yes, thought they could make a case for an open kind of socialism, but that was their own burden, not the burden of SDS. SDS, a democratic organization, was not a socialist one.

Another good reason for keeping the mass media's interest focused on what SDS had to say rather than on the organization itself was that we were experiencing great internal uncertainty about our structures of governance. This was borne of our explosive growth in membership, our sudden entry onto the stage of national politics, the awful growth of the war itself, and the rising anger of the black movement. The problems posed by these events were colossal, and we were young.

We lacked the infrastructure to handle what was happening. We had taken stage, as the actor in me would say, but beyond the basics of character, setting, and conflict, we didn't always know what we were supposed to do and often had to improvise our lines. Apart from explaining and debating the war in the voice of the teach-in, for example, some of us believed that we should be screaming about it in outrage. Sometimes we had to build bridges and sometimes we had to burn them down, and sometimes we couldn't tell the difference. We faced an internal chaos that in many ways mirrored the chaos we faced in the world around us.

So the SDS National Council called for a special back-to-the-drawing-boards conference before the regular NC meeting after Christmas, to be held that year at the Champaign-Urbana campus of the University of Illinois. The conference was attended by about 350 delegates from 66 chapters. It was our largest gathering ever.

It was an equally large failure, and not just because it didn't get anything done. In a delicious piece of prose published shortly afterward in the *Activist* magazine, SDSer Jonathan Eisen captured the spirit of this meeting perfectly:

> [It was] a morass, a labyrinth, a marathon of procedural amend-
> ments, non sequiturs, soul-searching and maneuvering, partying
> and arguing, plenaries which went nowhere, proposals unheeded,
> undebated, terminology which only the most in of the in-group
> could comprehend, much less care about, and a few who were too
> far gone to participate in anything but getting girls.[3]

And it wasn't just funny. Angry slurs flew back and forth. Someone accused the Texas delegation of racism, and it responded by walking out en masse.[4]

The NC that convened right after this conference was more sub-dued—or perhaps shell-shocked—but still could get nothing done. It was dominated by the old-guard community organizers, who operated under the philosophical leadership of Tom Hayden. In the face of the escalating war and the rising popular uneasiness about it, the Hayden bloc, the Economic Research and Action Project (ERAP), led SDS to reaffirm that its major task was to organize the white urban poor around community issues as a way to exert pressure on the Democratic Party. The ERAPers even attacked and defeated a proposal that SDS should formally call for the immediate withdrawal of U.S. troops from Vietnam, sneering that antiwar organizers were in the grips of a "Vietnam hang-up." Under Hayden's absentee leadership, this NC adopted a statement saying that "we should be prepared to reject activities that mobilize thousands of people but do not build constituencies." This statement continued:

> We should be prepared to argue with the antiwar movement that
> the real lever for change in America is a domestic social movement.
> And that the movement to end the war in Vietnam cannot end that
> war. Finally, we should also say that radicals have more important
> priorities than working simply to end the war.[5]

Hayden was not at this NC because, ironically enough, he was preparing to leave on December 28, along with Yale professor Staughton Lynd and the Communist Party theoretician Herbert Aptheker, for a nine-day trip to North Vietnam.

I thought this trip was a bad idea and had spoken quietly against it to several members of the leadership, including a dismissive Hayden. Maybe it was my blue-badge sensibility acting up. But here we were trying to get middle Americans to understand that the antiwar movement was not part of a Communist plot, that our criticism of Johnson's escalation policy was based solidly on core American values and had nothing whatsoever to do with the CP, and yet Hayden and Lynd had picked this moment to go to Communist North Vietnam in the company of one of the CP's principal theoreticians. If this be Red-baiting, make the most of it, but I felt that this was simply not the time to entangle the issue of the war with the issue of the CP's civil liberties and to hand our critics a way to put us on the defensive about our motives. It seemed to me lousy chess.

I turned out to be wrong about this. Nothing was ever made of the trio's having visited "the other side." Indeed, Lynd wrote a powerful essay about the trip, concluding justly that "no amount of military power can bring this dreadful war to an end."[6]

But Hayden's influence within SDS was still exerted through the ERAP bloc, and the ERAP bloc was still opposed to SDS's growing preoccupation with the war.

Thus, our Christmas NC rejected a proposal from the University of Michigan chapter calling for marches on army bases and induction centers. It rejected a proposal that we begin concerted protests against university war research. It rejected a proposal that we condemn student deferments as an unfair privilege of the middle class. The best the NC could do was to adopt a "freedom draft" campaign based loosely on our "Build, Not Burn!" statement.[7]

The NC's refusal to see that the war had become the preemptive issue of the day reflected the founding organizers' worries about how to remain active when they had left the campus to join the world. How could SDS escape the playpen of student politics? Should we rename ourselves Movement for a Democratic Society? Or perhaps create a new organization with that name? One group actually tried to do this, but the project failed.

And taken narrowly, the fear that SDS was becoming a single-issue voice was legitimate. The idea from the beginning was that SDS would offer an inclusive critique of American political life, addressing domestic as well as foreign-policy issues and trying to show the interconnections between militarism and poverty, between imperialism and racism, between superstate elitism and the two-party system. It was fair to worry that our growing hang-up on Vietnam might become self-destructive.

To add to the turmoil of our Christmas meeting was the emergence of what soon became known as the women's liberation movement. Many SDS women had been nursing an anger at their treatment in the organization, at being too often expected to assume roles that mirrored those of the larger culture. Women answered the phones, sent out the mailings, did the laundry, comforted the male heroes. By the end of 1965, their feelings about this had become raw.

So a workshop titled "Women in the Movement" was assembled at Urbana, the first of its kind in the sixties and off-limits to men. Many men were upset to be excluded and complained that this was a badly timed and destructive move. If SDS women were having problems, why not just quietly tell the men about it offstage? Why choose a moment like this to start bitching about, well, trivial complaints?

I wish I could say I'd been above this reaction. The women were right, and I knew it because Beth told me so. But was this the right time to make an issue out of gender? Didn't SDS have enough problems? Couldn't the women find quieter ways to voice their grievances? This was the era of the Pill and the liberation of women's sexuality, and SDS's breezily philandering studs were quite happy to support the pharmacies in this because, to put it technically, it made it easier to get laid. The one-night stand became all but presupposed as a part of our lifestyle. As long as that was what women's liberation meant, the men were fine with it.

But sexism was real. It was as destructive within the movement as outside of it. Once it had been recognized, it would not quietly wait for a more convenient time. By the end of 1965, women's liberation was already an irresistible force within SDS, whether the SDS men were prepared to cope with it or not.

And we were not. When it was all over and SDS lay writhing in its own gore, you could easily conclude that what brought us under the ax was precisely our inability to make the war part of a broader political agenda that included sexism as well as state repression, racism as well as poverty, the general corruption of the nation's political institutions as well as SDS's internal flaws.

AS SDS MET in Illinois after Christmas that year, 1965, there were almost two hundred thousand U.S. troops in Vietnam. Who could have guessed that this level was still to be increased by more than a quarter million more? That nearly fifty-eight thousand Americans and about three million Vietnamese and maybe a million Cambodians would be killed before it was over? That our troops would not start coming home until 1973? That for all the violence we laid on that country, Saigon would actually fall to "the other side" in 1975? That the cash bill for the whole U.S. adventure would total more than $120 billion?[8]

But what was clear by the end of 1965 was that SDS could not continue with its original strategy of organizing the white poor around economic issues. Whether we liked it or not—and many of us did not like it at all—the war had become the preemptive issue facing the nation, and students in particular. And students had no choice but to oppose it. As of SDS's Champaign-Urbana NC, the war had turned everyone's world upside down.

It did not help that many of us had grown sure about this time that we were being secretly penetrated by hostile government forces. Those who wanted to talk about this and try to conceive a collective response to it were typically dismissed as "paranoid." Even Arthur Miller was scoffed at when he warned the first teach-in at the University of Michigan in 1965, "You mustn't forget that the FBI is among you."

Freedom of Information Act and Privacy Act suits have established since then that this was not paranoia but simple realism. Precursors of the FBI's Cointelpro: New Left, the CIA's MH Chaos, and various provocateur actions by army intelligence's MI5 were already up and running. But SDS waited until 1968 to try to do something about it, and by then it was too late.

The stage was thus set for the toxic blend of road rage and comic book Marxism that would ultimately be expressed in the self-destructive violence of the Weathermen. How brilliant of us! We would cope with the FBI's attempt to destroy us by destroying ourselves!

BESIDES THOSE ON SDS's right wing who wanted us to go on organizing poor people's rent strikes, voices also emerged on our left wing to attack the "Build, Not Burn!" statement, despite its evident political success, because it wasn't fierce enough.

Many felt that the moment called for outrage. The thrust of the anonymous "Build Not! Burn!" counterstatement was that this was no time to try improving the evil empire but to hit it with everything we had. Neither the subtler nor the cruder form of the Booth-Oglesby rejoinder to this did anything to satisfy our critics, the subtler form being that to hit the empire with everything we had meant hitting it with its own broken promises because we didn't have much else, and the cruder being that getting violent would only make it easier for the prowar side to demonize us. To most SDSers, it seemed that what we needed to do in that confusing and difficult situation was to hold the course as well as we could. We needed to keep on trying to build a middle-class, campus-based, media-savvy youth movement against the war. We needed to use the moment to assert our democratic, populist ideals, to keep rebuilding our always shaky relationship with the civil-rights movement, and to start grappling with the demands of the emerging women's liberation movement. Yes, we had a lot to do.

Already attacked by the old guard for drawing SDS away from community work, we moderate Vietniks now came under fire from the other side of SDS for not opposing the war more militantly. There was something about the situation that put greater militancy on people's minds, that gave the more militant SDSers a glamorous panache and lent their demand for counterviolence a color of proportionality to the magnitude of the challenges we faced. The militant among us seemed serious. The nonviolent seemed to be caught up in a politics of children's games.

It would be another two years or so before SDS's ultimate venture into terrorism would come full bloom, but you could see it budding through the whole wild period from 1966 through 1968. And 1968 was the year of both the FBI's Cointelpro: New Left and the birth of SDS's Weathermen. Given that provocateurism is the favorite tactic for secret police attacks on dissent, we would be foolish not to wonder if the Weathermen and Cointelpro might be in some way connected, sharing a set of common causes. For me at least, Cointelpro and the Weathermen seem like twins, born of the same womb. I knew many of the Weathermen intimately and cannot bring myself to believe they were any other than honest if misguided militants. But it was they who planted and husbanded the seed of violence that gave the cops the excuse they were looking for to attack SDS full out.

This seed was in the ground by the end of 1965, though it would not come full blossom for nearly another three years. I still can only guess what drives it, having rarely seen violence close up and having never been in the least tempted by it either personally or politically. I can't pretend to know what made so many of our best and brightest minds, if hardly our most ripened ones, decide that it was "time to raise the level of domestic violence." Or that it might even be "time to pick up the gun," the slogan that migrated from the African Mau Mau to Malcolm X to the Black Panthers to the street-gang white Lefties who called themselves the Up Against the Wall Motherfuckers, and thence to the SDS Weathermen. As politics, this was a wretched idea. But as theater it was terrific. And it said a lot about how people felt.

Part of its appeal, I think, was simply that many of the most active among us had become impatient with mass rallies. These had become predictable occasions where a group of students, teachers, and church people would congregate in a public place, listen to a few speeches, chant a few slogans, then go home to see how it played on TV. We thought a little more militancy might tell the world of our rising anger, give the government a more tempting opportunity to overreact, and get the mass media interested again.

But we also realized that a formal SDS call for more militant protests would expose us to open attacks by various arms of federal and local police, which were already massing at our gates. Such tactics would also alienate the support we had begun to win in the mass media and the middle class.

Naively enough, I thought we should avoid that. I thought we might win our case against the war with the American people, steadily organizing a new kind of Left based on democratic values and within the framework of the Constitution. And that we would stop the war, help put an end to racism and poverty, crush male chauvinism, and then grow old together singing folk songs with Pete Seeger and dancing to the Beatles.

I could never have imagined in 1965 the oncoming decade, a decade that would include the violent implosion of SDS at the moment of its greatest strength as well as Johnson's decision not to run for reelection, the Democrats' nomination of the dovish senator George McGovern, the Republicans' landslide victory behind a cynical hawk like Richard Nixon, the escalation of the air war to Cambodia, then Nixon's scandal and virtual impeachment in the Wagnerian crisis of Watergate. And only then, at long, long last, the end of the war.

Who could have foreseen this conflagration in 1965? And that the SDS, which had wanted only to build, not burn, would be burning in the middle of it?

7 | Great Debates and Petty Spats

Salt Lake City and Chicago, 1966–67

IN MY FIFTEEN MONTHS since giving up my theatrical ambitions to take on the role of SDS president, I had spoken my new lines on dozens of stages, from New York to Los Angeles and in Puerto Rico, Canada, France, Italy, Cambodia, Laos, South Vietnam, and Japan. As 1967 began, I had tours scheduled for England, Scotland, Sweden, Denmark, and another to Japan. Soon there would be a trip to forbidden Cuba. I had moved with my family from Sunnyside to not-so-sunnyside in Ann Arbor, then to Yellow Springs, Ohio, then to San Francisco, and then, sans family, to Cambridge, Massachusetts. Being in the movement seemed to mean simply being always in movement. Home came to feel like a waiting room.

My reviews were generally good. I had even become a kind of star talking head. But it was not a good way to live.

This was hard for all of us and close to catastrophic for my family, as Beth and our kids struggled by themselves while I was either off making big-deal speeches or alone in my study writing big-deal articles. Beth and I had reached a kind of limit even before SDS took over my management, and the changes my movement life brought with it didn't do us any good, even though the new uncertainties kept us together a while longer because we didn't want to confront our kids with still greater confusion by splitting up against such a chaotic background. I had turned away from what was happening to my marriage and family because I had no idea of how to deal with it and had so many political things always on my mind. I had let my actor's ego take over my life. Scene by scene, I had lost myself in this splendidly demanding new role in which I had been cast, in these words of protest that I was called on to extemporize within the powerful themes by which SDS defined itself: participatory democracy, civil rights, antiwar. What actor would not be excited by the chance to take center stage in such a role? I could not have been more confident that my comrade cast members and I were saying things that needed to be said, but I never had the least idea of what would happen next.

The three years from the fall of 1965 through the fall of 1968 were my most exhausting and invigorating time, the time when the pressure to perform was greatest and when I had the strongest feeling that I was doing what I should be doing and doing it more or less right. I knew how to act the part—even, as a former student of Elia Kazan at the Actors Studio, how to become my role. All those days in high school and college speech contests and in the plays of Shakespeare and Arthur Miller were paying off—strangely, but for real. I had learned not to vocalize my pauses and how to let the silences speak.

There was an enlivening quality to it wholly at odds with its bloody subject matter. Pro- and antiwar voices quarreled all the time about the American body count versus the Vietnamese body count, and the prize went to the side with the more terrible numbers. The antiwar side won that awful prize over and over again. It was almost child's play. The prowar side had the mass media, a default patriotism, and a barely conscious fear of the government, a fear that was always just enough to awaken the whisper "Be quiet or you'll get in trouble with the Big Guys." But as to real arguments, a grasp of the history of the war, the economy of it, the strategy and tactics of it, the prowar side never had a thing but the chesty bravado of the brass hats and bureaucrats whose careers had come to depend on the system of lies that kept the war alive.

There was an excitement to this duel that I had not experienced before. The most gratifying scene out of those three years of watching the warriors tilt against windmills was the one played out on October 7, 1967, in Salt Lake City, in a debate I participated in organized by a joint committee of prowar and antiwar groups at the University of Utah and sponsored by the university, the Mormon Church, radio station KSL, and what the FBI report calls "other reputable organizations." This was the first and the last time that U.S. senators stooped to defend the war in a public debate with its critics.

Speaking on behalf of the war that evening were two Republican superhawks, Wyoming's senator Gale McGee, a twelve-year veteran of the Senate and an influential member of Johnson's foreign-policy brain trust, and Utah's senator Wallace Bennett, an archconservative with close business ties to the Pentagon.

McGee and Bennett had insisted that the topic be phrased to give them the affirmative side and thus, in standard debate format, the first and last speeches. Affirmative sides in formal debates usually argue for changing something, and negative sides for keeping it as it is. Normally phrased, the debate that evening would have been about getting out of Vietnam or not. But to satisfy McGee and Bennett, it was about staying in or not: "Resolved: that the United States should continue its support of the South Vietnamese government." So just to get the first and last speeches, McGee and Bennett ceded to our side the opportunity to ask *which* South Vietnamese government and thus make the point that palace coup followed palace coup in Saigon with the regularity of streetcars. And there was no last speech anyway, because the debate was followed immediately by a vigorous Q-and-A session with the audience.

I still wonder why McGee and Bennett agreed to this debate at all. No senator had done so before, and none would again. Maybe something territorial in their hawk's blood aroused them to rally against an opposition they no doubt visualized as the ineffective peacenik dove, fluttering with a bit too much freedom in their proud western skies. One of the debate's organizers on the Utah faculty told me that McGee had accepted the invitation first and then coaxed Bennett into taking part by telling him, "If we can't beat 'em in Salt Lake City, Wallace, the jig is up."

My partner in the debate was Robert Scheer, the high-energy young editor of *Ramparts* magazine, an independent, often impudent radical monthly published in San Francisco. At a time when it was the movement's style to dress in ragged jeans, Scheer delighted in British haber-dashery. That evening he wore a beautifully tailored, dark brown, three-piece wool suit with a red silk tie and pocket handkerchief, his hair shoulder length but well barbered. We were a movement whose patron saint was Demosthenes, but Scheer could make the rest of us look tongue-tied. His platform style differed from mine in that he never tried to thunder the way I sometimes did, but he could make Oscar Wilde seem a country bumpkin. He was quiet, cutting, and urbane, with a gift for quick, barbed asides. The FBI had designated him, like me, a "key activist."

I wasn't as glossy as Scheer, but I eschewed my normal blue work shirt and jeans and pulled out my old Bendix uniform of gray flannel suit, button-collared white shirt, and dark blue tie. I even got a haircut and wore clean underwear. Everything as in the old days but my blue badge of clearance. Compared to Scheer and me, the senators looked rumpled.

The debate was staged in the campus ballroom, which had a grace-fully domed ceiling, a state-of-the-art acoustics system, and a feeling of intimacy despite its huge size. The place was filled to overflowing that night, with standees crowded along the walls and many in the lobby lis-tening over a PA system, because the presence of the two senators had made it a special occasion and the faculty had encouraged their stu-dents to attend. The FBI report put attendance at 150 to 200,[1] but this is an order-of-magnitude copying error. There were more than 200 stand-ing in the hallway outside. The president of the university, Dr. J. D. Williams, was the moderator.

The senators presented a far-right version of the official picture of the war: We were defending South Vietnam against Soviet-inspired aggression from North Vietnam. We were fighting for the freedom of the South Vietnamese as well as for our own security against Communist expansion. If we lost in Vietnam, we would probably lose the Cold War. Our military forces were making progress. The nation should support our warriors.

Scheer's main theme was the deceptive way in which our government had escalated the war, constantly promising that there was, as Senator McGee said in his cliché-rich opening speech, "light at the end of the tunnel" while at the same time sending more troops and dropping more bombs. It was from Scheer that evening that I first heard the rejoinder that the light at the end of this tunnel was a locomotive heading our way. Most telling, he detailed from a professional journalist's perspective the ways in which the major media pliantly followed the Pentagon in consistently overstating American progress. A befuddled Bennett seemed to be hearing this for the first time. Scheer said, "I'm sure we are all eager to hear Senator Bennett's current excuse—pardon me, his explanation—for the administration's apparently systematic efforts to deceive the American public about the war."

My role was to make the case that our enemy in Vietnam was an authentic popular rebellion that had arisen in the cause of national independence against a long series of corrupt puppet governments controlled by the French, first, and now by the United States. I drew a parallel between what the prowar side was saying about Vietnamese nationalists and what the British had said about George Washington and the Sons of Liberty two centuries before.

The debate stayed polite through the ten-minute presentations but grew sharp in the Q-and-A session that followed, when Bennett made the mistake of trying to bully Scheer. With more than a touch of arrogance, Bennett said, "How can you pretend to be better informed about Vietnam than members of the United States Senate?"

Scheer answered, "Perhaps it's because I don't get my information from the National Association of Manufacturers."

This got a titter and moved moderator Williams to step in. "Your remark is inappropriate, Mr. Scheer, since Senator Bennett is a past president of that organization. I suggest that you apologize for that remark."

Scheer stood at the podium with a surprised smile on his face. Then he said with a little bow, "You are perfectly correct, sir. I should have said that understanding the Vietnam War must be difficult for someone who finds the Senate chamber such a great place for naps."

This got a big roar from the audience because Bennett had recently made the news for falling asleep at his desk in the Senate and snoring loudly during an important debate on funding the war.

Bennett wasn't used to being sassed this way. The audience response was our first clue that we might be winning.

My big moment came a bit later when I asked McGee, "If the Vietnam War is a legal war, Senator, please tell us when and by whom it was declared, and on what legal authority. And if the war has *not* been legally declared, then why is the Senate allowing the president to invoke war powers to fight it?"

McGee seemed uncomfortable with the question. This might have been either because he didn't know the answer or, more likely, because he knew the president was ignoring the law. So he sought refuge behind scoundrel patriotism.

"This is a time, Mr. Oglesby, when true patriots will support our men and women in Vietnam. I think you owe them an apology for the things you've said tonight about their mission."

The format prohibited rejoinders, but I had heard too much of that kind of crap by then. Of all the big-league proponents of the war, McGee was the quickest to drape the hall with flags and fill the air with fifes and drums. And the whole point of this debate was to cut through that. So I was quick to answer McGee's call for an apology by compounding my crime.

"Senator McGee," I said, not waiting for the moderator, "if you are truly so ignorant of this war that you can't answer the most basic question about its legal standing, then how can you justify your long string of votes to fund it?"

McGee and I glared at each other. There was a moment of uncertain silence in the hall. I wondered if I had been too blunt. Then the applause erupted like a blast. McGee looked stunned. I probably did, too. Scheer said afterward that it had been the deciding moment of the debate.

At the beginning of the debate the audience had given the senators a rousing welcome, with only polite applause for Scheer and me. The debate had been long and intense, with vigorous audience participation in the Q-and-A period. It had been scheduled to run from seven to ten-thirty, but when moderator Williams began to adjourn on time, the crowd shouted for more. Finally at twelve-thirty Williams stepped in to declare it over. Now it was McGee and Bennett who got the perfunctory applause, and for Scheer and me there was a long, standing ovation.

The worst of the war was still to come, but by McGee's standard, the Utah standard, the debate was over: two of the hawks' big guns had gotten shot down in flames in Salt Lake City. As even the FBI's inform- ant reported, "Oglesby and Scheer presented a much better case than did those who spoke in favor of the United States position in Vietnam."[2] The informant accompanied a group of us after the event "to a private home in Salt Lake City where the case against the United States policy in Vietnam was discussed until 4:00 A.M. on October 8, 1967."

So in one of the more conservative states of the Union, the children of the middle classes were starting to pay real attention to the war, and the more they learned, the less they liked what they saw. And McGee was right. After Utah, the jig was up.

BUT THE REAL QUESTION was whether winning the debate mattered very much. Despite its growing unpopularity, the war kept getting big- ger and worse. Working-class people remained committed to "support- ing our troops," and the more critical middle classes seemed to have no way to express their growing doubts. Middle America wanted out of Vietnam but could not decide whether the best exit path lay to the left or to the right, through truce and negotiations or through bombing Vietnam back to the Stone Age.

So a kind of tortured emptiness was opening up in the American cen- ter between the need to win simply because we were fighting and the need not to fight hard enough to do that.

A bitter acrimony fell upon the big-league hawks and doves. The hawks' heavy hitters were Senator John Stennis; the same Senator McGee of the Armed Services Committee whom Scheer and I wasted in Salt Lake City; the war's operational commanders, General William Westmoreland and Admiral Ulysses Grant Sharp; Secretary of State

Dean Rusk; and the most vocal of the hawks, LBJ adviser Walt Whitman Rostow, "whose saber rattled," writes the historian Stanley Karnow, "throughout Washington."[3]

The doves flocked behind Senator J. William Fulbright, chairman of the Foreign Relations Committee, and the State Department's W. Averell Harriman. Behind these doves, as Karnow reports, "were some lower-ranking generals in Vietnam who had learned the futility of the conflict from direct experience."[4]

Johnson appears to have embodied this conflict in that he saw the war as a troublesome distraction from his dreams of making the Great Society. "Bomb, bomb, bomb—that's all they know," he reportedly was saying privately.[5] Maybe our street chant was reaching him: "Hey, hey, LBJ! How many kids did you kill today?"

Yet he was always more strongly pushed by the hawks than restrained by the doves, constantly opting for still more bombing despite the fact that it was getting nowhere. A 1967 CIA summary of the previous year's air force campaign told him all he should have needed to know. Hundreds of bridges had been destroyed, reported the CIA, but they had soon been either bypassed or rebuilt. Thousands of transport vehicles had been destroyed, but supply traffic was still moving. About three-quarters of the country's storage tanks had been destroyed, but there were no shortages of fuel. And most important, North Vietnam's morale was still high.[6]

A senior assistant to Secretary of Defense McNamara, Alain Enthoven, was telling his boss exactly what he could have heard from the antiwar movement that was marching under his windows at the Pentagon, that what the United States was up against in Vietnam was not a Communist plot against the Free World, but rather, as Enthoven put it in a briefing document, "the strongest political current in the world today—nationalism."[7]

But Johnson could not hear this. Military and political interests were colliding. Neither side seemed strong enough to win or weak enough to lose. What to do?

Johnson's uncertainty gripped the whole country, which was becoming increasingly polarized.

We experienced this tension in the movement. We knew we had to do something more, but there was no consensus about what that was. Some of us were starting to look for answers on the edges. Maybe, to make peace in Vietnam, we had to make war in the United States? We had begun by saying "Bring the troops home." Now some of us began to say "Bring the war home."

There was always enormous admiration in the movement for Che Guevara and Fidel Castro and the July 26 movement that had grouped in the Sierra Maestra in the days of the iron-fisted Fulgencio Batista, only a few dozen strong, and announced to themselves that the days of the dictator were numbered.

I shared this admiration. I had even imagined that, had I been a Cuban of the 1950s, I might have been part of that small band of revolutionaries. Or in a similar dream, that I might have been one of the Sons of Liberty in our own nation's prerevolutionary time, writing fiery broadsides against the Redcoats with a musket on my back.

But I always saw that as an option for another time, another place. I could not believe that some of us were angry enough—romantic enough—to put guerrilla warfare on the SDS agenda. Sure, I had always known that there were people to my left in SDS, people far more militant than I, whether driven by temperament or creed. But I had always felt securely backed up by the mainstream SDS membership.

Now I was astonished to hear that I was under attack here and there by some of our key activists for taking what they saw as too timid a position. Some of them were passing around a tape of a talk I had given at Ohio's Miami University on February 6, 1966, and were upset by a number of things I had said there, such as the following:

"The New Left more than anything else is an attempt to take seriously the clichés of the American political experience, the aspirations for all people embodied in what we call the American Dream.

"The New Left is trying to ask, Can democracy work? The New Left is trying to ask questions about real power at all levels of government, not simply symbolic power. Who has real power in America? Where and how did they get it? What are they doing with it? Is this good for the people, or bad for the people?"

Said one of my SDS critics, "This is the kind of crap you can get from any big-party politician."

Compounding my sin, I had ended that speech with an appeal to the conservative campus group Young Americans for Freedom, to join with the SDS chapter in a campaign against organized crime in the Oxford ghetto. It was probably my good luck that YAF didn't take me up on it since, I later realized, not many in SDS thought the idea a bright one. Those who were starting to talk in Marxese called it one of my "errors."

But it didn't stop me. If it was an error, it was one I kept on making. I even put it into print at the end of my contribution to a two-part book *Containment and Change,* published in early 1967. The book had grown out of a "dialogue" with Professor Richard Shaull at Union Theological Seminary in February 1966. Shaull, whose specialty was the political history of Protestant theology, had recently discovered two historians who rang my bells and had talked about them a lot at the Union session. One was the liberal William Appleman Williams, and the other was the conservative Murray Rothbard. They were both libertarians, and that is what I had begun calling myself.

I still do. Libertarianism is a stance that allows one to speak to the right as well as to the left, which is what I was always trying to do. It was a venture in which Shaull had strongly encouraged me. So I had picked cherries from both Williams and Rothbard, favorably quoting a number of conservative critics of American imperialism. Why go to rightists on this theme when there were so many leftists to choose from? Because you made the strongest case against the war if you could show that both right and left should oppose it.

It was this approach that made me happy to quote General Douglas MacArthur: "Our country is now geared to an arms economy which was bred in an artificially induced psychosis of war hysteria and nurtured upon an incessant propaganda of fear."

And Ohio's senator Robert A. Taft: "Our Christian ideals cannot be exported to other lands by dollars and guns. We cannot practice might and force abroad and retain freedom at home."

To my mind, such statements were powerful weapons for our side. They gave us a cleaver that cut right through the Red-baiting charges that the prowar side was so hot to throw at us. They helped us get to the real issue without first having to peel a red star off our faces.

I made my centrist libertarianism as explicit as I could on regular occasions, and I did not think I was cheating on SDS in doing this. SDS's manifesto, the "Port Huron Statement," called to the right as well as to the left. That was what I liked most about SDS when I first met it. Its direct appeal to the populist spirit was for all lovers of democracy: "People should be involved in making the decisions that affect their lives."

BERNARDINE DOHRN, who would soon become an SDS national secretary and after that a leader of the Weathermen, had seen a transcript of my talk at Union. She kept quiet about her misgivings until *Containment and Change* came out that fall. But when I was staying with her in New York a little later, she confronted me.

"Carl, you're good on the war," she said, "but sometimes I'm not sure I know where you're coming from."

"Well, Ann Arbor, Kent, Akron, Kalamazoo."

We'd just had a nice time out with some friends and were back at her apartment, sipping an exotic tea. I felt tired and relaxed and I didn't want an argument with her.

"Then let me put it a little more plainly," she said. "Do you consider yourself a revolutionary or a failed liberal?"

I had to laugh. "Isn't that a distinction without a difference?" I said.

She didn't smile.

"And here in your book," she said, picking up a copy with a bookmark in it, "where you say that the New Left and the Old Right are 'morally and politically coordinate.' I'm confused."

"I mean that honest conservatives should oppose the war."

"Where will your honest conservatives be," she said, "when the barricades go up?"

"Barricades?"

"Come on, Carl," she said. "You know what I'm talking about."

"BD, I don't have the foggiest."

"Then let me help," she said. "Some of us are starting to wonder whose side you're going to be on when, you know, we get down to the nitty-gritty, so I thought I would just ask you."

I shook my head, trying to clear it, and sat up. "Why is this happening?"

"Terry Robbins noticed this strange little passage in a recent speech of yours," she said, reaching for a copy of the SDS newsletter. "Apparently, you actually said this," she said, and started reading: "'Inasmuch as the antiwar movement has never been able to dream up a threat which it might really make good on, this fiercer face-making has remained basically a kind of entertainment.'"

She looked up. "'Entertainment,' Carl? 'Face-making'? Is that what you think of your comrades?"

The flummoxed choose conventional defenses, so I said, "You're taking my words out of context."

But she was ready for that. "Context?" she said with an incredulous smile. "You want context? Here's your next sentence, and you're still talking about the movement: 'The main idea has always been to persuade higher authority—Congress, the UN, Bobby Kennedy—to do something. Far from calling higher authority into question, these wildly militant demonstrations actually dramatize and even exaggerate its power.'" She gave me a frowning, disbelieving look.

I didn't want this, but it was happening, and I had to rally myself. "BD, I was just trying to say that our threats of violence are really a kind of frantic call for help," I said. "I was trying to say that nobody's really planning to start making bombs."

"That's what you believe? Fair enough. So I'm asking: Where are you going to be when bombs start going off?"

"What's this about bombs going off? Isn't this a metaphor?"

"When it comes to fighting real battles against the empire," she said, "where do you think you're going to be?"

"Fighting? You mean like, what, with bombs and guns? Blowing things up? Shooting people?"

She just looked at me, very straight-faced. "This is what you refuse to see," she said. "We can't keep doing what we're doing without at some point encountering the armed power of the state. Okay? If we mean to continue the struggle, we have to be willing to pick up the gun."

"What gun? Who has guns?"

She stared at me and shook her head slightly. She said softly, sadly, "How could I tell *you* who has guns?"

It took me a few seconds to get a glimmer of what she meant. Was there a secret SDS group that I was not a part of? Within that group, were people thinking about "armed struggle"?

She waited, but I had no idea what to say. She went on in a soft voice.

"What began three years ago as a protest against a war," she said, "is changing into a resistance against a police state. Okay? We are facing a new kind of class warfare. The United States government clearly represents a heavily militarized plutocracy. You've made this point yourself in some of your stuff. As this plutocracy continues to escalate the war in the face of huge public dissent, our leadership challenge is to move from protest to resistance."

"No, Bernardine," I said, trying to focus another picture of what we should do in the hope that I could persuade her that she was wrong. Forget about it. BD was a great listener, so it could take you a while to realize you weren't getting anywhere. But she probably felt the same way about me. And as she had made her speech, I had to make mine.

"Our challenge, BD, is to move from protest to bigger protest. To turn more and more people against the war, not to turn some few of us into supermilitants. I think the comrades who have been talking about violence are just scared of talking to grown-ups. They just want to keep talking to young people, who are easily tempted by the romance of revolution. But as for dealing with cops, yeah, it's hard to know what to do. Our very success has put us in a tough, tricky situation. But we are definitely not going to cope with the threat of repression by handing the cops a hunting license on a silver platter. Okay? I'm done."

She seemed to listen carefully, her head tilted a little back, her eyes on mine.

"Listen, this is really basic. The key question about these grown-ups who are slowly turning against the war is, How much time do they have? Another is what they'll be willing to do about it. I think you've forgotten what you said in your SANE speech. 'We are dealing with a system,' you said, 'that does not want to change and is not going to change itself.' Do you want to take that back?"

"No."

"So how many options do you think that leaves us?"

"Comrade, I don't know any more than you do. But violence is not an option, it's a surrender. We've got to try to make democracy work."

Her smile was a cross between pity and condescension.

"Okay, BD, I know how that sounds. But if we can't make the law and the country's traditions and values and public opinion work for us, we're dog food. I mean, if our cause is going to be decided by guns, then we're going to lose. Okay? Do you deny this? There is no way that SDS can win a shoot-out with the palace guard. Am I getting through? No way."

"That depends on how you define winning, doesn't it?"

"All right, where's your *Webster's*?"

She flipped her hair and looked off.

How could I not be getting through to her about this? It seemed so simple. For all their brave rhetoric about "smashing the imperialist state" and "bringing the war home" and "picking up the gun," Bernardine and her comrades in the emerging Action Faction, the group that would evolve into the Weather Bureau, were only splitting SDS away from its strength and steering it into disaster.

"If it comes to shooting at people," I said, "or any variation of that, listen, BD, count me out. I hope I'm not telling you something new, but gunplay is just what the other side wants."

Quickly she said, "Is this how the July Twenty-sixth Movement or the Viet Cong looked on superior American firepower? With, you know, fear and trembling?"

"For probably a dozen really solid reasons," I said in my most professorial tone, a bad mask for my growing dread, "Johnson's America is not like Batista's Cuba or Diem's South Vietnam. SDS is not like the July Twenty-sixth Movement or the VC. We are not in the kind of situation that gave rise to Castro or Ho Chi Minh. We will make a fatal mistake if we try to emulate them. To try any such thing is to walk right into disaster."

She had put up both hands half through this. "Stop it, Carl. The point is not to emulate the Cubans or the Vietnamese but to follow their example. They faced superior firepower at every stage of their growth, just as we will, and they were still able to keep the empire off-balance and to move steadily closer to victory. We have to face our own disadvantages in the same spirit of ingenuity and determination, okay? And with the same willingness to act as enemies of the state. Do you hear this? We are not frustrated liberals, Carl. We are enemies of the state. Okay? *Enemies of the state.*"

We stared at each other. "Sounds like a rock band," I said.

She didn't laugh. Her face was not hard but set. I figured I had to keep trying. I said, "Violence, my friend, is exactly what the reactionaries want from us."

"Incorrect," she said with a little smile. "The hawks and their liberal allies want an America that's willing to accept the war even if it doesn't like it. Sure, they'll permit a few antiwar rallies to show the other tyrannies of the world how irrelevant free speech is. Okay? But they don't want American blood to be shed in American streets. The hawks do not want a turbulent America, an America terrorized—yes, terrorized—by the threat of violence from the revolutionary left. So the challenge for SDS leadership is to bring the war home. Okay so far? To accomplish this transition, SDS leaders will have to work in difficult circumstances. Some of us have been wondering if you're ready for that. For one thing, you've got Beth and your kids to think about. So there it is. What do you say?"

I should have said she made some interesting points and that I would have to think it all over but that I was sleepy now and wanted to go to bed.

But I couldn't stop. "So you're saying that SDS should turn itself into a terrorist organization to provoke the government into an overreaction, all on a gamble that this will embarrass the government somehow and pick us up some sympathy points with the middle class."

"Carl, God, this is not about the American middle class. It's about the Third World. It's not about the liberal reform of the empire. It's about the revolution. And whether we like it or not, that's the choice we in the mother country have to confront. Okay? Either we become revolutionaries opposed to the empire or we remain frustrated liberals hoping for a few cosmetic reforms. What don't you get? I'm simply asking if you're ready to be a revolutionary."

"And what if I think we should all be frustrated liberals?"

She shrugged. "Your choice."

I was as exasperated with her as she with me. "The only power we've got, BD," I pleaded, "lies in the credibility of our commitment to democracy and nonviolence. If we abandon that, we abandon everything that gives us any strength at all."

She snickered. "Sometimes you talk like a tour guide."

"Eat it, BD. The day SDS takes up terrorism," I said, with a hand on her shoulder to make her look at me, "it's dead!"

"So what?" she said quietly.

It stopped me. I said, "You don't care if SDS dies?"

She sighed. "Please try to listen," she said, holding up both hands and speaking softly and slowly. "SDS was created as an organization of protest. Okay? Partly because SDS did a good job, the need for protest has changed into a need for resistance. Okay? This requires a new kind of SDS, maybe a whole new organization, for a new phase of the struggle. Is this clear?"

"What, so we can all be outlaws?"

"Outlaws?" she said calmly, smiling slightly and seeming to relax. "Not bad. But the correct term is revolutionaries."

"You really mean this, don't you?"

She gave me a long, sad look.

Were we really not to be comrades anymore? We had started out together fighting for the same things in the same ways, then had drifted into fighting for the same things in different ways, and now were fighting for different things.

Maybe she was just braver than I.

I said, "Do you know what all this tripping on violence will mean in the real world? The feds will have an open season on us. They'll be able to attack us any way they want."

She finger-combed her hair. Her eyes wandered the room, then came back to me.

"Okay," she said. "I guess it's bed time."

8 | Running with Sartre
Copenhagen and Stockholm, 1967

EARLY IN MAY 1967, the French master Jean-Paul Sartre and the English master Lord Bertrand Russell decided to organize what they termed "an international war crimes tribunal," or "the Russell tribunal," as Sartre came to call it with a bit of a sneer. The tribunal's purpose was to investigate North Vietnamese charges that U.S. military forces were committing actual crimes of war. Were these charges mere propaganda, or did they have merit?

One day a call came to the Peace and Freedom Center in Yellow Springs. It was from Staughton Lynd, calling to tell me about the tribunal and to ask if I would accept an invitation to be a member of it. I was immediately disposed to do it because I admired Sartre so much. His plays, such as *No Exit,* were magnificent, and I had spent a term at the University of Michigan rapturously studying his great philosophical work *Being and Nothingness,* along with his novels *Nausea* and *Troubled Sleep.* I had even come to think of myself (no snickering, please) as something of an existentialist.

So the thought of spending some time with Sartre and his companion and great novelist Simone de Beauvoir, also on the tribunal, was irresistible.

But I had to ask, Why me?

"The organizers see American students as playing a key role in the antiwar movement," said Lynd. "They want people from SDS and SNCC."

And I became a member of the tribunal, along with two other Americans, Stokely Carmichael of SNCC and Dave Dellinger, who was at that time the leader of the umbrella coalition mobilization against the war, the "Mobe."

When we met in Stockholm in May 1967, Sartre was designated president of the tribunal and Russell its chairman. Sartre was a full-time participant, the practical leader of the project, while Russell remained a frail presence behind a glass of fine whiskey somewhere in Wales. Even at such a remove, however, Russell's presence was keenly felt in Stockholm, and a few months later in Copenhagen, at our second session, and not always happily.

His often displeased messages to the tribunal became no doubt needlessly abrasive in being delivered by his high-handed representative, the American expatriate Ralph Schoenman.

Schoenman was about thirty, a tall man with broad shoulders. He wore his black hair combed straight back and varnished down. His skin was pale, his dark eyes nervous and darkly shadowed. He was always in a black turtleneck sweater and dark blue blazer, always stiffly erect with his chest out, wearing a challenging frown, an air of brooding petulance. He was just the sort of guy to get Sartre's goat.

Nor was Sartre the only tribunal member to find Schoenman hard to deal with. Our chairman was Vlado Dedijer, a World War II adjutant of Tito's and a hero of the Yugoslav resistance. It was said that he had a metal plate in his head from a severe combat wound. He was a dark, beefy man in his sixties whose face wore a permanent scowl. Backstage gossip had it that Dedijer had taken the debate with Schoenman so far as to lift him off the floor by the lapels one day behind the scenes and slam him against a wall.

Schoenman and Sartre also had crossed swords well before I arrived on the scene in Stockholm, where the tribunal was meeting after being booted out of Paris, reputedly at the request of our State Department. Their mutual hostility was a fact around which the inner life of the tribunal was compelled to revolve. There were a few stormy scenes.

Example: In one closed meeting of the tribunal during our second session in late November in a town called Roskilde, about twenty miles from Copenhagen, Schoenman announced that Russell wanted the tribunal to take an affirmative position on the genocide question, one of several questions the tribunal was examining. The practical question was whether the United States was specifically targeting Vietnamese population centers. Attacks on civilians constituted a crime of war, technical genocide. Schoenman told us that Russell believed such attacks were happening and that the United States was therefore guilty of genocide.

Sartre disagreed. He saw American attacks on population centers as a consequence of the fact that Viet Cong and North Vietnamese combat units often stationed themselves in cities and villages. As Sartre saw it, such attacks were deplorable but nonetheless did not constitute genocide. In Sartre's view, one could not use that term without evoking memories of Hitler's assault on the Jews. Compared to the Holocaust, what the United States was doing in Vietnam was just fighting an ugly war in an ugly way. If the United States was in the wrong, he felt, that was because its effort to subdue the Vietnamese resistance was in itself wrong, not because the United States was trying to exterminate the Vietnamese people.

All day long Schoenman would say, on the one hand, things like, "Lord Russell says he expects the tribunal to find the United States guilty of genocide," where the subtext was that Russell was paying for this damned thing and did not want to be unhappy with its findings. And then on the other hand, when Sartre challenged him on the genocide issue, Schoenman would say, "Don't expect me to defend Lord Russell's positions because I would not think of speaking for him."

Apart from the, well, existential problems between Sartre and Schoenman, this split over the question of genocide was the one serious split among the members of the tribunal. In crudest terms, Russell wanted a guilty verdict on this question, but Sartre was determined to let the evidence speak for itself. And as Sartre saw it, the evidence did not prove genocide. He thought it essential that the tribunal demonstrate its independence by voting to satisfy its own conscience. And he had let it be known that he thought Russell in the wrong to push North Vietnam's line.

Schoenman didn't seem to care terribly about the quality of the evidence. He had already harangued several closed sessions of the tribunal about this and was now doing it again.

"Lord Russell was unhappy to hear of the recent attacks upon him by certain tribunal members," Schoenman said. "He is all the more distressed by these attacks in that they are occasioned by large differences within the tribunal on the issue of genocide."

"No one has attacked Russell," said Dellinger, who acted as the tribunal's secretary and occasional peacemaker. "We simply disagree with him on this question. Why does he consider disagreement a personal attack?"

"That is for Lord Russell to say," said Schoenman. "I would not presume to speak for him. I am here only to say that Lord Russell believes the United States guilty of genocide in Vietnam, and that he will be disappointed if the tribunal continues to attack him for this view. He believes it imperative that—"

"*Première!*" thundered Sartre in his powerful, raspy, Gaulois-seasoned bass. "Our findings will be significant only if they are supported by facts! *Deuxième!* It is *you* who are under attack, Schoenman, not Lord Russell! *Troisième!* You cannot both stand behind Lord Russell and put him in your pocket!"

Schoenman was stunned. Sartre rarely spoke in English, a language he seemed to spurn for political reasons. That he had used it now in this sudden eruption showed that his dislike of Schoenman was not merely political.

It was not a knockout. Schoenman bowed his head slightly but kept his composure. "I will see that Lord Russell receives a faithful account of your statement," he said.

Sartre glared at Schoenman a moment more, then turned to look at de Beauvoir, whose face was sternly set. She lowered her eyes and nodded briefly, then Sartre turned back to Schoenman. *"Merci,"* he said quietly, and the clash was over.

Sartre's star had shone even more brightly in my eyes after 1964, when he declined the Nobel Prize for Literature as an act of protest against the war. Much of the appeal of the tribunal for me had lain in the chance to see something of this short, round cannonball of a man at work. Other members, too, were well worth an Ohio boy's attention—the remarkable novelist, de Beauvoir herself, for example, who never left Sartre's side and who said *"sacre bleu"* a lot.

I was particularly struck by the Swedish playwright Peter Weiss, author of the international hit *Marat/Sade,* and a new play that had just opened to critical acclaim in Dusseldorf, *Trotsky in Exile,* the opening of which had been disrupted by young ultraleftists. Weiss had gone onstage to denounce the use of police against the ultras and to agree with them that the theater was a haven of the privileged and that there might be something contradictory about doing a play sympathetic to Trotsky in a pricey theater instead of, say, in the streets.

"What is permitted cannot be subversive!" Weiss told me the ultras had shouted at him. "What is not subversive cannot be revolutionary! Only that which is forbidden can be permitted!"

Weiss said he had chosen to stand mute against this line of attack, although he knew perfectly well that he was not without defense. The publications of the ultras were themselves "permitted," he pointed out.

Or to bring the point home: If the performance of Weiss's revolutionary play by a theater company in Dusseldorf were an advertisement for the government of Willi Brandt, then the acquittal of the Oakland Seven must also be an advertisement for Ronald Reagan's California.

Well, maybe it was. The deal is that the same rules are supposed to apply equally to all. When the other guy actually does what he's supposed to do, why shouldn't he advertise?

These ultras of Copenhagen thought about politics in much the same way as did the ultras I'd begun running into around the movement that year, 1967, in New York, Chicago, and San Francisco. Not just Bernardine and her cohorts. The movement suddenly seemed rife with militants for whom each victory was a defeat and each defeat a victory. Yes, because our victories just made the other side, generally a college administration, look good, while our defeats proved that we were forbidden, that we were true revolutionaries and not just playing games in the schoolyard.

Weiss told me that he had tried to draw the ultras into a discussion, both Trotsky and co-optation being highly interesting subjects, but couldn't get past the one-sided shouting match the ultras seemed to prefer. To make matters worse, the microphone failed, Weiss told me, and he couldn't make himself heard. He had to wonder if an ultra had pulled the plug. He said he dreaded the thought but had to voice it: "If they are to be judged by their fruits," he said, "one has to ask if the ultras were in fact a creation of the secret political police."

Also sitting on the tribunal was the Polish historian Isaac Deutscher, author of major biographies of Lenin, Trotsky, and Stalin, a short, bald, rotund man in his sixties with a pointed gray goatee. Next to him sat the dark, powerful, scowling Dedijer, author of an acclaimed biography of Tito. He chaired some of our meetings. Japan, India, Pakistan, and West Germany also had representatives, but they were essentially silent throughout.

The other American besides me and Dellinger was Stokely Carmichael, a SNCC field secretary. Dellinger played a large role in the affairs of the tribunal, but Carmichael was hardly ever there. He was well represented, though, by three other SNCC field secretaries, Charles Cobb, Courtland Cox, and Julius Lester.

We held a few public sessions, mainly to put some Vietnamese statements on the record. At the first of these we met on the stage of a Stockholm theater. The stage had been fitted with a long row of tables for the dozen or so members who were present. At far stage right was the rostrum from which our witnesses presented their statements and answered our questions.

The first order of business was to stand and state our names and nationalities. This seemed straightforward enough, but I immediately screwed up.

I stood up, fumbled with the wires of my table mike, said, "Carl Oglesby, American," and sat down. Simone de Beauvoir, sitting next to me, began to stand up, and I started helping her with her microphone.

Then Dedijer thundered, "I object!"

We all froze.

"Many people are Americans who are not from the United States!" he said angrily. "People from Cuba are Americans! People from Canada are

Americans! People from Brazil, from Ecuador, from Peru, from Mexico, these are all Americans!"

I couldn't believe he had chosen to confront me publicly over something like this, and in the first minutes of the tribunal's first public session. I didn't know what to do. I thought of saying something moderately sassy like, "I take note of Mr. Dedijer's curious view of geopolitical nomenclature," but I didn't want to make a scene in the first moments of our first public session. Nor could I imagine what he wanted me to say. So I returned his stare for a moment, then turned over my nameplate and pushed my chair back a little way from the table. The introductions went ahead without further incident (e.g., "David Dellinger, from the United States"), and we proceeded to the first presentations, me with my nameplate turned over and my head buzzing.

After getting past the embarrassment, I settled down to being pissed off. I could see no reason for Dedijer to have publicly challenged me about something so trivial. He and I had a private discussion about this behind the scenes later on.

"Look, Vlado," I said, glaring upward as fiercely as I could into his black, always-angry eyes, "people from Mexico are Mexicans. People from Canada are Canadians. And whether you like it or not, people from the United States of America are Americans, and everyone in the world knows what you mean when you call yourself an American."

"You are all nothing but imperialists and warmongers!" he said with a sneer, turning away.

"You can believe what you like," I said, pursuing him, "but the next time you allow yourself to lecture me in public about a trivial thing like this, you will need another plate in your head."

"Do what you please. I am indifferent."

Luckily for me, since the guy outweighed me by a hundred pounds, we avoided a physical showdown, but we stayed on each other's bad side the whole way through.

In November we had a second session, sitting from the nineteenth through the thirtieth, this time in Copenhagen. By chance, I ran into Sartre and de Beauvoir and their retinue at the airport coming in. They had snubbed me throughout the first session, rarely exchanging more than that little French nod of oblique recognition and dismissal, though I sat next to them at the left end of our table. I didn't know if this was because they supported Dedijer's view that I'd been wrong to call myself an American or because I actually was one.

But now at the airport Sartre and de Beauvoir made a great show of greeting me warmly. Sartre even spoke in English, made eye contact with his one good eye, smiled, gave me a two-handed handshake, and congratulated me for my article on the tribunal's first session. This was a piece titled, "Vietnam: This Is Guernica," which had been published in the *Nation* of June 5. It was nice to make some points with him, to be the "American" who had written something he liked about the thorny genocide issue. Except for big Dedijer, all the other members warmed up, too. As far as I know, I was the only one to have published anything on the tribunal's doings, at least in a magazine as well regarded as the *Nation*. It gave me a bit of status. And I liked it.

Our second session was much like the first. We heard more witnesses and finally produced a "verdict" that surprised no one, namely that the United States was indeed guilty of crimes of war in Vietnam. This finding was of trace effect in the United States, where the tribunal was largely ignored, but many European intellectuals thought our work might be of some significance in Western Europe, where the war was already strongly opposed.

The U.S. government naturally disliked this tribunal and had done what it could to keep it from having a venue. Secretary of State Dean Rusk conducted an especially mean-spirited attack on Russell, calling him a "doddering old fool." Russell's relationship with the tribunal, said Rusk, "shows how far past his prime he has fallen." In a written response sent through Schoenman, Russell disdainfully answered that Rusk was "in no position to call anyone a fool."

Both the Copenhagen and the Stockholm sessions were often circuses. Intense media attention clustered around our international stars Sartre, de Beauvoir, and Weiss, and whenever they presented themselves, to the three middle-aged, erect, reserved North Vietnamese officials to whom so many West European governments, under State Department pressure, had denied visas. They were perfectly groomed, polite, and quiet, always dressed formally in gray military uniforms with high-necked jackets with epaulets, striped, creased trousers and polished black shoes, always together, and always with a cluster of admiring Europeans nearby. For all their reserve and modesty, they were treated as though they were the latest rock band.

Especially in the Copenhagen session, there was a heavy social scene around the tribunal. Sometimes we gathered to sip champagne in a mansion with ivory-trimmed spiral staircases and a string trio playing Mozart, sometimes in a huge, luxurious houseboat with a rock band playing music to twist to. De Beauvoir actually left Sartre's side to dance with Weiss, though Sartre kept to the wall, surrounded by his admirers. There were lots of gorgeous young Danish radicals running about, always energizing and beautifying the scene. The Vietnamese officers went to one of the parties at the mansion but kept religiously together and never sipped from their champagne glasses, never abandoned their distance from it all, and left early in a limousine.

Circus that it may often have been, however, the Russell-Sartre tribunal also pulled together what was for that time a novel reconception of the Vietnam War, one totally at odds with the conception upon which the United States based its policy.

The tribunal knew its findings were all but certain to be seen as a purely partisan statement and that the Western media and the American media in particular would be simply dismissive. It therefore made a real attempt to anticipate the American point of view and either to meet or to accept American objections. It documented its findings in a prodigious film and paper record. It sent several fact-finding teams separately into Vietnam to investigate particular Vietnamese charges, most especially the charges that the United States had attacked civilian population centers and that it had used illegal weapons. The tribunal relied extensively on U.S. government policy documents in establishing the tenets of U.S. military doctrine.

And the tribunal broke several important stories on the war.

For example, the tribunal was the first to report that the United States was using a special kind of bomb, called a guava bomb by the Vietnamese and by the United States a cluster-bomb unit, or CBU, a weapon that seemed spectacularly vicious and arguably in violation of the rules of war.

The distinctive feature of the CBU was that its purpose appeared to be maiming its victims rather than killing them. An expended CBU was presented to the tribunal by the Vietnamese and explained by a British arms expert who was cool and technical in his manner and who seemed fair-minded.

The CBU was a three-stage weapon. The first stage, which the expert called the mother bomb, consisted of a set of stabilizer fins mounted at one end of a slender five-foot tube. This was dropped from a low-flying aircraft on the end of a stall parachute, the chute's purpose being less to slow the mother bomb's descent than to ensure its proper vertical orientation.

The mother bomb was fitted with a barometric arming device designed to fire at low altitude and pop open the two halves of the mother bomb. This released the CBU's second stage, which consisted of about thirty cast-iron bomblets, each one about the size and shape of a hand grenade and packed with a high explosive. These bomblets were flanged in such a way that they started spinning when they hit the airstream. This spinning action oriented each bomblet vertically to the earth and armed a spring-loaded triggering device inside. When the spinning bomblet struck something, it of course stopped spinning. This relaxed the tension on the internal spring, and that closed a circuit that set off the main charge, detonating the bomblet and thus deploying the third and final stage.

This final stage consisted of hundreds of BB-like metal pellets embedded in the outer skin of the bomblet in such a way that they would fly out in a dish-shaped pattern around the blast. They were a threat to anyone within several hundred yards, and thirty of them would be going off all at once.

From the air force "use doctrine" document that the British arms expert produced (this was a secret spec and I have no idea how he acquired it), the tribunal's panel of European military experts concluded that the purpose of the CBU was not to kill people but rather to produce many nonfatal wounds, thus overloading the other side's medical facilities and in this way inducing despair and defeatism in the population. Its target, in other words, seemed to be civilian morale. And that, at least arguably, is a war crime.

Through the tribunal's research, the world also learned for the first time about a chemical defoliant called Agent Orange, which the United States was using to denude rain forests and thus expose VC trails. Agent Orange inevitably seeped into rice farms and poisoned food supplies. The tribunal saw evidence that this was happening in Laos as well as in Cambodia and Vietnam. This practice violated the United States' pledge to abide by the Geneva accords. It posed grave health risks not only to Vietnamese civilians but to U.S. troops as well.[1]

The tribunal's main conclusion was that U.S. military strategy had resulted in actual, technical genocide in Vietnam and Laos. This conclusion was important. It was soberly presented, and it asked for a sober hearing.

A sober hearing was given to a great extent in Western Europe, but on the commanding heights of the U.S. government as well as in the broad shallows of the mainstream U.S. media, the idea that the United States might be committing actual war crimes was dismissed out of hand as mere propaganda. We Yanks were good guys. We didn't do things like that.

I CAME HOME to Yellow Springs, and I remember trying to settle down, but the findings of the tribunal obliged one to pull up one's socks and get busy. As the pace of the war was quickening, so was the pace of the protests against it, so this was no time to get personal about life. Victory and defeat still seemed equally possible, as well as equally indefinable.

9 | One Way to Skin a Cat

Cowpens, 1968

NOT LONG AFTER I got involved in the antiwar movement, my father retired from the rubber mills of Akron. He had worked at Goodyear for thirty years to end up with emphysema and lung cancer and had then retired to an apartment in Spartanburg, South Carolina, about ten miles from the old-fashioned cotton farm near Cowpens where he had grown up, the site of a major American victory in the Revolutionary War and where most of his eleven sisters and brothers still lived.

My trip to see him had been set for a while. It would be my first visit to South Carolina since running off with the movement, and I was nervous about it. I knew he was not likely to be as proud as I was of my book or my speeches or my world travels. It was all nonsense to him if it wasn't making money. "Damn it, you ought to get yourself a real job where you can settle down and take care of your family and quit all this unpatriotic horseshit."

Nor did it matter to him that elsewhere in the country, among media and midlevel government people, the tide of opinion on the war was starting to run the movement's way. He didn't know nor did he care to know that the CIA had begun openly quarreling with the Pentagon's optimistic predictions of an early victory. If we hadn't yet won a clear-cut victory, like our victory in World War II, that was probably the fault of protesters like me. If I tried to talk to him about why the war had stirred us up, he would turn away, scoffing.

Senators George McGovern and Ernest Gruening were a little less lonely in opposing the war from their chairs in the Senate when Senator Eugene McCarthy announced on February 1, 1967, that he was running for president on an antiwar platform. This didn't get McCarthy anywhere near the Oval Office, and he often seemed less interested in attacking LBJ than in distancing himself from the antiwar movement, calling us a "fringe opposition" and saying that we were "protesters for the sake of protest."[1]

Thanks, Gene.

But we could take it. His candidacy lent a new air of urgency to dissent and helped us build the movement. More and more, it was possible to question the wisdom of the war without being called a traitor—except to some of my family in Cowpens.

As of spring 1967, nine months before the Tet Offensive, the Cowpens Oglesbys still supported the war strongly, and even more strongly favored getting tough with those like me who were actively opposing it. The men of my family especially thought it was time to knock some sense into some heads. This had nothing to do with any concept of Vietnam's place in American security. It was purely about authority and what it meant to be a patriot.

"If our boys are getting shot at," as my dad had told me on a previous visit, "you do what you can to support them."

"Yeah," I had answered, "like bring them home."

He had glared at me for hours, just like when I was a kid.

So I had made up my mind not to talk politics this time. I was off for a visit with my down-home family. My mission was to make reunions, not to win debates.

I happened to be in the D.C. ghetto on April 4, 1968, a day before my schedule had me off for South Carolina. I'd been hanging out with my SNCC friends when the word came that Rev. Dr. Martin Luther King Jr. had been murdered, shot down in Memphis by a single assailant, James Earl Ray, at point-blank range. As all around the country, riots at once broke out in Washington. I soon found myself in the streets with my friends. Not that we knew what to do, but you couldn't stay away from a scream like this. If not even a peacemaker such as King would be

allowed to pray for us, we must all be condemned. If we were all condemned, all we could do was gnash our teeth.

So a few SDSers and I found a small crowd of black friends to gnash
our teeth with. We ran up and down, looking for some way to engage
with the force responsible for this, but encountered only other such
groups and police barricades. Up and down, up and down. We saw
many flames but never got out of the ghetto.

The day after this, my plane to Spartanburg took off from Washington National Airport. For his own reasons, the pilot flew us in a leisurely
circle around the columns of thick black smoke that rose straight up
into a smiling blue sky.

"That's your nation's capital burning down there, ladies and gentlemen," said the captain in a deep, calm, almost amused tone of voice. "If
my history is correct, that has not happened since the British set it on
fire in 1812."

MY FATHER AND I made a tacit agreement not to fight about any of
this. The murder of King and the riots it ignited had taken place in a separate world, a separate reality. I would be in Cowpens for five days. I
would not voice my antiwar thoughts. I would go on Sunday to the family Baptist church and pass around snapshots of my kids to be admired
by my aunts. I would go to church again for a Wednesday-night prayer
meeting. I would pitch horseshoes with my uncles. I would hear a touch
of drawl return to my speech. I would smile and agree that it was great
to be back home. If I were asked what I was up to these days, I would
say something vague about teaching. I wasn't there to speak truth to the
powerless.

One morning seven or eight of my uncles took me down to the Pacolet River, a mile or so below my grandfather's farmhouse, to "phone up
some cats."

Yes. Phone, as in telephone. Cats as in catfish. Some unknown time
before, someone, maybe a local practical genius or an importer of outside technology, had introduced a new idea in catfishing.

You need a portable power generator for a World War II–vintage army field telephone. This generator is housed in a wooden box about ten inches to a side and light enough that you can carry it at your chest, slung around your neck on a heavy-duty canvas strap. It has two electrical wires running out of it. In normal use, these wires connect it to a field telephone. On one side of this box is a hand crank that you turn when you need to generate some power.

Suppose you cut the generator's electrical wires down to a length of maybe ten feet, wrap the ends of these wires around some short links of chain to make them sink, and drop them in the river at a shady spot where you think some catfish might be spending a quiet afternoon hanging out together. Your partners carry fishnets and spread out twenty to forty feet downstream of you. When everyone is all set, you start turning the crank.

No other sort of fish seemed to care, but the local catfish seemed to care a lot. One theory was that this was because catfish have skin instead of scales. Others disagreed, pointing out that people also have skin but don't react, and said the reaction you were about to see was caused by the catfish's whiskers. Whatever the reason, putting a little current in the water with that generator never raised any of the bass or perch that you might catch in the same spots the low-tech way. But catfish within fifteen or twenty feet of the lines will rush to the surface and swim in mad circles on their tails like speedboats, as though to keep their skin or their whiskers out of the water. At a good spot, you might raise a few dozen this way.

Spread out several yards downstream of the guy with the generator, the half dozen or so other members of your fishing party, armed with fishnets, would take off frantically after the cats, turning the water white to scoop up as many as they could in the half minute you had before they swam away.

My job that day was to carry the big burlap bag that we kept the catch in as we got what we could from one spot and then went on to the next, always moving upstream because the fish that escaped seemed to carry a warning to the fish downstream. In no more than an hour or so of this, we had the main course for the fifty people who would come together later that day for a feast in celebration of my homecoming.

We'd have caught what we needed even sooner if it hadn't been for being surprised halfway through our expedition by a guy I knew as Shorty, an amiable, potbellied friend of the family who also happened to be a local game warden. One of my uncles noticed him standing on the forested bank with a camera in his hand, taking pictures of us. Phoning for cats by this technique is not a legal way to fish, and Shorty had just taken a few pictures of us doing it. Things quickly came to a halt.

"What say, boys?" said Shorty. "How they runnin' today?"

It seemed a well-rehearsed situation. Shorty had a bag with him, and Uncle Paul told me to hand over the bag with our catch in it, so I waded up to the bank to do as I was told. Trading small talk with my uncles about how sweet the catfish were that summer, Shorty picked out a dozen or so of our best ones, put them in his bag, then took the film out of his camera and tore it up, said he hoped we all had a good time at our family get-together, and was on his way.

It is a famous truth that there are many ways to skin a cat, so I should note the way preferred on the Oglesby farm. The fish are still alive when you get them back to the farm and throw them in a washtub with a lot of well water in it. Wearing work gloves because the cats' spiked fins can cut, you grab one by its tail, slap it against a tree stump to get it to be still, then chop its head off with one stroke of a big meat cleaver. You leave its tail on because the tail is what you will hold it by when you're eating it. You slit its belly open and scoop out its innards, tossing these to the hounds. Again, one stroke is best, both in the slitting and the scooping. The squeamish will have trouble here, but if your knife is sharp and your spoon is the right size, you get used to it.

Then holding the headless, gutted fish by the tail with one gloved hand, you grab a piece of skin near the tail with a pair of pliers and, in one single motion, pulling downward, divest it entirely of its skin. This is the method favored on the Oglesby farm, although it's of course well known that there are many ways to skin a cat. This method is possible, of course, only because a catfish has skin rather than scales.

The cats are now ready for Granny and a crew of sisters and aunts to southern-fry them.

Southern-fried catfish go beautifully with southern-fried chicken, so while we fishermen were skinning the cats, Granny took to the barnyard, where the chicken flock ran free, to chase one down for dinner. She had to be nearly eighty, but she was still strong, skinny, and agile, with bright blue eyes and quick hands. She had no trouble cornering a madly squawking, white-feathered bird. She grabbed it by the head with two hands and slung its body around and around in a tight circle until its body flew off. She tossed the head into a slop bucket and let the headless chicken run in crazy circles, its blood spurting out. It flapped its wings for a few minutes, then finally keeled over, twitched for another moment, and then was ready to be bled, feathered, gutted, sliced, and cooked.

The bird's next public appearance was in nicely fried pieces next to the fried catfish on a big platter on one of the heavy wooden picnic tables in the farmyard under the huge old shade trees that stood around the house, served with freshly picked boiled corn on the cob, homemade biscuits and hush puppies straight from the oven along with Aunt Thelma's famous stuffing, Aunt Lorene's famous mashed potatoes, Aunt Loree's famous iced tea, Aunt Betty's famous green beans, Cousin Rita's famous sweet potatoes, and Cousin Cora's famous dumplings, with the feast topped off with Aunt Winnie's famous apple pie and Granny's famous peach cobbler.

Where was Vietnam?

Two days later was yet another family feast, this one at Boop and Loree's house a little way up the road from Pop and Granny's, the warm afternoon sweet with magnolia. Uncle Boop was another hero of my youth, a lanky, taciturn man who had seen combat in France in World War II and had returned to a lifelong job at the Draper cotton mill. Loree was a vivacious, girlish woman only a few years older than I. She had become a crush of mine when she came to Akron to marry Boop right after the war, just after he was mustered out.

I had gotten through almost four great days with Dad and my family and was looking at a noon departure the next day. Boop's grandson, twelve-year-old Jimmy, had just been baptized at the Wednesday night prayer meeting at the family church, and now his grandmother, Loree, was giving a family feast in his honor, her little house packed with family and friends.

Jimmy was still in his starched white shirt and red clip-on tie as Loree called us to the long dinner table that she had fashioned out of several card tables set up in her living room. Jimmy had delivered a little memorized sermon in the big church that evening on the text, "Blessed are the peacemakers, for they shall inherit the earth." He had spoken from the pulpit, standing on a little wooden box, and in front of the whole congregation. He had sailed through it and now was light-headed with success, glowing with innocence and victory and all the attention he was getting. We all stood at our places while he said grace. "Dear Lord, may we be worthy of thy many blessings. Amen."

We all said amen and smiled as we took our seats, and then Jimmy suddenly sang out, "Hey!" We all stopped and looked at him. "Did you all hear they caught the guy that shot Martin Luther King?"

It startled me. "Really?" I said, all ears.

"Yeah!" Jimmy piped back. "They charged him with killing a coon out of season!"

Big laugh, during which many eyes cut around to see how the Yankee member would react. I grimaced and got through the moment by mumbling that I would say a prayer for them all. But it was the sort of moment that you tend to replay.

Another such moment came the next morning. I was alone with Dad in the yard, where bursts of Granny's yellow forsythia were in bloom. It was a crisp, clear day with a delicate breeze lifting off the Pacolet. I was waiting for my ride to Atlanta, about to start my first big speaking trip through the South and a little nervous about it.

Dad seemed nervous, too. He knew in his heart that I was going off to blame his beloved Old South for all the ills of America and his beloved America for all the ills of the world.

He thought he had raised me better. Once when I was a kid in Akron, ten or eleven years old, having heard Mom and him worrying about making ends meet, I had shoplifted a ten-cent bottle of food coloring from a downtown market where Dad had taken me to help carry the groceries home. I didn't steal it because Mom colored food but because we were poor and it was there and nobody was looking. Once back home, with a big grin, I produced the little bottle for Mom and Dad, thinking they would praise me.

I was stunned when Dad gave me a furious, unbelieving stare, then said grimly, "All right, come on, let's go."

Saying not a word all the way, he marched me back up West Street hill to the bus stop on West Market Street, took me all the way back downtown to the store, and asked a clerk to see the manager.

The manager was a heavy-set middle-aged man in a white shirt and purple tie. My Dad said, "My son has something that belongs to you. Buddy, tell him what you took and give it on back."

I was cringing with shame. "I took this from your shelf," I mumbled, "and I'm sorry."

The manager seemed more surprised than angry. He said to my father, "Well, if everybody did like you, sir, I guarantee this town would be a better place."

Yet I had grown up to be a traitor.

And now as I was about to leave Cowpens, Dad turned that same kind of glare on me.

"So you're gonna go out yonder and speak up for that damn nigger, ain't you?"

"You can curse him all you want to, Dad, but King was still—"

"Gimme my rights!" he said in his ugliest imitation of black country dialect. "I wants my rights! Shit, I'll give him his goddamn rights, right up his goddamn black asshole!" It was the only time I ever heard him swear like that.

I put on my normal incredulous voice for such disputes with him, saying in a cross between disbelief and vexation, "Dad, a man is a man. What difference does the color of his skin make?"

"I'll tell you something," he said. "If I'm working with a man, the color of his skin sure in the hell makes a difference to me! You got to watch your back with a nigger!"

"Don't you remember little Harold Steel when I was at Crosby grade school? He was one of the best pals I ever had. Mom called him the sweetest kid she knew."

"I also remember that gang of niggers that tried to kick your white butt 'cause you wouldn't pay 'em no protection money!"

"Good and bad people come in all colors!"

"You look and see who's making them riots in all them big cities," he snapped. "Niggers, niggers, niggers! And you can't say it's just in the South, neither. Where'd they have that first big one? Yeah, in Chicago! Where's Chicago? Huh? Tell me, is Chicago in the South? Is Detroit in the South? Is Cleveland in the South?"

The student from Emory University arrived in the middle of this, right on time, to drive me to Atlanta, so Dad and I didn't have time to cool off. I poked my head out the car window on the way out the driveway, thinking we might at least wave good-bye. But he was already walking back to the house with his hands in his pockets and his head down.

10 | Banned

Atlanta, 1968

THE SOCIAL-STUDIES prof who had arranged this gig met me at a coffeehouse near the Emory campus. Fred was a dark-skinned black guy in his forties, nearly bald and with a short, frizzy beard and bright, quick eyes. When I'd called him from Cowpens the day before to get the details of my ride, he had seemed eager, but now he seemed nervous.

"I have bad news," he said when we sat down. "You've been banned."

"Banned?"

"Our president says he can't allow you to speak on the campus."

"You're kidding me."

"He just told me this morning. He called me to his office. He said there's too much smoke in the air. That's how he put it. 'Too much smoke in the air.' We'll cover your fee and expenses, of course, but he says he can't let you speak on campus. Maybe later this year, he says, but not now. He said to tell you he's sorry, and I think he really is. He's a pretty liberal guy. I think some of the trustees may have leaned on him. They think you may be here to cause some trouble."

"Trouble? Me?"

Emory University is a Methodist school founded in 1836. It has always been proud of its liberal tradition, a kind of Arminian populism, right up my alley. The Methodist motto is "Open minds, open hearts, open hearts, open doors." But even the most gracious host has to take care of the house, and the SDS of that moment and against the background of all the riots could hardly have inspired the benefit of a doubt.

"Nobody can remember a thing like this," Fred said.

"It's because of the King riots, right?"

He took a deep breath. "Yeah, mainly the riots. But also the Tet Offensive. Everybody's been a little uptight."

"Me, too."

"But I think it's more than that," he said. "How can I put this? SDS has been pretty busy lately, you know what I mean? A lot in the public eye."

He had a point. When I stepped back from it, I could see that Emory's officials might well wonder if this SDS guy had come to make trouble.

SDS and other campus activists had grown sharply divided between those who believed we should stick with nonviolence and those who believed it was time to kick some ruling-class ass. The persuaders were the huge majority, but the militants had more energy and were making more noise. This dispute had been onstage that fall and winter.

The huge group of activists at Berkeley, for example, the Free Speech Movement, had recently gone through a contentious and highly public split. The larger group was still committed to nonviolence, but the more newsworthy group favored militant tactics.

We could still be nice guys, and for the most part were. At the State University of New York at Binghamton, for example, our SDS chapter's big project that fall had been to buy Thanksgiving dinners for North and South Vietnamese children.[1]

The SDS chapter at Southern Methodist University in Dallas had made some news when it turned away an antidraft organizer because it preferred legal means of protest.

Our Pennsylvania State College chapter believed that SDS's proper role was to make life better for students, so it had concentrated on getting the price of football tickets lowered.

The Queens College chapter in New York City had joined peaceful picket lines with striking transit workers.

In Boston, many chapters peacefully organized against higher transit fares.

Many chapters in the Midwest and West were busy trying to establish alliances with steel, copper, and farm workers.

An SDS group from Columbia and CCNY had started a peaceful draft-resistance project in a Puerto Rican neighborhood.

And despite SDS's official position that mass marches were like yesterday, many SDSers from around the country had joined the National Mobilization Committee's avowedly peaceful mass march of October 21, 1967, on the Pentagon.

But even if Emory's president had not read the "Port Huron Statement" lately and did not have its paeans to nonviolence ringing freshly in his mind, it would have been hard for him to miss our presence all over the place as a serious disturber of the peace.

Suppose that you are the president of this school. You are all for free speech, but you want to keep things peaceful. It's an especially restless time because King has just been killed and a lot of cities are on fire. Here comes this guy to give a talk on your lovely, quiet campus. All you know about him is that he is a former president of SDS. Here is what you might know about SDS:

Early in 1967: Two SDS national officers, Greg Calvert and Carl Davidson, publicly said they admired the tactics of Guatemalan guerrilla forces.

June 1967: A *New York Times* report on the SDS national convention noted that some of us were talking of guerrilla warfare and the "guerrilla mentality" and were studying how to oppose "counterinsurgency techniques."

August 25: SDS activists used nonviolent but aggressive means to disrupt the National Student Association's congress in Washington, attacking NSA's ties to the CIA and denouncing it as a front for "corporate liberalism."

Summer: SDS proclaimed its support of the Revolutionary Action Movement, a group of black militants in New York. Police had charged sixteen members of RAM with conspiracy to murder moderate black leaders Roy Wilkins and Whitney Young.

Summer: In the same breath, SDS supported the eleven SNCC members who had been arrested for "criminal anarchy" following a police raid of SNCC's Philadelphia office. The police said they had discovered a cache of several pounds of dynamite. SNCC people assured SDS that the dynamite had been planted, and since SDS knew from experience that blowing things up was not SNCC's style, SDS believed them. But if you're Emory's president, you don't know this. And anyway, it seems paranoid to think that police officers in America would plant evidence.

Fall: In an account of the NSA action in *New Left Notes,* SDS officer and future Weatherman Jeff Jones first used the expression "Build not! Burn!" This was Jones's incendiary restyling of the Peace Corps–like phrase "Build, not burn!" that, just two years before, your would-be campus speaker had proposed as SDS's defining slogan. But you don't know this.

September: SDS officer Carl Davidson, speaking at his alma mater, the University of Nebraska, argued that student riots were "a legitimate form of protest and disobedience." Try negotiations first, he assured, but "when nitty gets down to gritty," the activists' position should be: "Either give us what we're asking for, or we'll shut this school down."

September: A University of Illinois SDSer told a reporter that "draft-card burnings were not accomplishing any change in the course of the Vietnam War," so "the time had come to move SDS efforts into the streets."

October 16–21: SDS sponsored a national program, Stop the Draft Week, targeting induction centers for shutdown. There were mass sit-ins and some clashes with the police. The big one was on the seventeenth at Oakland, where demonstrators blocked busloads of inductees headed for their first army base. The police tear-gassed thousands and arrested hundreds.

October 18: A big SDS issue that fall was campus recruiters from Dow Chemical Company, which manufactured the napalm and defoliants that the air force was using in Vietnam. Hundreds of SDSers sat in against Dow recruiters at the University of Wisconsin, chanting, "Dow shalt not kill!" Demonstrators threw rocks when the police moved in to stop the disruption. Sixty-five demonstrators and policemen were hurt.

October 20: At Brooklyn College, eight thousand students led by SDS boycotted classes to protest police intervention and arrests on campus the previous day in an SDS protest against U.S. Navy recruiters. SDS had wanted to set up a literature table near the recruiters' booth, but the administration had refused permission. Things got physical.[2]

October 21: Among the many nonviolent SDSers who joined the Mobe's old-fashioned peace rally at the Pentagon were five to ten thousand who suddenly broke through the fences bordering the rally area, pushed through the first line of startled soldiers, and made it all the way to the walls of the Pentagon itself before they were finally stopped by troops with fixed bayonets. There were fistfights with the police, many injuries, and hundreds of arrests.[3]

Late October: In SDS's postmortem to the Pentagon action, according to published reports, some SDSers began openly to formulate a "guerrilla" tactic of operating in small, mobile groups that would not passively await arrest but would directly and physically challenge the police.[4]

Late October: The guerrilla approach to protest was championed by SDS officers Davidson and Calvert and an SDS founder, Tom Hayden, who had left community organizing to join the antiwar cause about a year before. Their thoughts were beginning to take form as the strategic line that became known as "resistance," as in Calvert's phrase "from protest to resistance."

Late October: Harvard SDS physically denied Dow recruiters access to the campus. University of Colorado SDSers physically blocked CIA recruiters. Princeton SDSers physically blockaded a military research building to protest university relations with the Institute for Defense Analysis.

November: Stanford SDS blocked CIA recruiters. University of Iowa SDS blocked Marine Corps recruiters. University of Rochester SDS blocked Dow recruiters and followed up with a student strike protesting disciplinary suspensions imposed after the sit-in.

And Emory's president was entirely right in thinking that more of this was on the way, so why should he not fear that it was coming to Emory?

So nonplussed as I was at being banned, I had to admit that the Emory president did not have to be a crazy fascist pig to be worried about a traveler from SDS. SDS was stronger and angrier than anyone, including me, yet knew. A lot of rough stuff had been happening, and I could easily have agreed with the Emory people that it was probably going to keep on happening.

And it did. May was a month of mayhem. In Boston, Northeastern University SDS led a forceful takeover of a meeting room to protest ROTC. In Hanover, New Hampshire, Dartmouth SDS struck against ROTC and military recruiting. In Baltimore, Johns Hopkins SDS led a sit-in against militarism in university contracting. NYU SDS cosponsored a sit-in demanding abolition of the grading system and open admissions for area high-school graduates. Brooklyn College SDS "broke down the door to a dean's office" in protest of campus military projects. University of Cincinnati SDS led students on a window-smashing and furniture-breaking "spree" against military projects. Seattle Community College SDS, supporting "various militant black student demands," got into "street-fighting with police."[5]

Yes, SDS was busy. There was a lot of smoke in the air. And more was to come.

"So what's our next step?" I said to Fred.

He said, "Well, if you don't mind speaking from a pulpit, there's a Methodist church right across the street from the campus, and the pastor there says you'd be welcome."

"Perfect. I already have a text in mind."

Predictably, getting banned was the best promotion I could have hoped for. It was like *Time* magazine's cover-page attack on SDS. It had only made us seem important. All the pews in the church were filled. Church members, townspeople, reporters, and teachers were there as well as students who would otherwise scarcely have noticed my presence. I'm sure many of them had come less to hear some SDS guy waste their time than to make a point about free speech, or else out of simple curiosity. Or to water me down if I tried to light a fire.

The church was lovely in its plainness, all white and glowing with morning light. I thanked the church and the pastor for their generosity and all the people for coming, then took hold of the pulpit with both hands, took a long pause and a deep breath, and said, "Blessed are the peacemakers, for they shall inherit the earth.'" The audience—congregation?—murmured "amen," and I started out. I wanted my talk—sermon?—to be about being banned, how it felt, what it might mean. But I couldn't help wandering off to peacemaker King and his murder and the riots still smoldering in cities all over the country, and about the one time I'd met King maybe two years before and been honored to give a brief talk from his pulpit in Atlanta.

But I had to talk about what was really on my mind, and that was my young Cowpens cousin Eddie and the way he seemed to glow with innocence at the big family dinner two days before, right after he'd been baptized and had given his little sermon on that line about peacemakers, and had then cracked his nasty little joke about King's assassin. And my bitter quarrel with my dad about it just before coming to Atlanta, to discover I'd been banned from the campus.

I kept my "sermon" brief because I wanted to hear what the congregants were thinking. Our dialogue was intense, many-sided, and respectful. We ended with a moment of silent prayer. There were smaller meetings that afternoon and evening in the church's basement. Toward the end of the day, Fred told me that the school president had withdrawn the ban and that I would be in certain classrooms the next day and then a guest of the Methodist student group at their retreat in the country for the two days after that.

Ye masters, lords, and rulers in all lands, consider this. Had I not been banned, I'd have met for a few hours with a handful of students and then been gone.

11 | Cointelpro, Anyone?
U.S.A., 1968

IT WAS THE BEST of years and the worst of years, a time when masses of people freed themselves from silence and spoke up to power, a time when power let the people know what it thought of such nonsense.

The first big blast was the Tet Offensive, launched in the early morning hours of January 30, 1968.

I was just dozing awake from a nice sleep on a pallet on the floor in Missoula at the home of Peter and Lucille, he a middle-aged history prof at the University of Montana, she a young painter in the manner of Georgia O'Keeffe, their walls hung with giant canvases of yellow and mauve buttes and canyons.

"Carl, wake up," said Peter, "something big's happening in Vietnam. Coffee's hot."

"I thought we had a Christmas truce," I mumbled.

"Well, a Christmas truce to some is a Christmas goose to others," Peter said.

The TV news was scant, but the BBC had some guys on the scene. More than seventy thousand DRV and VC combatants had appeared from nowhere to strike at once in all of South Vietnam's thirty provincial capitals. In Saigon they had hit the U.S. mission and even briefly penetrated the Presidential Palace.[1] For the first time, a DRV-VC unit had stood their ground to fight the Marines in a regular combat mode.

Since the DRV had pledged to observe a truce until the lunar New

Year, this sudden attack wound up costing Uncle Ho considerable sympathy in the West. Even France denounced the attacks as a violation of a formal truce agreement. But what it cost in goodwill it seemed to make up for in military shock and awe.

The Tet Offensive was soon "repulsed," as the hawks chose to see it, although it is equally conceivable that North Vietnam's military chief, General Vo Nguyen Giap, having made his *political* point, simply chose to draw his regular forces back across the DMZ and to dissolve the VC among the people.

The hawks' line was that the offensive had been a desperate, last-ditch effort that failed despite its surprise. But it moved the army to ask for 206,000 more U.S. troops, and it was not hard to sense at the time what the world later learned for a fact: the attacks had staggered Washington. The mere fact that Hanoi could prepare and coordinate so many attacks came as a shock to the public. As one of Johnson's "Wise Men," Clark Clifford, was later to write, the Tet Offensive's "size and scope made a mockery of what the American military had told the public about the war, and devastated American credibility."[2]

Clifford is less clear on what top presidential advisers such as himself had been told. In his 2001 book based on declassified National Security Agency files, *Body of Secrets*, James Bamford cites a warning from the theater commander, General William Westmoreland, strongly indicating that the Tet Offensive was not really all that much of a surprise. Nine days before Tet, writes Bamford, Westmoreland had cabled the Joint Chiefs of Staff: "I believe that the enemy will attempt a country-wide show of strength just prior to Tet, with Khe Sanh being the main event."[3] This is exactly what happened.

The previous JCS chairman, General Earle Wheeler, had warned on December 18, 1967, six weeks before Tet, that "it is entirely possible that there may be a Communist thrust similar to the desperate effort of the Germans in the Battle of the Bulge in World War II."[4]

And as to whether the big people were paying attention, Bamford writes that LBJ was all but micromanaging the war and even "had a sand model of Khe Sanh built in the Situation Room." Clifford was about to be made defense secretary at this time, so it is inconceivable that the

Westmoreland report was not made known to him. So when he echoes Walter Cronkite's famous cry "I thought we were winning the war," maybe it is just his stab at the ancient art of covering one's ass.

Most Americans, whether they supported the war or not, believed that our forces could at least win it without trying too hard. But many antiwar activists and a few reporters realized that this was not the case, that our foes in Vietnam were militant nationalists who would fight to the death. Their basic combat style was to emerge from the civilian population, fight quick battles in our forces' rear, then dissolve back into the population. Tet deviated from this scenario in that, for the first time, the other side stood its ground and engaged American and South Vietnamese units for several days like a regular infantry.

The principal VC combat mode, however, remained that of the guerrilla. And in those days, this simple fact seemed beyond the comprehension of those who were running the war. Whatever their closely held worries might have been in the fall and winter of 1967, as General Giap was putting his forces in place for the Tet Offensive, our South Vietnam ambassador Ellsworth Bunker and military chief Westmoreland continued to assure Johnson that "we are making solid progress and are not in a stalemate."[5]

These "proud assertions," Clifford came belatedly to understand, "were among the most erroneous ever made by field commanders." He quotes a West Point textbook as expressing his own view of Tet: "The first thing to understand about Giap's Tet offensive is that it was an allied intelligence failure to rank with Pearl Harbor or the Ardennes offensive in 1944."[6]

Self-criticism is good to see in the likes of Clifford and the authors of West Point textbooks, but they seem to be wrong about this. The intelligence take prior to Tet appears to have been more than adequate. Our side knew that the other side was coming and had a very good idea of where and when. Perhaps our side failed to see the scope of the Tet Offensive, but that was less a result of intelligence failures than of ordinary overconfidence. True, the Tet Offensive was not a Pearl Harbor or a Battle of the Bulge. It was a Tet Offensive.

Nonetheless, as with McNamara's tardy mea culpa, I think Clifford's words are valuable because they are the second thoughts of one of the foreign-policy "experts" to whom LBJ turned for advice. And Clifford could not be clearer when he writes that Tet "was a turning point in the war."

Johnson pretended that Tet was a victory for our side. He and General Wheeler could hardly help conceding that the Vietnamese had scored a "propaganda" victory, which they were quick to blame on the media and U.S. dissenters. But "contrary to right-wing revisionism," Clifford writes, "reporters and the antiwar movement did not defeat America in Vietnam. Our policy failed because it was based on false premises and false promises." He concluded that "the most serious casualty at Tet was the loss of the public's confidence in its leaders."[7]

Clifford's words are so fascinating to me on this point because of his high place in the pyramid of power at the very moment all this was happening, and because, as his predecessor McNamara has also done, he paints the same picture that we, in the antiwar movement, were being jeered at and Red-baited for. What I had been banned from the Emory campus for wanting to say, what I and scores of others in the antiwar movement were routinely Red-baited and attacked by the FBI for saying, was that the United States was up against an army of highly motivated patriots fighting for their own nation's independence, and that it was simply not possible to defeat such a force without a lot more blood and money than the United States could afford and a sickening change in our own sense of national identity.

Clifford's revelations are important because they show that it wasn't just those of us on the antiwar side who knew the American effort was doomed. Johnson and his staff knew it, too, and if Clifford is right, they knew it in their bones, where such knowledge hurts. "It is hard to imagine or re-create the atmosphere in Washington in the sixty days after Tet," he writes. "The pressure grew so intense that at times I felt the government itself might come apart at the seams." And again: "There was, for a brief time, something approaching paralysis, and a sense of events spiraling out of the control of the nation's leaders."[8]

Nor were Clifford and McNamara alone among those at the top in understanding the significance of the Tet Offensive. For example,

Undersecretary of the Air Force Townsend Hoopes, a staunch conservative, sent Clifford a "long personal letter arguing that 'the idea of a U.S. military victory in Vietnam is a dangerous illusion.'" Clifford continues: "At the end of February [1968], General Wheeler returned from his three-day visit to Vietnam and submitted a report that was to frame the most dramatic policy debate of March. Wheeler's report contained an assessment of the situation so bleak, and a request for additional troops so large, that it had a profound effect on the course of the war and American politics."[9]

Wheeler wanted 205,179 additional troops. In his last day in his DoD office, McNamara told Clifford, "The goddamned Air Force, they're dropping more [bombs] on North Vietnam than we dropped on Germany in the last year of World War Two, and it's not doing anything! We simply have to end this thing. I just hope you can get hold of it. It is out of control." Clifford writes, "We were all stunned."[10]

As to who made things hard for American forces in Vietnam, Clifford is equally forthright:

"In fact, it was the hawks, not the doves, who weakened America by pursuing the war so long. . . . Then, after the failure of their policies, they sought to blame America's defeat on those who had opposed the war, instead of accepting responsibility for the poor strategy and poor leadership they themselves had offered in Vietnam."[11]

It is certainly good of Clifford to take the onus for the Vietnam War's outcome off our much-maligned opposition. But as one of the antiwarriors, I have to say that I think he makes two important mistakes here.

First, a voluntary withdrawal is not the same as a defeat. The United States left Vietnam because it chose to, not because it was forced to. And it chose to because its own cost-benefit analysis persuaded it that the game was not worth the candle.

Second, when Clifford blames the war's outcome on the hawks' "poor strategy and leadership," he implies that a victory might have been achieved if the hawks' strategy and leadership had been better. But this is wrong. There was no way to derive a winning strategy from a false belief and contradictory assumptions.

The false belief was that the other side was fighting as the tool of an outside power, that the VC was the puppet of the DRV and the DRV the puppet of Moscow. No. The VC was fighting on its own, for a while even against the wishes of Hanoi, to win South Vietnam's independence from the United States.[12]

The contradictory assumptions were, on one hand, that we could crush the other side with heavy metal, while, on the other hand, in the lapidary phrase of the sixties, winning "the hearts and minds of the Vietnamese people." Succeeding in either of these objectives would preclude succeeding in the other. Crushing the other side's military power required bombing Vietnam "back to the Stone Age," which inspired hatred of us in the people. Winning the loyalty of the people required embracing the cause of Vietnamese nationalism, which would be a de facto concession of the war's basic argument.

But I must agree with Clifford's observation that the hawks "were greatly aided by the nature of the antiwar movement in the United States, much of which took on an ugly, unpatriotic and anti-American tone." I was saying as much inside the movement when a supermilitant, pseudorevolutionary rhetoric began to exert a fatal charm over many of our best people.

Of immeasurably greater aid to the hawks, however, was Clifford's own silence about what he knew at the time to be the war's colossal folly. Along with his predecessor secretary of defense, McNamara, Clifford appears to have been guided by the words of Santiago Ramón y Cajal, who said in 1906, "To be right before the right time is heresy, sometimes to be paid for with martyrdom." Martyrdom seems not to have been an option for Clifford. Like McNamara, he picked his moment to tell us that he, too, had been a closet dove, a moment long after the folly of the war had become the consensus view. He is in no position to find fault with those whose inexperience, idealism, outrage, desperation, and, yes, courage sometimes drove them beyond the bounds of "permissible" dissent.

Nor does Clifford seem to have noticed that discoveries made public well before he published his book make it distinctly probable that many—not all but many—of the incendiary acts of our "violent doves" were the work of federal provocateurs. Since the Army Intelligence

Corps had carried out many acts of provocateurism during the years in which Clifford was secretary of defense, he could hardly have been unaware of them. If he was unaware, the complaint against him is even stronger.[13]

One final objection to Clifford's tardy apologia. He writes that "the war was not lost at home, as is so often stated. It was lost where it was fought, in the jungles and rice paddies of Southeast Asia, and in the offices of a corrupt and incompetent ally."[14]

Wrong. The war was "lost" where it was begun and managed, in the offices of Johnson, McNamara, and Clifford themselves, who saw the secret daily summaries of the killed and maimed, yet managed to stifle their tears so as not to stain the bombing orders they were signing. The only difference between Johnson's crew and Nixon's crew is that the latter had no taste for ambivalence.

Yes, as with McNamara, Harriman, Hoopes, Nitze, and the other closet doves in high places, I think it is to the good that Clifford at last came out. As one of his foes in the streets of that era, I'm glad he finally set the story straight by telling us of his late-blooming qualms about the war.

But I can't forget that Clifford and the others had the price of their ghastly narcissism updated every morning with their coffee. They knew *at the time* that they were parties to a deception of an unprecedented scale in our history. Yet they so prized their high places in that palace of lies that they would wait until doubts of the war had become de rigueur among the foreign-policy elite before telling us that they, too, had been queasy about it. Compared to the stench of deceit in Washington, the stench of corruption in Saigon was perfume.

WHATEVER THE CAUSE of my banning at Emory, whether the school president acted on his own instincts or because of pressure from the school's trustees, and whether or not the trustees were themselves under pressure, 1968 was the year of the FBI's "Cointelpro: New Left," a program whose purpose was not merely to gather information on the antiwar movement but also to destroy it. The program specifically targeted SDS.

For those not conversant with spookspeak, let me note that "cointelpro" is a contraction of "counterintelligence program." It significantly differs from intelligence-gathering, which entails bugging phones and the like and aims merely to collect information. Counterintelligence, on the other hand, entails active disruption of the targets' activities, organizations, and lives. One technique is to plant false stories with "assets" or collaborators, often in the media or with a target's employer, or through the use of penetration agents. Another technique is to spread false gossip about the targets to turn them against one another. A favorite method, known as "black jacketing," is to spread rumors that targets are informers.

More aggressively, trained provocateurs take the role of ultramilitants and try to lure protesters into felonies, or simply commit the felonies themselves, preferably on camera, to bring an organization into public disgrace.

We had certainly had agents among us from the beginning. An FBI report released decades later revealed that the FBI had actually placed an informer, identity unknown, in SDS's Chicago national office as early as May 1966.

The FBI's original mission in placing agents among us was possibly just to find out what we were up to. We had no big problem with that. We, too, sometimes wondered.

But altogether different was the infiltration of our ranks by provocateurs whose explicit purpose was to destroy us. Their tactical premise was that we would grow less sympathetic to the public the more violent we appeared to be. As presidential adviser McGeorge Bundy told Johnson in November 1967, "One of the few things that helps us right now is public distaste for the violent doves."[15]

This points up a basic lesson for the politics of protest: A commitment to nonviolence is not merely a moral imperative, but a strategic one as well. This is true for a very simple reason: The less sympathetic a protest appears to the public, the more daring can be the repressive forces mobilized against it. The provocateur has not the least difficulty figuring this out. Do you want to whack the antiwar movement? Okay, don't whack it outright, at least not until the movement's reputation has been blackened, because that will only fire people up and make you look bad in the morning news. Instead, just grow long hair, put on an SDS uniform (ragged jeans and a T-shirt with a Grateful Dead logo will do fine), and do something stupidly violent, where it will be sure to be picked up by a reporter and a camera.

But by no means do I claim, of course, that all among us who came to adopt violent tactics were cops. Sometimes we went crazy. Why? Maybe it was the daily diet of video news from Vietnam, the first war to be televised. Maybe it was just an ungovernable rage at the war machine, the deceits of the government, the mindless apathy of the great American public. Maybe it was our growing fear that whatever our level of self-control, however prudent we were, however large our numbers, we would simply never have the strength or the time to do what had to be done.

Sometimes going crazy can seem the only sane thing to do.

JOAN M. JENSEN, a professor of history at New Mexico State University, is one of several academic researchers into the problem of federal penetration and the only one I know of to focus on the army. Her remarkable *Army Surveillance in America, 1775–1980*, remains sadly under-appreciated. She notes that the sixties movement, unlike the pacifists of the 1920s, seldom complained of army surveillance, apparently because we knew so little about it.

We might have paid closer attention. Jensen tells us that a military intelligence captain infiltrated the SDS chapters at both the University of Denver and the University of Colorado in Boulder. A sergeant who worked with this captain attended our National Council meeting at Boulder in October 1968 along with at least four other army agents.[16]

Army agents posing as New Leftists staged several ugly incidents, as when one threw a chair at San Francisco State University president S. I. Hayakawa during a speech at the University of Colorado. Just to make us look tough, no doubt.

Controversy about army infiltration of SDS only developed in January

1970, when a former military intelligence officer, Christopher Pyle, published an article in the *Washington Monthly* titled "CONUS [continental United States] Intelligence: The Army Watches Civilian Politics." Evidently an honest man, Pyle had become troubled by excesses in the army's domestic intelligence program. His article, Jensen writes, "opened the first full-scale public debate on Army intelligence in more than seventy years of its existence." By then, of course, it was too late for SDS. Secret agents had already taken it out of the game.[17]

Another perceptive student of this period, Tom Wells, writes in *The War Within* (1994) that during the spring and summer of 1965, after the antiwar movement had come onstage, Johnson took the kind of action he believed in: Following a talk with the president, who had "no doubt" that Communists were behind the dissent, J. Edgar Hoover directed the FBI to prepare a memorandum linking SDS with communism. FBI agents infiltrated SDS chapters.[18]

I suppose most of us in the opposition assumed that Johnson had launched his massive escalations of the ground and air war in confidence that an American victory was possible, and that he was siccing Hoover on us because he thought we impeded a noble effort he believed could succeed. In August 1965, as he sent the first large contingent of ground troops into combat, he assured a Washington audience: "America wins the wars she undertakes. Make no mistake about it!"

But in *Reaching for Glory,* historian Michael Beschloss presents evidence from Oval Office tapes that Johnson believed no such thing. Throughout the months in which he persistently raised the table stakes, like a poker player with a flat hand who has simply decided to go for broke, throwing in more bombers and exhorting the troops to "nail the coonskin to the wall," Johnson was telling his advisers that "America could never win the war." The Johnson of this period was "a driven, frightened, angry and suspicious man," Beschloss writes. "Over and over he moans to those around him that he is 'depressed' and 'scared to death' that the war will end in catastrophe."

To one adviser, Johnson said, "If you let a bully come in and chase you out of your front yard, tomorrow he'll be on your porch, and the next day he'll rape your wife in your own bed."

Johnson's bizarre idea that Vietnam was an American "front yard" and that American troops whom he himself had ordered into combat were being "bullied" by an adversary whose homeland they were savaging with every weapon short of nuclear bombs and his reduction of the conflict to a macabre sexual metaphor cast doubt on his sanity. But he was perfectly sane in realizing that the United States could not win the Vietnam War.

I think his consciousness of his predicament is the one thing that allows us to believe that he was not simply nuts. There is something of a tragic figure about him when he cries to his wife about the war, "I can't get out, and I can't finish it with what I have got. And I don't know what the hell to do!" He tells her, "I am not temperamentally equipped to be commander in chief." There is something sane in him at this moment.

But the madman reappears in his craving for proof that we who also opposed the war must have been subversives. Many of us in the streets were driven by much the same line of reasoning that tore at him. We knew what he knew, that there was no way for the United States to win the Vietnam War.

Yet he grasped at straws to persuade himself that we protesters must be Soviet pawns. *Newsweek* of November 12, 2001, reports that he told Lady Bird, "One of the boys in this . . .[antiwar] youth organization? His mother . . . is one of the leaders of the Communist Party in this country. . . . Hoover was very upset about it. He brought over the files last night."

What can one say about the quality of this reasoning? This man was president of the most powerful nation on earth. At the very time when he himself had lost faith in the war, his only explanation for those of us who had also lost faith in it was that we were traitors. Did Johnson see himself as a traitor, too?

The FBI of this period appears to have been led by people of the same level of dementia.

To any who may think this melodramatic, I recommend a remarkable study by Ward Churchill and Jim Vander Wall, *The COINTELPRO Papers: Documents from the FBI's Secret Wars against Domestic Dissent.*

Making skillful use of the Freedom of Information and Privacy Act, Churchill and Vander Wall have assembled a story of official crime against the Constitution that can boggle even the most jaded minds.

As I lose no opportunity to repeat, the story of Cointelpro is as basic to an understanding of the Vietnam War as is the story of the war itself. As with Jensen's study of the army's domestic counterintelligence operations against the New Left, Churchill and Vander Wall have assembled the story with scholarly care, attention to detail, and a willingness to face frightening facts.

An especially intriguing subplot of their story concerns not the FBI but the CIA.

Early in 1967, about a year before the FBI's Cointelpro: New Left got going, Johnson ordered the CIA to start spying on us dissenters. CIA director Richard Helms at first refused to do this because the 1947 National Security Act that created the CIA forbids it from engaging in domestic operations. But Johnson somehow forced Helms to bend to his will.

So the CIA put together a program, ultimately titled Operation MH Chaos, to see if the movement had ties to hostile foreign states. In a series of reports to Johnson titled "Restless Youth" in 1968–69, the CIA presented its conclusion that there were no such connections, and this despite the fact that several SDSers had traveled to North Vietnam and Cuba. It would have been easy for the CIA to trump up a case against us. It is forever to Helms's credit that he refused to do this.

There was a whisper around SDS at the time that the CIA was within us and that some of its agents objected to this mission and were even sympathetic to our cause. Some wondered, as did I, if this whisper was floated by the CIA agents themselves. If Churchill and Vander Wall's research is as solid as it seems, this whisper had substance. At the time, of course, we could not credit it because it could easily have been a bit of disinformation designed either to make us suspicious of each other or to put us off guard, or both.

The FBI's program seems much the more serious of the several government operations that targeted us. Cointelpro was a huge operation. As one of my FIPA documents shows, FBI headquarters in 1968 was demanding "aggressive and imaginative" action by the more than two thousand agents assigned to us full time and the more than two thousand informers whom these agents hired, at three hundred dollars a month, to support their work. In November 1974, shaken by the Watergate scandal, the Justice Department admitted to having mounted 2,370 specific separate actions against us.[19] But we still don't know what a single one of them was.

We assumed that the feds were boring from within. Generally we tried to keep cheerfully quiet about it because we saw no need to add paranoia to our other flaws, although, at our 1968 convention in East Lansing, we posted a workshop on sabotage and explosives to draw the agents out of our serious workshops, a stratagem that apparently worked. One agent came from the sheriff's office of Jefferson Parish, Louisiana, attended the sabotage workshop, and later told a Senate committee, "everyone who didn't fit the mold, who appeared to be agents, undercover workers, FBI or local police intelligence units, all went to the sabotage and explosives workshop."[20] For the most part, we confined ourselves to quiet crash-pad gossip about turf struggles between the FBI and the local Red squads.

We were intuitively aware of a significant change in 1968 when the FBI fused all the municipal Red squads into what was in effect a secret national police force dedicated to our destruction. We also assumed—there was really no way not to assume—that army intelligence branches had gone beyond mere spying to launch their own operations against us, especially around military bases.

My banning that day at Emory University could well have been the result of an early Cointelpro action. The FBI agents shared a reactionary worldview and a mutually reinforced image of us in which the greater our villainy, the greater their heroism in fighting us, and the fatter their budgets. Oglesby was a leader of SDS. SDS was a villainous group. Therefore Oglesby was a villain. Q.E.D. Ban the rascal. But finally we just do not know much about all this. We don't know how well the FBI was coordinated with the CIA and army intelligence. Could they always recognize each other? Or was one agent's provocateur another's terrorist?

I know of no direct evidence that the secret campaign against SDS, a campaign that was fully up to speed in 1968, was a prime cause of our destruction. Certainly the elected national leaders of SDS made two fatal mistakes in 1968 that seem to have been entirely of our own doing. One was to abandon the SDS commitment to democracy and nonviolence. The other was to disband the SDS national office when SDS most needed a coherent national voice.

And yet the evidence is pat that the destruction of a surging SDS exactly coincided with the onset of Cointelpro. One moment we were the brightest thing on the political landscape. Then came the charge of the secret brigades. Within a year, we lay in little bloody shards all over the map. Should we assume it was mere coincidence that our collapse coincided so exactly with the onset of Cointelpro?

No assessment of the collapse of SDS can be complete without some account of the still-secret FBI, army intelligence, and Red Squad programs whose specific purpose was to destroy it.

That account, if we ever get it, is still to come.

The demise of SDS is therefore still a mystery.

12 | Finding the Radical Center
New York, 1968

SDSERS BEGAN SHARING gossip about a Robert Kennedy presidential campaign early in the spring of 1968. RFK wasn't as openly dovish as Wisconsin's senator Eugene McCarthy, whose hat was already in the ring. But we all believed that McCarthy's bid was dead in the water, just to get the kids off the streets, whereas RFK had a real chance to win.

And as mainline politicians went, RFK was generally a good guy, although you couldn't say he was great. He had a strong anti-Mob record. He had gone after Teamster boss Jimmy Hoffa with a will. But he'd been only a tepid supporter of the civil-rights movement. He had ignored SNCC's appeals for help against organized racist attacks.

But he seemed better on the war. We knew that he had floated the notion of U.S. withdrawal as early as 1963 when JFK's White House was struggling with the assassination of South Vietnam's president Ngo Dinh Diem.[1]

The buzz of an RFK campaign went to a rumble in March, when LBJ said he would not run for reelection. This excited a good many antiwar people, including me, although most SDSers still affected a lofty disdain for liberals and big-party politics.

Shortly before the possibility of an RFK campaign became a public noise, a New England SDSer named Rick Dodge asked me a good question.

Rick said that his girlfriend's father, Eldredge Haynes, was chairman of a New York–based consulting firm called Business International,

Inc., which collected and analyzed data on foreign markets and sold the product to corporate subscribers. Rick said that he had been talking about SDS with Haynes for several months. He had given Haynes copies of the "Port Huron Statement" and several pieces of mine, including my SANE speech. Haynes told him that he had come to agree with SDS about the war, racism, and urban poverty. Haynes said he admired SDS for its commitment to politics and its energy. He said he might have been an SDSer himself had he been born a few decades earlier.

Haynes had recently asked Rick to see if I would be willing to meet with him to discuss a project he had in mind. Rick put the question to me. I said, "Sure. Why not? The guy sounds interesting."

So Rick played go-between and set up a meeting within the week for lunch at an overpriced restaurant at the Gotham Hotel in New York.

Eldredge Haynes was, I guessed, close to sixty, a tall, stooped, slender man with thinning white hair combed straight back over a high, peaked brow, a long, pale, troubled-seeming face, and steady, colorless eyes. He was wearing a blue blazer with gray slacks, a wrinkled white shirt, and a gray bow tie. As for me, I was in my basic movement working clothes, jeans and a brown corduroy jacket, having come to the meeting from a big outdoor rally at Columbia University.

Through lunch, I answered Haynes's questions about me and SDS, and he answered mine about himself and Business International. He was a Harvard man. He had spent much of his career in the foreign service but had left government during the Kennedy years to become a consultant to businesses operating in the "frequently turbulent" countries of the Third World. This work had grown into Business International, Inc.

CIA, right? I kept my suspicions to myself not only because my curiosity was up and running, but also because I actually hoped he was. I'd come to think the CIA, or at least a significant part of it, its analysts, had broken with LBJ on Vietnam.

I did have to play my own role, however, so I said as politely as I could that much of the "turbulence" of the countries in which BI and its customers operated was the work of the very companies that BI represented. Haynes, after all, sat before me as a spokesman for exactly the sort of multinational-corporate plunder of Third World countries that was the theme of my SANE speech and my book *Containment and Change*, which had just come out.

Urbane and diplomatic, Haynes didn't try to rebut my complaints. On the contrary, he said he had read the SANE speech and agreed with much of it. "You are to be congratulated," he said, "for helping Americans realize that a good many of today's crises lie in their own hands to resolve." A major purpose of Business International, he said, was to deliver this message to the companies that most needed to hear it.

Thus, his question: Would I be willing to present my views and discuss SDS at one of the round-table meetings that BI organized "for people from the private and public sectors who have a special interest in foreign affairs"?

"Like who?"

"Our participants include executives from General Motors, AT&T, General Eclectic, IBM, Ford, and the Associated Press. We also have a man from the State Department."

For easily one full second I pondered the complex political implications of meeting with such people. Then I said, "When do you want to do it?"

The next morning I sat at a long table at BI's office in the Gotham Hotel with nine white middle-aged men in suits and talked about corporate imperialism and the Vietnam War. It was bizarre but polite, no screaming.

Haynes introduced me: "Our guest today is a former president of the group that has currently shut down Columbia University."

I talked for fifteen minutes and outlined the themes of our protest. Big American corporations routinely pillage the Third World both abroad and at home. A current domestic example is Columbia's attempt to acquire and raze black neighborhoods for space to build a gym. As to the Vietnam War, our government's policy is inherently imperialist in that any conceivable military victory would leave us mired in Vietnam for decades. The VC's cause is one of national independence, poses no threat to American security, and in any case cannot be suppressed.

The other guys conceded a few points about the war and racism but said I was being unfair. They said our businesses brought much good to the Third World. They transformed backward populations into organized, trained, productive workforces. They modernized undeveloped economies and introduced isolated states to the world community.

We went around and around for a couple hours, then Haynes said, "Thank you, Mr. Oglesby. We have appreciated this opportunity to exchange views on these vexing problems."

I was thinking that was that, but then he said, "Perhaps you would be good enough to join us again and bring some of your friends from SDS."

This happened. I was at the Gotham again in two weeks with half a dozen SDSers from Columbia and CCNY. The "dialogue" was much the same but more vigorous and more focused on the militancy of our protest. SDS groups without me continued these meetings, sitting down with BI people four times that spring. Everybody seemed to find it a useful experience. No one's mind was changed, but I think we stopped demonizing each other.

Haynes and I kept meeting. A little later that spring, he popped the big question.

"Suppose Robert Kennedy were to become a presidential candidate. Do you imagine, Carl, that SDS might be inclined to support him?"

"No way. Impossible. Forget it. You can't get there from here."

"Why do you seem so uncertain?"

"Two reasons. One is that our founders were traumatized in the cradle by liberals." I told him about the bitter dispute in the early sixties in Ann Arbor when city officials denied a permit to a free school created by early SDSers, including my wife, Beth. The free school reached out to university liberals for support. The liberals turned their backs, even though some of them had kids in the school. "This left some scars. The first rule of SDS politics is that liberals can only be trusted to betray you."

"And the second reason? Is it equally tentative?"

"Less angry," I said, "more tactical. RFK needs New Left support like a hole. Hawks would feast on that. Many of us do want RFK to run and beat the hell out of Nixon, but we know better than to say it out loud."

"I hadn't noticed that SDS is often reticent," he said.

"But we're not always nitwits. We know that only a president can stop the war."

"So why is Eugene McCarthy not your candidate?"

"He seems less a candidate than a stalking horse. And he's too interested in getting the kids off the streets. Only RFK has a real chance to beat Nixon. His record of solid ambivalence on the war would play well in middle America. As president, he would probably stop the bombing, make a truce, start negotiations, and get the troops back home without blowing the roof off the Pentagon, and then turn the country's attention to poverty and racial discord. This is good enough to pray for."

He mulled it over without saying anything, so I added, "And among our heavies," I said, "Tom Hayden seems to have a high regard for RFK. So I probably wouldn't be alone in arguing that SDS should just stand aside and let him do his thing."

He still seemed unconvinced, so I said, "Besides, we're too busy trashing banks and draft boards and college presidents' offices to care much about the games grown-ups play." At last he smiled silently and nodded.

Popular support for the war had stood at 75 percent at the end of 1965. By the end of 1966, it had fallen to less than 50 percent.[2] It continued to fall through 1967, and the Tet Offensive of January 1968 gave it another big blow. The prowar side was reeling.

This is why I was so intrigued by the feeler from Haynes. I had been arguing from the beginning of my trip with SDS that we needed to organize toward the center—to our right, not to our left. It was perhaps my addiction to irony, perhaps my political innocence, but I had decided early on that it made sense to speak of "the radical center" and "militant moderation." I meant that we should be radical in our analysis but centrist in reaching out to conservatives.

This had become a main theme of mine right after I joined SDS. My speech at the 1965 SANE antiwar march on Washington, for example, had called on liberals to join our fight against an unconstitutional war. I took my ideas even more explicitly toward the right in 1967 in the last chapter of my part of *Containment and Change*, where I sang the praises of anti-imperialist conservatives such as Murray Rothbard, Robert Taft, Frank Chodorov, and Dean Russell, as well as the remarkable Garet Garrett, who warned in 1952, "We have crossed the boundary that lies between Republic and Empire." My argument that "the Old Right and the New Left are morally and politically coordinate" had bothered SDS's conventional leftists, but I had held to it and by 1968 had grown all the more convinced that SDS's strongest path lay toward the center.

And this is why it seemed to me in early 1968 that a quiet but friendly attitude toward an RFK presidential campaign was very possibly the movement's only way to help stop the war.

THIS QUESTION OF what SDS should do in view of its gathering victories in the great Vietnam debate began to boil when Johnson announced on March 31 that he would not seek reelection. Vice President Hubert Humphrey was still the Democrats' presumptive nominee, but now an RFK campaign could unfold without cracking the Democratic Party in two.

Our cause had grown more powerful after Harrison Salisbury, senior editor of *The New York Times,* filed the first of a long series of dispatches from Hanoi confirming what we protesters, as well as several of America's European allies, had been saying all along, that the U.S. bombing of North Vietnam had caused massive civilian casualties. The Pentagon denounced Salisbury's reports, but popular revulsion against the Strategic Air Command's bombing campaign grew palpable. It was with an awful cost in blood, but the antiwar tide was becoming a tidal wave.[3]

I thought we could see the end.

FOR A WHILE I allowed myself to see my experience with Eldredge Haynes as proof that victory could actually be ours, that SDS could become a builder of the radical center.

I must confess, too, that I'd been scared of heavy-metal politics from the beginning, whether you called it acting up, as our supermilitants called it, or acting out, as I called it, or simple rioting, as the police and the media called it. My fears of SDS's leftward inclinations were strengthened by my sense, as of the BI meetings, that an alternative to a politics of rage was within our reach, and that it was essential that we choose it. Big as we might have become on our own stage, that stage was still only a tiny part of the great theater of the real world. There was no way for us to achieve our objectives, I thought, without at some point establishing a sotto voce relationship with mainstream grown-ups.

Now this seemed on the verge of happening. I thought I could make out the glimmerings of the City on the Hill. SDS would establish itself as a serious force on the political scene, a voice for the growing body of young Americans who wanted a seat at the table.

BERNARDINE DOHRN was one of SDS's three national secretaries in 1968. I wanted her to meet with BI, my hope being that a face-to-face encounter might open her up. But she was certain that BI was not our kind of crowd. Our paths happened to cross at LaGuardia Airport a little after I'd suggested that she go with me to meet Haynes. We found an empty waiting room to sit down in.

"From what you tell me, Carl," she said, "this BI thing has got to be a front for the CIA. Okay? And even if it isn't, it seems to be looking for a way to manipulate us. How can you want SDS to play footsie with imperialist pigs like these guys?"

"Yes, my friend, it has occurred to me that Haynes might have a CIA tie. But if Haynes or the CIA has a secret agenda, I believe it's not to screw us up but to use us in some way to help make RFK president."

"Well, it could be both, couldn't it?" she said. "You say this BI's thing is to gather intelligence on Third World countries and sell it to the guys you once denounced as corporate imperialists. I don't understand you, Carl. It seems like you talk one way and act another."

"I've always believed we should organize toward the center."

"What would you hope to gain by this?"

"I'm not sure, BD," I said. "But what I am very sure of is that there's nothing to our left but chaos and oblivion."

She gave me a puzzled, frowning half smile.

I said, "Well, what? Are we only preaching to the converted now? If we could open up the Haynes crowd to some kind of dialogue, maybe we could learn something. Maybe we could even teach them something."

"Like what? That the Chase Manhattan should stop financing apartheid in South Africa? That General Electric should stop making stun guns for the pigs in Brazil? That Dow Chemical should stop making napalm for Vietnam?"

"Yes, to all of the above," I said. "We should keep on saying what we have to say. And we should say it to anybody who will listen to us, including BI, the CIA, Chase, GE, Dow, whoever."

"All right, let's play a game," she said. "What's the best thing you think we could get out of this?"

"Okay. We could find out that some influential people in the foreign-policy community are turning against the war. They're starting to see Bobby Kennedy as the way to go. We can show them that SDS is not a bunch of crazies, and that they should pay attention to what we have to say. Okay so far?"

"I understand your words, but I don't think you understand yourself what you're saying," she said. "But anyway, then what?"

"Damn it, Bernardine, I don't know. Maybe we could help the country get a president who cares about the things we care about? Maybe we get the FBI off our ass? Maybe the war ends a split second sooner? One or two bombs don't get dropped? A hundred fewer people get killed?"

"Good luck."

"I really wish you'd meet with these people. You could tell them to their faces that the revolution is coming and their days are numbered. And they would fall madly in love with you and do anything you told them to do. Wouldn't that be a trip?"

She chuckled and shook her head. "You're a strange man, Carl."

"So what?"

"I can't connect your dots, that's what. First you make this really good speech at the SANE march against the war. A lot of us, me included, thought it was really good. Okay? You describe in this speech a form of colonialism that's run more by big companies than the state. Okay? Corporate imperialism. Cool. Then you write this book about it, a good, pissed-off book. Same argument, lots more evidence. Very cool. Because we read this stuff and were moved by it, a lot of people got busted for sitting in at the Chase Manhattan Bank. Okay? Now you want SDS to sit down for a friendly political chat with the types that just had them put in jail." She laughed. "Carl, what am I not getting here?"

"Bernardine, no plausible reading of that speech could take it as a call for revolution, or even for rejection of liberal values."

"What values got us into Vietnam? What values keep trying to knock off Castro?"

"People betray their values all the time."

"Was John Kennedy a liberal?"

"Yes, and somebody killed him for it."

"Is Lyndon Johnson a liberal?"

"He's a lying crook."

"Oh. So liberals can be crooks."

"Go back to school, BD. This Haynes guy is exactly the kind of person we don't ordinarily get a chance to talk to."

"So we're trying to talk to warmongers now?"

"We're trying to talk to people who make decisions about war and peace, yes. I think we're saying things they don't usually have to hear. I think they're starting to doubt the war. Look, we all changed to get where we're at. Why can't you imagine that these guys might change, too?"

She looked at me with a bemused half smile, her arms folded.

"Bernardine," I said, "you've heard of dialogue, right?"

"I've also heard of taking a stand."

"Suddenly I'm not taking a stand? Look, if you think we can win this fight with what we've got, without finding new sources of support or neutralizing some of the opposition, you're even more naive than I am."

"New support is fine. New ways to get fucked over are bad."

"How is it getting fucked over when the other guys say they heard what we're saying and want to talk? We'd be nuts not to hear what they have to say."

She gathered her jacket and bag and stood up. "Friend, I'll tell you what they'll have to say. They'll say: Get the kids off the street, vote for

Bobby Kennedy, and we'll consider you for, you know, like dog catcher. Okay? Now I've got a flight to catch." She blew me a kiss and split for her gate.

There was no way to resolve this argument. She thought like the ultras who attacked Peter Weiss's play about Trotsky: Only the forbidden can be permitted.

Things didn't get more brutal between us yet because we liked each other. BD had brains, bravado, and beauty. She embodied the part of a many-sided SDS that was most charismatic, most willing to take risks.

But timid liberal that I was, I also thought this was SDS's most dangerous side, a flaw with a real chance of going fatal. Like a number of SDSers, BD had a bit too much confidence in her own anger. She could seem easily as fierce a fundamentalist as the folks in my South Carolina family. She had the word. She knew the truth. There was one god, the dialectic. The savior was Marx. Salvation was the revolution. End of discussion. The saved might disagree about tactics, but the revolutionary goal was fixed. A lot of ink was spilled in those days, and I spilled a good bit of it myself, on the question of what the New Left was, what made it *left*, what made it *new*. But for Bernardine, the question of our essential identity was settled and fixed. The New Left was SDS, and SDS was what she and her cohorts chose to do. Her SDS discussed its philosophy in the streets. Action was all. The American system was evil because it was killing masses of people for the profit of a few, and our task as revolutionaries was to do whatever we could to hasten its overthrow. As for dialogue, you don't have dialogue with the Devil.

But hell was my favorite hangout. The Devil was my favorite dinner companion. Surely I was damned.

I COULDN'T DENY that the BI-SDS meeting was politically risky for me. It was a big gamble about my future with the movement. For some SDSers, I knew I'd been a little suspect from the start because of my background in defense, and my new fascination with BI would hardly still the doubters.

But I just had to say to hell with worrying about that. To my mind, one of SDS's best qualities was its experimental attitude, its willingness to cut through received assumptions and try to turn conflict into dialogue with anyone who would listen and talk, including imperialists. So for me, an SDS conversation with the BI people was at least an interesting experience, maybe useful in helping to pull the center toward us, maybe even exciting.

Because for me the revolution was not god. It was a howl of all-too-human pain and rage, and it was provoked by the behavior of the master countries of the advanced world, by the imperial West, in big part by the United States, whose policies sucked the natural-resource wealth out of the nations of the Third World and corrupted their political systems to ensure that this pillage would go on.

The black upheaval in our inner cities, in what some leaders of the black rebellion were calling "internal colonies," was analogous to this. The common theme linking the rebels of Vietnam to those of Harlem was a need for power over one's destiny, for control of one's identity.

Yes, the 1960s revolt of America's black ghettos was more complex than the rebellion of, say, the Vietnamese in that it was in one part a struggle for racial equality within the American nation but in another part a struggle for independence from it, for black power, a struggle partly for integration and partly for separation, its voice partly that of King and partly that of Malcolm X, partly a demand for a share of the America Dream and partly a demand for escape from the American Nightmare.

Yet American politicians insisted on demonizing the people who were fighting this revolution as threats to American security, people whom they saw as motivated not by a need for national freedom but by a malicious need to bring America down. Revolutionaries were therefore *evil*, diabolical enemies of God-blessed America whom the right-thinkers among us were mandated to attack with napalm and guava bombs.

As one white American among the many who came to see the VC as fighters for Vietnam's liberation, I believed it was not impossible for other white Americans to see things this way, too, even businessmen, and through this recognition perhaps to change the way they lived in the world. Why was this crazy?

The alternative was an abysmal future of continual unrest and insecurity and the constant threat of violent impotence and an erosion of our civil liberties as an unavoidable result.

Even a businessman could see this, I believed. If SDS could get some corporate VPs to open their minds to this perspective, and to see that we who had taken to the streets to oppose the war and racism were campaigning not to destroy America but rather to rescue its vaunted commitment to freedom and equality, would that not be a good thing?

Should we not leap at an opportunity to get this message across to businessmen such as Eldredge Haynes? If we could encourage some of them in their growing uncertainty about the war, wouldn't that be good? Wouldn't it be good if some of them realized that police brutality was bad for business? And if a mainstream politician like Robert Kennedy was ready to carry such a message, wouldn't that be good?

This was so simple! Why the hell could a smart person like Bernardine not see it? She was probably right in assuming that BI and Haynes were tied to Kennedy and very possibly to the CIA. We knew we had informers among us, that our phones were tapped, our bedrooms bugged. So how could we assume that BI's apparent friendliness was not deceptive?

But who cared? As far as I was concerned, the more the CIA knew about SDS, the better. We had nothing to hide! Some of our snoops, of course, especially the ones from the FBI, wouldn't have been deterred to find our signatures on the Declaration of Independence. Some of them were out to crush us no matter how legitimate we were simply because we operated outside their system.

As to the provocateurs among us, all we could assume was that they would cast themselves as supermilitants. I thought there was nothing to do about it but make sure people were aware of the threat and stay immovably committed to our basic message and our open, nonviolent, democratic style. People who strayed from that into violence thereby turned in their membership cards. Violence was wrong and always counterproductive.

Admittedly this was getting harder to say in view of the rough confrontations that were becoming increasingly common ever since our attempt to shut down the Oakland induction center the previous October. Or at Madison that same month, when SDSers defended themselves aggressively against police attack. Well, I could say, we didn't bomb the army buses at Oakland, we just sat down in front of them. And as to struggling with the cops in Madison, no commitment to nonviolence cedes the basic human right of self-defense against illegal attack.

For sure, J. Edgar Hoover himself seemed crazy, but maybe some of his agents could see the truth about us, maybe hear the truth of what we were trying to say. I lived on Maybe Street.

But we were to learn much later that there was at least a shred of substance to this hope. In his 1975 book *FBI: An Uncensored Look behind the Walls,* Sanford Ungar documents a clash between Hoover and one of his top officers, William Sullivan, precisely over the question of the legitimacy of SDS and the antiwar movement as a whole. As Ungar reports, Hoover directed his investigators to tell him that the movement was a creature of the American Communist Party, that we were funded and controlled by secret agents of the Soviet KGB. Sullivan managed the FBI's surveillance of us from his position in charge of the FBI's Domestic Intelligence Division. He came to believe that we were straight. Even as he reported that the Weathermen were preparing to adopt a strategy of "urban guerrilla warfare," Ungar writes, he also "flatly declared that there were no links between the Communists and the student radicals."

This report angered Hoover and led to a lengthy feud between him and Sullivan.[4] No one could have known about this at the time, of course, but I wasn't surprised to find out about it. Good for Sullivan! The more such family feuds the better!

Given that we were targeted, I believed that our only feasible defense was our innocence, a view that made Bernardine scoff.

"My dear friend and comrade," she said, "you cannot make a shield of naïveté!"

WHETHER HAYNES was a defector from the prowar consensus or not, the first half of 1968 was a period of storm surge in antiwar sentiment throughout American society, a surge that swept several of Johnson's top foreign-policy advisers with it. No one outside the administration could have known it at the time, though several of us suspected it, but the rebels against LBJ now included his secretary of defense, Robert McNamara; his foreign-policy adviser Clark Clifford, who took over as secretary of defense when McNamara left in February; his UN ambassador, Arthur Goldberg; his generally archconservative undersecretary of the navy, Paul Nitze; and his undersecretary of the air force, Townsend Hoopes.[5]

These defections stayed concealed for years, but others, perhaps of even greater political weight, emerged in plain view soon after the January Tet Offensive.

The *Wall Street Journal,* for example, had supported the war from the beginning. But shocked by the Tet Offensive, its conservative chief editorial writer, Joseph Evans, wrote on February 23, "We think the American people should be getting ready to accept, if they haven't already, the prospect that the whole Vietnam effort may be doomed. . . . We believe that the Administration is duty-bound to recognize that no battle and no war is worth any price." Evans concluded that "everyone had better get prepared for the bitter taste of a defeat beyond America's power to prevent."

Then four days later, with even greater weight, came Walter Cronkite of CBS, the dean of TV anchormen and the voice of the American middle class. Cronkite had gone earlier that month to South Vietnam, where he spent two weeks interviewing hundreds of officials and military people. Back in New York, he presented a half-hour CBS News special on the war on February 27. He ended the program with a rare personal statement:

It seems now more certain than ever that the bloody experience of Vietnam is to end in a stalemate. This summer's almost certain standoff will either end in real give-and-take negotiations or terrible escalation; and for every means we have to escalate, the enemy can match us, and that applies to invasion of the North, the use of nuclear weapons, or the mere commitment of one hundred or two hundred or three hundred thousand more American troops to the battle. And with each escalation, the world comes closer to the brink of cosmic disaster. It is increasingly clear to this reporter that the only rational way out will be to negotiate, not as victors but as an honorable people who lived up to their pledge to defend democracy, and did the best they could.[6]

Nine million Americans heard him.[7]

The statements of the *Wall Street Journal* and Cronkite were major defections from the prowar media consensus. The Cronkite broadcast especially, by report, "shocked and depressed Johnson."[8] Antiwar protesters might circle the White House, but this was a new kind of siege.

Our national debt was up, our taxes were up, our inner cities were up in flames, our war strategists were up a tree, our kids were up to their necks in killing and getting killed in a lost cause, our North Atlantic allies were almost up in arms against us. The war had to come to an end. Johnson had to go.

And the man who seemed uniquely positioned to do the job was RFK.

I had my answer ready for the SDSers who would liberal-bait me for my relationship with Haynes and my support for RFK.

It was baby simple. The argument for revolution was an expression of hopelessness in the "system." It was therefore least defensible when some of the system's people were trying to turn it around. And this was happening: McNamara, Clifford, Nitze, Hoopes, Cronkite, Haynes, RFK. The war that would drag on for another seven years seemed on the verge of being ended. I thought the in-house effort to stop it obliged us to give the system a bit more rope.

Today I look back on this spring of '68 as the last time at which SDS might still have gone more or less straight and come out of it all healthy enough to establish itself as a long-term presence in American education.

A scenario: RFK wins the nomination, wages an implicitly antiwar campaign with the passive or even quarrelsome support of the antiwar movement, wins office, moves the war to some kind of internationally brokered truce, and gets America's attention focused again on domestic problems.

And maybe SDS would get the dog pound!

THERE WAS NO TIME to think about any of this. Not far from the BI meetings at the Gotham Hotel, an SDSer named Mark Rudd was leading one of our larger and more militant chapters in a sit-in at Columbia University to protest its war-related research and its plan to build a gym in Morningside Park, despite the objections of the people who lived there.

Rudd had persuaded a reluctant SDS chapter to make the move from protest to resistance. Hundreds of students broke into Columbia president Grayson Kirk's office, occupied it, and refused to leave. The energy level among the SDSers reached a powerful high. Tom Hayden was drawn to the scene, going inside to encourage the occupation. I was there, too, back at the steps of Low Library to do a turn on the bullhorn, with a police unit forming an attentive part of the crowd.

All during the days of the occupation, self-forming working groups of student rebels and supportive teachers were mapping out the foundations of the Columbia Free University that would come into being in the months after the sit-in. The free-university movement, a signature product of SDS, was born in those months. It was to have a deep impact on American education. It broke down traditional barriers between teachers and students, forced prolonged reconsideration of the grading system, toppled the ivory tower, and focused the schools' attention on the problems confronting society.

And Chicago cops were already busting heads in the Loop, as though in training for August, when the Democrats' national convention would be in town.

This period was the high tide of the student movement. The Education Testing Service estimated that SDS membership at this point, the spring of 1968, stood at about 140,000. We had well over 400 chapters. Many of them were at that point leading campus strikes. We were present in every state.

And in Paris and Nanterre in May and June, behind the leadership of Danny "the Red" Cohn-Bendit, the French student movement was threatening to reach critical mass.

West Germany's Rudi Deutschke was leading an equally militant student demand to "tear down the wall."

Masses of students were on the move in Spain, Sweden, Denmark, Brazil, Guatemala, and Mexico. I made speaking trips to England, Scotland, Wales, Italy, and Japan. The New Left had gone global, ever more confident of its power and certain of its cause.

Fortune for June 1968 editorialized, "You can't argue with success, and SDS has yet to lose a battle." And after a good afternoon session with yet another BI group, I could still flatter myself that my case for the radical center was being stated by events themselves. My gamble was going to pay off. SDS was becoming a player. We would not destroy ourselves in an orgy of play-school Leninism. The hawks would be caged by the RFK coalition, which would capture the presidency, end the war, and move the country on to welfare reform and the burning problems of the inner cities.

Fathers and mothers would smile and open their arms. Sons and daughters would return to the bosom of the family.

And a minor playwright would find a money job somewhere and go back to his wife and kids and his basement study.

What was so crazy?

LATE ONE WARM June night in New York, I was on the subway headed uptown. As the train stopped at the Thirty-fourth Street station, I noticed an elderly black man on the other side of the platform scurrying from car to car. He crossed over to the car I was in and stuck his head in the door.

He was short of breath and his eyes were wide and wet. He was wearing a narrow-brim hat. His beige shirt was buttoned at the wrists and collar. His face was round with precise features. His cheeks wore a few days' growth of gray stubble.

He looked around the half-empty car, then fixed his staring brown eyes on me. In a loud stage whisper, he said, "Bobby Kennedy has been shot and killed!"

13 | The Whole World Is Watching
Chicago, 1968

AFTER MIDNIGHT two days later, RFK's coffin arrived in New York to lie in state at St. Patrick's Cathedral. In the crowd of several hundred that met the body and sat all night in silent vigil were SDS's Tom Hayden and Chicago's Mayor Richard J. Daley. In two more months, Hayden and Daley would be the opposing field generals of the great week-long battle of Chicago's Grant Park, a confrontation that was in a strong and complex sense the Tet Offensive of the antiwar movement, a battle that ended with both sides in tatters.

But this night in early June, in this huge and beautiful cathedral in midtown Manhattan, Hayden and Daley were united in mourning for the one man who might have united them in politics. Imagine Hayden walking down the aisle to find Daley on his knees in prayer, then joining him.

When Hayden heard of RFK's assassination at two or three that morning, he had "immediately freaked out," as someone put it, first phoning all his friends, including me, to call us to arms, summoning everyone at last to real rebellion in real streets. No more fun and games! This was it!

Masses of impassioned citizens and equally impassioned police were soon rushing up and down Greenwich Village's narrow, twisting streets, each side sometimes chasing and sometimes being chased. Mayhem.

Something like this scene was enacted with variations that night in Washington, Akron, San Francisco, Ames, Milwaukee, Detroit, Baltimore, Tucson, Roanoke, and on and on, more than a hundred spontaneous demonstrations varying in scale and violence but as to message always the same: If RFK can be killed, any of us can be killed!

"Look what black people did when King was murdered!" a furious Hayden had yelled at me. "They tore the place up! Now what will we white people do when the victim is another Kennedy?"

Even Eldredge Haynes was outraged. He called me that morning to say, "All bets are off, Carl. Get your people out and tear the goddamn place into pieces!"

A lot of us tried, and with no need for marching orders from me. But I felt sadness, not anger, when I saw the smashed windows. *Come on,* I thought, *this little shop owner didn't kill anybody.*

But the Southern Baptist in me felt some sympathy for the Catholic in Hayden. I can already hear him scoff, but I think he had seen the RFK of June 1968 as a kind of savior, the only politician among us capable of offering a way out of the impasse, the one all-star in the Democrats' bullpen who could be relied on to strike out the side, clean up after Johnson, beat back Nixon's assault, end the bloodshed, bring the troops home, calm the tumult, reconcile the dissenters and loyalists, create a functional governing coalition open to civil-rights and social-rights causes, and restore that ineffable sense of legitimacy that American government had begun to lose with the assassination of his brother almost five years before, and which the news from Vietnam shredded anew every day.

Hayden might fairly object that I'm projecting my own hidden hopes onto him. But whatever his reasoning or his instinct that night, news that RFK was dead seemed to explode something in him. Frustrated, outraged, wild with grief and impotence, he went bellowing out into the early morning Village night, calling people to the streets, looking for a riot to join.

"First King, now another Kennedy!" he screamed at me. "How long are people gonna sit still for this kind of shit?"

The stance of the Chicago organizing group did not change after the RFK murder. The promise of nonviolence in Chicago was not taken back. And because movement activists had always been so dismissive of

RFK to begin with, there was no need to ask if his assassination changed anything.

At the same time, movement people did notice that the MLK and RFK assassinations had in fact changed the whole lay of the land. And from the movement's standpoint, the change was vastly for the worse. Now there was no strong, well-established liberal hero whom we could look to in furtive glances as we pretended not to need him, no one who could get real things done in the real world that we pretended to ignore. We would still pretend to be above conventional politics. We would still support nonviolence. But I could feel an anger and a desperation in movement people that I had not felt before.

"We've been challenged," said a future Weatherman I was close to. "We've got to show them we can fight back."

The new anger seemed almost to welcome the looming prospect of Chicago violence. Not because silly people had begun to think of street fights with well-trained, well-armed, well-motivated cops as a fun way to spend a few days in the City of Big Shoulders. No, it was welcomed because it was no longer avoidable. It was unavoidable because the police wanted it, convinced it was time for a showdown. Mayor Daley wanted it, ready to show that his was the fist that ran Chicago. FBI director Hoover wanted it, tired of playing games with these crypto Commies. The Republicans probably wanted it, too. How could it fail to amuse them to contemplate the problems a riotous convention week would create for the Democrats? And the media people smelled hot copy.

Hayden could see this. Why did he keep saying, "See you in Chicago"? Did he not know that wise guerrilla warriors avoid confrontations they know they cannot win? We could not win the pitched battle that Mayor Daley was preparing for and in fact seemed to be trying to provoke, as with his refusal until the very last minute to issue park permits.

But I didn't see anything in the Loop group's organizers but a stubborn pressing ahead with no thought to the changed situation. They kept promising a week of nonviolent protest when they very well knew the week could in no way be nonviolent.

I learned sometime in July that our organizers were indeed expecting to be attacked by the Chicago cops. People were told to start training in techniques of nonviolent self-protection. We were advised to go to Chicago in small "affinity groups," cells of a dozen or so people prepared to look after each other, so that no matter what happened, no one would ever be alone or unaccounted for.

And some SDSers were getting ready to make the most of whatever was coming.

"Until it comes to a physical fight," I recall future Weatherman Jeff Jones saying to me, "it's all just a game. And it will be all to the good if the fight starts with the TV lights on." Jeff was then a lean, good-looking, warmhearted young college man with long blond hair and a constant smile, not the kind of guy who goes looking for a fight.

"But what if we lose?" I said.

Jeff chuckled. "We can't lose. Just by getting into a fight, we win. You don't see that?"

"You're losing me, Jeff."

He shrugged. "Whatever happens, we show the power elite that's running this illegal war that it can't continue without paying a price."

"And that price is what?"

"That price is a rise in disturbances in American streets. This shows the people that our rulers aren't all-powerful, that they can't guarantee the security of the domestic rear any more than they can stop the rebels in Vietnam."

"Jeff, don't you realize that this will just bring harsher police repression?"

"Maybe, but so what? Our answer to that is more anger, more angry people. This is how the dialectic works, right?"

"Where does this end?"

He grinned. "The revolution, man."

"And then the counterrevolution?"

He laughed. "Really, Carl, this has to happen. We have to get ready for it. We have to welcome it."

"Why not keep building, like, sideways? Building the *size* of the protest?"

"Great," he said, "but the war is so obviously bad by this time that antiwar feeling will keep growing with or without SDS. Let SANE and the Mobe do more mass marches. You keep on making your speeches."

"Making speeches? I thought I was organizing."

"Face it, Carl. Somebody's got to raise the stakes."

"You don't think you'll just scare people off?"

"Maybe some, sure, but it's just as likely to make others come out. And the ones who do come out will be all the more committed."

As with Bernardine, there was no last word.

So partly as a result of my hung debate with Bernardine and Jeff and their friends in the group that would soon be styled the Weathermen, and partly because I just didn't think we could win in that arena, I'd begun shamelessly arguing to anyone who would listen to me that we should not go to Chicago at all.

In March that year, at the SDS National Council meeting in Lexington, Kentucky, five days before King was murdered and the grief riots erupted in eighty cities, I had actually argued, as Hayden himself once had argued, that SDS needed to get over its fixation with the war and return to its original concerns with racism, white poverty, and the reform of education. In particular, I had thought we needed to find ways to support the black-power movement and help keep it from getting isolated.

I don't doubt that my own fixation with the war contributed to SDS's. Of course, it was the daily news reports that overwhelmingly fed this fixation, but I had spent my time as SDS president and the nearly two years since then in constant argument against the war. Racism and poverty remained core issues for SDS, but the war was preemptive and we had no choice but to help build the opposition.

But I didn't feel good about the way many of the most committed SDSers seemed to be moving, especially since the RFK assassination. Many shared Jeff's conviction that the stakes had to be raised. And many, Hayden among them, saw the Democratic National Convention as an opportunity for the eruption of something new and big. Well and good, but the bad guys were waiting for us, ready to rumble, and the right wing would rejoice.

So my line was that what would be really new and in its own way bold would be to greet the DNC with total silence.

"Evacuate Chicago!" I implored that summer. "Make Chicago a ghost town in August!" If we were there, confrontations would happen. They would be sharp because the cops were being pumped up, as by Gerald S. Arenberg, founder of the American Federation of Police, who told his crowd, "We are at war with an enemy just as dangerous as the Viet Cong in Southeast Asia."[1]

And sharp confrontations at the DNC would inevitably play better for the right than the left. Democrats would suffer and Republicans would prosper. That "bitch of a war," as Johnson was privately calling it,[2] would just keep on worsening.

And if we just had to do something at convention time, why not go to Miami to play with the Republicans? Or why not hold small counter-conventions in other cities to critique the two-party system and update our objections to the war?

In the absence of Robert Kennedy, who might have made demonstrations almost a lovefest, massing in Chicago was the worst strategic mistake the antiwar movement could make.

Thus did I embroil myself in a one-sided running debate with the Chicago demo's key proponents and organizers, Tom Hayden, Rennie Davis, and David Dellinger, the Loop offensive's strategic high command. One-sided, I call it, because none of them paid the least attention to me.

The organizers were in a bind. SDS had decided on the DNC action while RFK was still alive. To cancel it after his death would have come too close to confessing that the real purpose of the action had been to celebrate his anointment.

No matter how RFK's death had changed the situation, the Chicago action was simply going to happen. Hayden, Davis, and Dellinger had decided, and movement culture made it impossible for them to admit that RFK had had anything to do with it. Their lives in that frantic summer were filled with the enormous detail work an effort like theirs entailed, chartering buses, begging for funds, setting up contacts, finding paper clips. The big picture was fixed. Hayden spent some time in Paris that summer helping with North Vietnam's release of three American POWs, but his mantra always remained, "See you in Chicago!"

My mantra remained "Evacuate Chicago! Chicago is a trap! Chicago can kill us! Stay out of Chicago!" But there was a magnetism about the DNC action that many found irresistible, maybe because the premonition of high drama was so acute. I still think my "ghost town" strategy might have worked, might have kept us strong without wounding the Democrats badly just before their coming fight against Nixon. Our Chicago action was an anti-Republican protest wrongly delivered to the Democrats' door. It gave the prowar Republicans a peace they didn't deserve. All SDS got for it was a face-off with some very muscular people.

For all its talk of "involving people in making the decisions that affect their lives," SDS had held no formal discussions of the merits of staging demonstrations against both conventions, against one or the other, or against neither one. The decision to join the Mobe in ignoring the Republicans in Miami and bringing people to Chicago to bother the Democrats had simply appeared full blown sometime before RFK was killed. Hayden, Davis, and Dellinger were working on it, so that's what we were going to do.

I was wholly out of the Loop group, and I was galactically outside of Hayden's mind. The main thing I knew about Hayden was that he was the only SDS heavy who had originally scorned SDS's decision to take up the antiwar cause. Through most of 1966, he remained dedicated to organizing the white poor. When he came over to the antiwar movement, my doubtless too cynical impression was that he did so because he realized that the war was where the action was, a classic case of the leader running to catch up with his followers.

As for his Chicago field generalship, I have yet to see what he thought our Chicago objectives really were beyond making a big scene. I never saw the reasons for SDS's sudden, uncharacteristic interest in big-party politics, or why we should harass the Democrats instead of the Republicans.

The decision to go to Chicago was doubly absurd, I argued, because we didn't do party politics and because the passion to fight the Vietnam

War burned most fiercely on the Republican right wing. The only justification for a big rally at the Democrats' convention that I could see
had been to help set the stage for the appearance of a coalition among
RFK's party liberals, King's civil-rights liberals, Senator McCarthy's
peace liberals, and the antiwar movement's closet liberals, but such an
argument was never made.

If it had been, it certainly would have been worth talking about.
SDS's main problem with such a scenario probably would have been
that it looked like co-optation, but that was a problem we could happily
have dealt with when the war was over, when black people and poor
whites had a friend in the White House, and when students could feel
that they had fought their way into a place in the nation's political life.
A Kennedy-King alliance would have offered the most realistic possibility that liberal Democrats would take power and open up these possibilities.

Then bang, bang. The MLK and RFK hits threw the whole national
left into disarray, from the Democrats to SDS. And I think the RFK hit
especially changed everyone's sense of the movement's purpose in
Chicago. Before June 5, we were going there to say something about
hope. Afterward, we were going there to scream our hearts out.

WHEN FRIENDS ASKED me if I was planning to be in the crowd during the Democrats' convention week, I answered that I'd be far away in
Cambridge, celebrating ambivalence, starting my new column for
Boston Magazine, and getting ready for the coming semester as a visiting lecturer at MIT.

Then one day early in August, my editor asked if I would go to
Chicago to cover the streets.

All my arguments against being anywhere near Chicago during convention week flashed through my mind, as fresh and strong as ever.

So naturally I said, "Why not?"

I easily found a group of half a dozen people to go with.

We piled into somebody's station wagon for the long trip, me with
my notebook and pencil in hand.

That's why, on August 28, 1968, I was standing with my Cambridge friends, my "affinity group," near the band shell in Grant Park. Mayor Daley had granted the protest organizers a permit at the last minute. The permit was only for rallies in the park, but the people wrote their own permit when things got heavy and went where they thought they should go. The park was a few blocks from the Hilton Hotel in downtown Chicago, where most of the Democratic Party delegates were staying.

It was the third day of the rally, a warm, gray afternoon, when I heard Dellinger call my name over the PA. If I was in the audience, he said, would I please come to the front.

My group and I worked our way to the stage, and I asked a nervous-looking parade marshal to tell Dave I was there.

Dave looked frazzled. He was the MC. It wasn't easy to keep an event running smoothly in a situation like this.

"Carl, we need speakers," he said. "Please, will you take a turn?"

So having promised myself not even to be there, certainly not to tread the boards, trying to improvise lines in a play I didn't know, I was soon behind the microphone on the low-platform stage looking out on the scene before the battle.

The crowd numbered in the low thousands, not nearly the turnout the organizers had hoped for. We were surrounded by a line of several hundred stone-faced policemen standing shoulder to shoulder in black riot uniforms and white helmets. Some of them wore what I took to be Mace and tear-gas canisters on their belts, along with their regulation handguns in black holsters. All of them held their sticks at the ready in two hands across their chests.

Everyone in the crowd was standing. Their attention swung between the stage in front of them and the police around them. A heavy police presence had been expected, but being surrounded like this in a peaceful rally was new. The police cordon's purpose seemed to be to keep us from spilling onto the streets and bothering the delegates.

Our people were visibly crawling with anxiety. The vibes were as dissonant as vibes can get. You could hear the crowd rumbling in low quarter tones.

There were two narrow openings in the police line to get in and out by, one at the far end of the crowd and one at the side farthest from the hotel. Several of our people had already been roughed up. No one could have been surprised to see the heavy police presence, but no one could have expected to be surrounded this way.

I was maybe two minutes into the kind of talk you give when you don't know what to say, agitated like everybody else, my thoughts jumpy, when I saw two or three dozen cops collect off to my right behind the circle of cops who surrounded us. I saw a lot of people watching them uneasily, looking all around them at the police encirclement.

I stumbled along for another half minute. Then a guy in the middle of the crowd, maybe fifty yards straight out in front of me, threw something toward the cops. From the way it fluttered and lost speed in the air, I could tell it was something light, certainly not a rock. It looked like the core of an apple. I could see it clearly in its arc over the crowd. It flew well over the cops' heads and dropped harmlessly to the ground.

But as if this harmless missile were a cue, the separate squad of cops formed immediately into a double line and came marching through the cordon and into the crowd toward the guy who had thrown whatever it was, clubbing people to their left and right, people who didn't know what was happening and had nowhere to run because they were hemmed in by the cordon. People screamed and tried to pull back, but they got in each other's way and tripped over each other. Many in the line of the attack were trapped. I saw a young couple I knew from Columbus fall right at the feet of the cops. Both of them took serious jabs to the ribs and blows to the head as she tried to pull him back.

Yes, good old true-blue American cops were clubbing innocent, unresisting, helpless people who had committed no crime and had nowhere to run. They were doing it in the light of day in full view of hundreds of witnesses.

Did I rise to the occasion? Did great streams of passionate oratory come welling up out of me? Standing helplessly at the mike, I screamed, "Look at this! Where the hell are the media now? Look at this!"

A crowd can do little in the way of expressing itself actively but surge or chant, and now that it was penned up, this one could only chant.

And all it could find to chant was the slogan under which this entire demonstration might have been organized: "The whole world is watching!"

So the crowd began to chant this, even though at this particular place and time, the whole world was not watching at all, not any of it, because there were no cameras there. I could see that from where I stood. I knew how quickly the media's cameras normally react to a photo op like this, and I knew where the TV crews had been grouped only a few minutes before. They were not there now. Had they left to meet deadlines? Had there been a word to the wise? For whatever reason, this part of the week-long Chicago "police riot," as it came to be called, was not going to be on the evening news, no matter what the crowd chanted.

I stood there before this unfolding scene with a sense of staring into the abyss. In helpless counterpoint to the crowd's chant, in fear and outrage, in a certainty that we were beholding here the collapse of reason and the triumph of madness, a scene from hell itself, I could only shout into the microphone, "Where are the media now?"

"The whole world is watching!"

"Where are the cameras?"

"The whole world is watching!"

"Who keeps law and order when the police commit the crimes?"

"The whole world is watching!"

Dave came up beside me and said, "We've got to help these people get out of here."

I was glad to stand aside. Dave got on the microphone to start organizing a retreat as still more policemen charged into the crowd and got busy with their clubs.

My affinity group was calling to me from the side of the stage. I joined them, and we started looking for a way out. The bridge we had used to come over was now barricaded by National Guard barbed wire. But a bridge north of that was still open, and we followed the crowd pouring over it.

The police were at that point still trying to block Michigan Avenue in front of the Hilton Hotel, but fate intervened with the arrival—script this!—of a team of mules! Yes, a mule team in downtown Chicago, drawing an old-fashioned farm wagon!

The wagon, we later found out, was part of a civil-rights demonstration organized in the South and given a parade permit by the city long before. The National Guard opened the barricade for the wagon and then couldn't close it again as the crowd pushed through.

That night the media were present again as the angriest physical confrontations between protesters and police took place in front of the Hilton Hotel and in the streets around it. Even a few of the DNC delegates got chased and clubbed by the police. Lit off and on by the blue-white glare of the police and TV lights and often with gauzy clouds of tear gas hanging in the air, Michigan Avenue and the park across from the Hilton became a phantasmagorical blending of two very different but very American visions: The whole world was watching, all right, but mostly on a different channel.

14 | At Maggie's Farm
Indiana, 1968

IN THE IMMEDIATE AFTERMATH, I shared most movement people's feeling that the police riot would play well for us in middle America, all the more strongly so because Soviet tanks had just rolled into Prague to suppress the Czech rebellion. We started calling Daley's city "Chi-Prague-o."

But the actual denouement was not so clear.

The few print reporters on the scene at Grant Park and that night at the Hilton seemed to have been deeply affected by the experience. Their drawn notepads had seemed to make them special targets of the police. They could hardly keep assuming it was all by mistake that they were repeatedly clubbed, and they could not help being hurt. I mean physically hurt. Bruised. Bloodied. If they had never been certain how much to credit demonstrators' claims of unprovoked police violence, they were perfectly certain how to credit their own experience. They had been special targets. Cops had hit them on the head, hard, seemingly just for being there.

In that great born-again New Left concept of the soul, many reporters were in this way "radicalized." They realized that just getting clubbed by the cops didn't prove you were guilty of something.

But the TV coverage diminished the events that night to the dimensions of the medium that packages and delivers them, as one news item among others. The protest's enormous scale gave way to the size of the TV screen.

Moreover, what most reporters *did* report, the "story" of the police riot, seemed to strike much of middle America as the story of long-suffering fathers finally getting down to business with their spoiled brats. About time, too.

So, yes, the whole world was watching, but it saw only what the medium had taught it how to see.

OUR NATIONAL INTERIM COMMITTEE held a special meeting right after the DNC encounter at a place called Maggie's Farm, a house in the country in Indiana not far from Chicago. The meeting's purpose was to consider the question of movement strategy in view of the recent events. It would have been better if this meeting had happened two months earlier, because these events, at least in general form, had been well foreseen by then. We knew that Mayor Daley had drawn a line in the dirt and that we would cross it at some peril. This is why the organizers had urged us to form affinity groups. It's why they advised refresher sessions in techniques of nonviolent resistance.

Yet we failed to deal with the big strategic questions. We didn't ask what a fight with Daley's cops might mean politically. We didn't try to think through our options in responding to it.

One of our basic beliefs earlier in 1968 was that the antiwar side was winning the national debate, and nothing revealed by later studies has undermined that belief. On the contrary. Minus the assassinations of King in April and Kennedy in June, the summer of 1968 would very probably have seen the ascent of a strong antiwar coalition within the Democratic Party. We, of course, did not know it for a positive fact, but we easily sensed dramatic inner-circle defections from Johnson's attempt to force surrender on the Vietnamese through a strategy of brutal aerial bombardment. Johnson himself may have wearied of this at the end when he halted all bombing of North Vietnam and announced that he would not run for reelection.

But after the RFK assassination, no massing of antiwar forces was to be. Vice President Hubert Humphrey would become the Democrats' nominee, and he had long since committed himself to the war. The certain Republican nominee, Richard Nixon, would tell the Joint Chiefs of Staff that he wanted a victory in Vietnam and would give them whatever they needed to achieve it.

The mainstream liberals' central command had been destroyed. There was no longer a national focus for the wider antiwar cause.

How to deal with this? That's what the group of about fifty of us were meeting at Maggie's Farm to try to discuss. The troubled mood hanging over from Chicago quickened tempers. I came out of a reverie to hear a combative Mike Klonsky, one of the three SDS national secretaries, barking out my name.

"What is Oglesby trying to prove with this outfit called Business International? A company with a name like that has got to be a CIA front. Right? And even if it's not, it's still a voice for big business. I thought Oglesby was against these guys. Now here he comes organizing SDS meetings with this outfit and this big shot named Eldredge Haynes. What about it, Carl? I think it's time you tell us."

I started fumbling for an answer with an acute sense that I was in trouble. Klonsky was a spare, broad-shouldered, rugged man of close to thirty with an angular face and a strong nose, a strong, close-shaven jaw, his brown hair cut factory short. I knew from our games of touch football that he was a solid athlete. As I recall, he said he came from a family of Communist Party labor organizers on the East Coast docks, so he had grown up in a tradition that knew the physical side of politics. I'd found him surly and a bit of a bully, but he was a bulwark for SDS against the Progressive Labor Party's attempted intrusions, and in any case there he was, one of our key national officers, so I'd kept my mouth shut. And now I had to open it. What to say?

A few weeks before the Chicago action, Hayden had told me with a little grin, "Klonsky is going around saying, 'Oglesby is the most dangerous man in the movement.'"

"Coming from Klonsky," I said, "that's high praise."

Klonsky held me to be dangerous, Hayden said, because of my ability to persuade unformed minds that my liberalism, my extreme moderation, was okay.

"Come on, Carl," Klonsky said. "What's going on here?"

What could I say to this man? If I'd had my fighting gloves on, I'd have said: Mike, my friend, how many people have *you* brought into SDS? How many people have *you* turned on to movement actions? How many prowar experts have *you* faced in public debate? Who are *you* to call *me* to account? And yes, I might have said, I do try to reach out to people who are not like us, to people on our right like those in Business International who lead other kinds of lives. I want them to hear what we have to say, and I want SDS to hear what they have to say. What the hell else is building our base of support all about? Is turning leftward and demanding prescribed beliefs the way to bring new strength to our cause?

But I did not have my fighting gloves on, and I just sat there, growing older.

"We're all waiting for an answer, Carl," said Klonsky.

I was, too. So, completely befuddled, I opened my mouth to see what might come out.

And just then the phone rang. I know, I know, it's crude dramaturgy, but it happened.

The phone had a loud, old-fashioned bell that could call you in from the fields. It made us all stop. A guy on the other side of the room picked up the receiver. We all waited to see who it was.

"Hello?" he said. Then a brief pause. Then he turned toward me. "Carl, it's some guy for you. Long distance."

My thought was, "Please, God, not more trouble." I said, "Find out who it is and get the number. Tell him I'll call back later."

The guy said into the receiver, "Could I ask who's calling?" A brief pause, then he looked back to me.

"He says his name is Eldredge. He's calling from New York." I wasn't the only one in the room to gasp.

Klonsky said, "Ha!"

"Surely you jest," I said.

"No, he says Eldredge. He says you know him."

I couldn't believe such a coincidence, to be getting skewered about my BI connection at the very moment that Haynes should give me a call. A little titter fluttered around the room. And so chummy! "Eldredge," yet! Couldn't he at least have said "Mr. Haynes"?

Well, there was nothing to do but take the call. So I crawled over people's legs to get to the phone. Everybody was going to listen, so I didn't even try to talk in a low voice.

"Hello," I said. Static. "Hello? Eldredge?"

"Hey, Carl, my main man! How you doin'?"

The voice was deep, a little husky, the words spoken with a ghetto lilt.

It was like that moment in Chicago when the mule team appeared.

This was not at all Eldredge Haynes of Business International, Inc. It was Eldridge Cleaver of the Black Panther Party. Instead of one of the whitest men in the world, it was one of the blackest.

Some demon in me exulted. I felt a huge grin spread throughout my body.

"Hey, my man!" I said loudly. "Good to hear your voice! What's happening? How's life on the barricades?"

No one in the room could have expected this sort of reaction from me. One second I was mounting the gallows and the next I was vibing hallelujah. And I was not above feeling an inner glee in watching Klonsky's sneer dissolve. A little confusion in one's adversary is wonderful to behold.

But besides being grateful that this was Cleaver and not Haynes, of course, I was also full-out curious. I had admired Cleaver's book *Soul on Ice* and had met him briefly through SNCC friends after the King riots that spring. I followed most SDSers in seeing his purported crimes as acts of political rebellion. We didn't know yet that his record included several rapes. As of the moment of that phone call to Maggie's Farm, we knew Cleaver as an eloquent improviser from the soapbox with great personal charm and vitality. His emergence in a leadership role in the Black Panther Party had marked the black movement's transition from the rural South to the urban North, from an integrationist demand for civil rights and racial equality to a separatist demand for black power. His militant, confrontational political style had won him and the Panthers the admiration of most SDSers.

But surely Cleaver wasn't calling just to talk about life. What could this be about?

"Listen, my man," he said. "You ever hear of this Peace and Freedom Party?"

"Sure."

"They any good?"

"Yeah, they're good people. Why?"

"They want me to run a write-in presidential campaign this fall in a couple states."

"Hey, cool! Are you going to do it?"

"I think so, man."

"You ought to do it, Eldridge. That would be a strong move."

"All right, but there's one problem."

"Raising money, right?"

"Well, all right. Two problems."

"What's the other one?"

"I need a running mate," he said, "and it ought to be a white dude. And I can think of a thousand reasons, man, why this white dude ought to be you."

"Really? Like what?"

"Well, like everybody else on my list has turned me down."

"I'm flattered, my friend," I said. "It would be a great privilege to work with you."

"Way cool, man. So I can tell my guys you'll do it, right?"

"Tell them I *want* to do it, but something like this, you know, I've got to talk it over with my people."

"So talk. I'll hang on."

"No, it'll probably take a little while, okay?"

"How long?"

"I'll call you back tonight. You at your number?"

"Yeah, but don't fuck around, dude. I need this."

"Be there after dinner."

"All right, but do this, my brother! Just, you know, like *do* it!"

"I'm a disciplined man, my friend. I've got to see what the committee says. I'll call you as soon as I get a take."

My first thought was that the NIC people would be all for it. We all thought the black-power movement, a gift of the slain Malcolm X, was healthy for the black cause. But we were worried about black separatism, which had won support that spring from a former integrationist leader, SNCC field secretary Stokely Carmichael, who had become convinced after King's murder that blacks and whites could no longer work together.

And the leaders of the black-power movement, Cleaver and the Black Panther Party, were in serious trouble. The Panthers' chairman, Huey Newton, was in jail in Oakland on a charge of having shot and killed a policeman. The Panthers had organized a "Free Huey" campaign, and SDS had supported it in an effort to keep black militants from isolating themselves.

We knew that much of the Panthers' trouble was of their own making. Their slogan "It's time to pick up the gun" and their "off-the-pig" rhetoric was nothing more than empty posturing, since they knew they hadn't the remotest chance of surviving any serious firefight, and it infuriated the already hostile "pigs," many of whom had adopted "Oink!" as a greeting. Such impotent saber rattling was indeed just what their fiercest enemies wanted to hear. It conceded the moral high ground that was one of the great strengths of the civil-rights cause under King's leadership. It frightened away potential supporters. It picked up the gun only to hand it to their enemies. If the Panthers were to have any political future at all, they badly needed to get back to reality. They needed white allies.

And running a political campaign around a black-white ticket seemed to me not a bad way for the Panthers to start sending a healthier message. They must have decided they needed to bring their cause to a wider audience and that their adopted faith in Chairman Mao's dictum that "power grows from the barrel of a gun" was not the way to do it. And if Cleaver wanted a nonviolent white guy like me to run with him on a Peace and Freedom Party ticket, that seemed like a good thing.

But I'd been elected to the National Interim Committee that summer on a call for discipline that I myself had raised. SDS had grown too important and its situation too volatile for it to continue with the hang-loose attitude of its earlier years. If you couldn't agree to do what the NIC thought was good for SDS and not to do what it thought was bad for it, then you shouldn't be a member of it.

So it followed from my own argument that I should submit Cleaver's request to the NIC and abide by its decision. After I'd hung up, I turned back to the group. Klonsky still looked puzzled.

"That was Eldridge Cleaver," I said. Klonsky's smirk froze. There were a few gasps of astonishment in the room. Ham that I am, I couldn't help taking a few beats.

"Cleaver wants us to know that the Peace and Freedom Party has asked him to be their candidate for president in a few states this fall," I said. I took another moment, all eyes on me.

Only when all breath was held did I say, "He wants me to be his vice-presidential running mate."

My stock soared like a rocket. A few laughed at the over-the-top irony of it. Klonsky furrowed his brow and shut up. I'm sure I didn't completely suppress a little look of relish.

But now a really intense debate got going. Intense because it involved three difficult questions at once, each one independently hard, harder in its resonance with the other two, and then all the harder again because they all bore on SDS's uncertain conception of itself, including its relationship with white liberals and black militants, and its role in the great world.

First, should SDS continue the dialogue that I had begun with Eldredge Haynes and Business International, Inc.? The big underlying question here was whether we saw ourselves as socialist revolutionaries or as process-oriented democrats. If the former, we could have nothing to do with BI. If the latter, we could at least be open to the dialogue that Eldredge Haynes appeared to want.

Second, should SDS form the explicit relationship with the Black Panther Party that my joining with Eldridge Cleaver on a Peace and Freedom Party ticket would entail? The underlying question here was whether we wanted to go beyond the integrationism of King's civil-rights movement to support the separatism of the Panthers' black-power movement.

And third, a question basic to the first two: Should SDS, as it continued to grow, welcome opportunities to form relationships with groups unlike us, with militant far-left groups like the Panthers as well as with conservative groups like BI? Or should we reject all such relationships and continue to keep our independence pure?

In the debate of Eldredge and Eldridge, the Maggie's Farm group tried to figure out what the BI and Black Panther Party overtures meant, both in terms of each one in itself and in terms of the two of them occurring together.

My views on all three questions were baby simple, stress *baby*.

First, I thought we should accept BI's request for a continuing dialogue because that would help us convince the great American middle class that SDS's values were those of democracy and the Constitution, that it was on behalf of those values that we opposed the Vietnam War and supported black liberation, and that the middle class should call off the cops and get with the program.

Second, I thought we should accept the Panthers' request for an alliance because that would help counter the disturbing tendency toward reverse racism, a dangerous racial isolationism, that was becoming increasingly attractive to many black activists. The black movement needed white allies, and it needed to acknowledge this.

And third, I thought we should form relationships with all groups that came to us willing to share our basic democratic values because that would help us broaden our front and give us access to the widest possible array of constituencies.

I lost on all three questions.

Steered by Klonsky, the NIC decided that SDS would have nothing to do with either the Black Panthers or Business International. The Klonsky faction said that SDS must learn to be more guarded rather than more open in its external relations.

It hurt to lose, and it pissed me off. The SDS leadership, I thought, had been presented with golden opportunities to move SDS out of its rut and had instead chosen to dig the rut deeper.

And it was tough to tell Cleaver that evening that our answer was no. He didn't want to hear my explanation. He just said "Shit" and hung up. Jerry Rubin of Berkeley, one of my friends and a founder with Abbie Hoffman of the Youth International Party, the Yippies, ultimately joined with Cleaver on a Peace and Freedom ticket.

When I cooled down enough to get my vanity out of it, I came to think that the NIC's decisions were probably right, or at least not insanely wrong. Informal personal talks with a group like BI were marginally okay, but I'd been naive to push for anything more formal. Such a relationship would have drawn us far too deeply into a political arena in which we had not the least idea of the game, the rules, who was playing for whom, or what the stakes were.

A formal organizational relationship with the Panthers, on the other hand, would have drawn us too far into the sometimes violent and often lunatic fringe of Panther politics, where there had never been much more than over-the-top rhetoric to begin with. We would have put ourselves on the defensive with our middle-class base and invited even more aggressive Cointelpro attacks.

And in a time when our own growing pains were confronting us with serious identity problems, it seemed to make sense to stay within ourselves, on pain of getting pulled apart. My eagerness for dalliances with Eldredge and Eldridge was not wise. Such things were not what I meant when I said that the left and the right could find a common cause in the radical center.

And I came to wonder if Klonsky wasn't on to something when he called me the most dangerous man in the movement. Good actors—good leaders—need good lines and the ability to speak them well. But they also need to know that the play began before their entrance and will continue after their exit, and that the "meaning" of it all awaits a higher criticism.

A FEW WEEKS after my string of fortunate defeats at Maggie's Farm, I was outside a large hall in East Lansing, a few blocks from the Michigan State University campus.

I'd gone there to help the MSU chapter deal with the appearance on campus of several prowar politicians at a big awards ceremony. A few fraternities and football patriots had organized what they called "a peacekeeping committee" to hold us protesters beyond a certain line outside the hall so the great men would not be offended by the sight and sound of us.

There was more than the usual shoving back and forth in the course of the evening, sometimes as physical as a football scrimmage, with lots of vigorous jeering on both sides.

Then at about 10:00 P.M., SDS's campus traveler for this area in Michigan and northern Ohio, Billy Ayers, not yet a Weatherman but with the instincts brewing, found me at the side of our crowd of several hundred demonstrators. He pointed out a certain TV camera team busily taking pictures of our crowd, one guy with a heavy camera on his shoulder and another with a battery pack and a big set of lights. Other crews had come and gone, but these two had stayed and were keeping at it. Unlike the other crews, they liked to work our crowd from the inside, getting the camera right up into people's faces for lingering close-ups.

At this point Billy was a close family friend from Ann Arbor days. He and his future wife, Bernardine Dohrn, would be fiery militants within the year. We would be driven apart by our political differences. But now he was still warmhearted, full-of-fun, handsome Billy who just a few years before had delighted in giving my young son, Caleb, piggyback rides.

"The thing about these two guys," said Billy, "is that they routinely turn their tapes over to the cops."

"How do we know a thing like that?" I asked.

"Through a contact in local TV," said Billy. "They're media people, all right, but they're also doubling for the pig."

"So what's to do?"

"What do you think?" he said.

Actually, I thought we should all smile broadly for the camera. But then I thought of all I'd heard lately about my lack of taste for militant struggle, and I had to admit it was true. I hated to see politics get rough. Yet ever since Chicago, I'd been shaky about this. How could I be sure that my rejection of violence wasn't just a character flaw? Maybe I was less a dove than a chicken. Maybe if you weren't willing "to raise the stakes," as my militant comrades were starting to put it, you shouldn't try to stay in the game.

So I took Billy's question as a chance to experiment with raising the stakes. I said, "We should show them they're not welcome here."

"I agree. So what's your plan?"

"We might show them how fragile their toys are."

"I think you're right," he said. "Let's do it."

So Billy and I got together with Diana Oughten and Terry Robbins. Diana and Terry were also close family friends. They would kill themselves with a bomb they were making in less than two years in a famous explosion in a town house in Greenwich Village. We assembled a very simple little plan. Diana, Terry, and Billy would distract the cameraman and his assistant by staging a squabble right in front of them. Then I would step in from behind and give the obviously heavy camera a push, hoping it would slip off the cameraman's shoulder, fall to the pavement, and break, and that the four of us in the attack party would melt away among the people.

This pretty much happened. It went even better than planned because we got a second target, too. The people in the crowd reacted especially well. Without the least foreknowledge of this little guerrilla action, they instantly opened escape lanes for the four of us, allowed us to melt into them, then closed behind us so we couldn't be chased.

But one little detail, unforeseen by the playwright, emerged in the staging.

When I grabbed the camera and shoved it off the cameraman's shoulder, he shouted, "Hey! What the hell are you doing?!" and turned toward me, staring straight into my eyes even as he was stumbling sideways trying to catch the camera. We had all tied handkerchiefs around our faces as outlaw-style masks, so I wasn't afraid of being identified.

But I had not foreseen the guy's shock and fright in that instant when he looked at me. He turned away to snatch at the camera, but it fell to the street with a fine, satisfying crash, mangled by its own weight. The camera lights had not been in the script but happened to be vulnerable, and as the Bard says somewhere, "as well be hanged for a hawk as a handsaw." It took me just one quick second push to send the lights crashing down, too, with an even greater racket, the broken bulbs fizzing and sparking wildly.

And yet not nearly so wildly as that burst of fear in the cameraman's eyes. Sorry, but that was terrible to see.

15 | My Cuban Fling

Havana, 1968–69

SO WHERE DID this leave me? As things stood in late summer 1968, my rep had gotten a boost from being asked to the prom by pick-up-the-gun Panther heavy Eldridge Cleaver. And the guerrilla action against the TV crew had shown some doubting comrades that I could be, under the right conditions, a street-fightin' man, that I was not a wimpy liberal, that I could be less extremely moderate, that I could dare to struggle, dare to win.

But I had picked up a memory I didn't like living with: the fright in that cameraman's eyes when he first realized that something bad was happening and looked straight at me.

I made Beth listen to my confused and bitter rambling about this.

"Is this what it's all coming down to at last?" I asked. "Just being nasty enough to go around scaring the shit out of people? Just daring people to hate us?"

Beth shrugged. "I can't pretend to know, Carl," she said, almost sadly. "But you were thinking about what this might say to the kids, right?"

In fact, I hadn't thought about that. It would never have occurred to me that my three kids might reprove me for it or feel threatened by it.

But I was coming to worry about what it meant to the kids to have to move so much. Our oldest, Aron, was then a twelve-year-old, Shay was eight, and Caleb six. Now a reflective middle-aged professional woman, Aron says she didn't see anything amiss in all our moving because, she says, she "had nothing to compare it to." But she had some anger to flush out once she got grown up.

"Don't mistake me," she says now, "I'm not blaming you and Mom for what you did. You had to do it. But it was good to have the regular family life in the nice middle-class neighborhood where Daddy goes off to work in the morning and comes home for dinner, and where you make friends that you play with and go to school with and grow up with. And it was not good to lose that. Yes, we got things from the life we led. But in the four years after you joined the movement, we moved four times! And that was kind of rough."

BETH AND I had had several difficult talks about this. We were in the backyard of the roomy house we were renting near Yellow Springs. We had moved there from Ann Arbor when Antioch College offered me a part-time teaching job. But the Antioch gig would soon end. Beth and I had spent a good deal of the fall of '68 wondering where to go next and how to get there and had not come up with a good plan.

And then that mule team showed up again, this time on the telephone, calling me at my campus office.

It was a guy from the SDS chapter at San Francisco State. He was calling on behalf of SDS chapters in the Bay Area. They could arrange for me to give talks or seminars at several schools in the area over the winter school quarter. They could promise pretty good fees. But they couldn't afford to keep flying me back and forth between Ohio and California. Would I be willing to stay in the Bay Area for the whole term?

"Interesting," I said. "Would you help me get my family there and help us get resettled?"

"Sure. That's part of the offer."

"Sounds great. Let me call you back tomorrow."

I hurried home. "Hey, Beth! Guess what?!"

So Beth and I were soon loading up our red and white '57 Chevy wagon with children and belongings. By late fall, we were living on a hill.

I WAS MORE and more troubled by the rising extremism in SDS, an egregious example being the December 3, 1968, firebombing of the ROTC building at Washington University in St. Louis by an SDSer named Michael Siskind.

But I made myself concentrate on being a good husband and daddy and getting the family settled into a funky apartment in the Mission Hill district with a great view of the expressway. Things got better. Beth and I and the children had a good fall season meeting new people and learning our way up and down the city.

Then came a call came from Bernardine Dohrn. She was calling from our Chicago office.

Despite my political differences with her, she was still one of my favorite SDSers. She would say, when asked her political philosophy, "I consider myself a revolutionary Communist," but I saw this less as politics than theater, less a creed than a splash of *frappez-les-bourgeoisie*. Now I know she was just saying what she meant.

"You guys doing all right?" she said.

"Thanks to Beth, the children might survive. How goes the revolution?"

"Speaking of which, we've just been contacted by Cuba's UN office in New York."

"Uh-oh."

"No, listen. I think you'll like this. Cuba is about to hold an international festival to observe the tenth anniversary of its revolution. Okay? And they've invited SDS to send a delegation to stay for two weeks as their guests. All we have to pay for is travel. The Cubans want one of our group to be a current officer or a past president of SDS. I've talked to the NIC people and we all agree that this nominates you."

"Me? But I thought I was, you know. . . ." I broke off and there was a little pause. At that point I did not know where I stood with Bernardine and her group. They knew I dismissed their "revolutionary analysis" as preposterous at best and dangerous if taken seriously. And I knew that

BD saw my "liberalism" much the same way. Our blind spots over-lapped. Each of us thought the other had to be kidding.

She broke the pause. "Carl, we think you might be radicalized by the experience of revolutionary Cuba. You might become an asset of the revolution. We all hope that you will. Any problem with that?"

Yes, namely, the picture of NIC people weighing my value to SDS, or lack of it, in terms of this hallucination they had come to share, the "revolution." The certainty of this revolution had been revealed to them through what they called, without irony, their "correct analysis," which they imagined was based on Marxism-Leninism jazzed up by some Mao, some Uncle Ho, a dollop of Che. They believed in the revo-lution with the same almost erotic fervor with which my South Carolina family believed in the Second Coming, and on basically the same stan-dard of evidence. No, I didn't like being considered the potential asset of the national-office collective's collective hallucination.

But then, hey, a free two-week trip to Cuba? I figured, let Cuba radi-calize me as it may. Who wouldn't want to be radicalized by a Cuba dancing in the streets?

So I said, "When do we leave?"

"Right after Christmas."

"How are we paying travel?" I said.

"You'll have to raise it," she said.

That meant finding a magazine that would pick up the travel costs in exchange for a story. None of the New Left magazines that I had pub-lished in could afford it. But I'd recently met an associate editor at *Life,* Roger Vaughn, who had done a mostly friendly piece about the student movement. He had invited me to pitch some story ideas. I called him to see what he thought of my doing a piece on Cuba's celebration. He called me back within the hour.

"Do you think you can produce a story right away?" he asked. "Before the tenth-anniversary peg is old news?"

"Definitely."

"Do you promise to come back to New York from Havana and work with me here in our office until we've got a story out of you?"

"Sounds like fun."

"All right. Let's do it."

I called Bernardine back.

"Good news. The funding's taken care of. I'm going to cover the Cuban thing for *Life* magazine."

"No way," she said mildly. My first thought was that this "no way" was of the "wow" category. I'd been surprised myself that *Life* would retain a writer like me, someone it had to assume would write sympathetically about Castro's Cuba.

But I had it backward.

Bernardine picked up the pause in a stern voice.

"Carl, you know as well as anyone that *Life* magazine is a front for the worst imperialist regime in history."

Gulp. "Well, but I mean, even so," I stammered, "wouldn't that just make this all the more significant? You know, that even *Life* is willing to billboard a New Left take on the Cuban revolution? Isn't there some valuable, I don't know, legitimation in that?"

"For your information, Carl, SDS is not asking *Life* magazine to legitimate it. This is a classic case of co-optation. But I'll poll the NIC and get back to you."

"Bernardine, you should at least hear my argument."

"I could look it up," she said. Click.

Given her opposition, there was little chance that the NIC would say yes. I said to Beth, "She'll get the votes of the national office in Chicago and maybe she'll call two or three others and talk them into saying no."

Beth said, "Obviously you should sound out some other SDS people, see if you'd have any support. I mean, if you still need that. Or want it."

"Need it, no. Want it, yes."

So I called up some others, seven older SDSers with roots in the days when "participatory democracy" was still a treasured term.

All my friends believed that I should take the assignment.

Bernardine called back in a few hours. She said, "The NIC people all agree that you cannot go as an SDS rep and at the same time as a reporter for *Life*. So it's one or the other, Carl. Your choice."

"Honey, Marxism has clogged your pipes. If you're saying a person can't use a big media outlet and still represent SDS, you're propounding a new doctrine. We'll have to deal with that later. We could have a lively debate about it in Austin."

"Some things don't have to be debated."

"Yeah, like your foolishness. As to co-optation, the people I trust agree with me that we can use *Life* as much here as *Life* can use us, and that it can be good for Cuba to be shown some understanding in a mass-market outlet like this magazine. So I'm taking the job."

"Fine," she said. It was easy to tell when she was angry. Her voice got thin and hard. "But you will not be going as an SDS rep. You cannot represent *Life* and SDS at the same time."

I was angry, too. "You do not have the authority to make such a decision, BD. Okay? So *viva la revolución, mi compañera.* And *adiós.*"

My turn to hang up.

This disagreement between me and the national office's increasingly Old Left–sounding faction was still a problem I thought we could handle. Despite our growing political differences, Bernardine and most of the other ten or so people in the national office collective, many of them future Weathermen, were still friends, even if not comrades. And friendship always trumps ideology, right? Besides, BD was in all other ways a smart, sane person. When she saw the finished piece on newsstands everywhere, she'd be glad I'd taken the job.

I really did believe that.

THEN CAME a strange diversion.

One day earlier that year, I'd shared a New York cab downtown from a Hunter College forum with the political writer and jazz critic Nat Hentoff. He'd heard, he said, that I played a little guitar, sang a little, that I had written some songs, that some of them weren't too bad. Hentoff had mentioned this to a friend of his, Maynard Solomon, president of Vanguard Records. Solomon was intrigued enough to ask for an audition tape.

So I'd gotten together in San Francisco with a country-blues band named Mad River, also migrants from Yellow Springs, rented a studio for a few hours, and taped three songs. Solomon came through San Francisco on other business and we met briefly in the lobby of his hotel. I later heard that he can be hard to get along with, but we had a good hour together. Hentoff had told me that he was a serious radical scholar and an accomplished writer on Beethoven. I don't know what Hentoff had told him about me, but I thought we took to each other easily, even though we could not have looked more unlike, skinny me in my neobeatnik attire and pirate whiskers and Solomon a robust fiftyish man with a flowing gray mane down to his collar and a dark suit with ruby tie and silver stickpin.

After a few minutes on the sorry state of the world and a rich hour on Beethoven's Great Fugue—which we agreed was the greatest single piece of music ever written—he looked at his watch and said, "So Nat tells me you have some songs?" I handed over the tape, thanked him for offering to listen to my stuff, saw him off to the airport, and went back to getting ready for my trip.

I was headed for Havana through Mexico City under circumstances that remained fretful to the last. Would my Cuban travel visa be ready where I had to get it in Mexico? How would I contact the other SDSers in Havana, and how would we get along? Could *Life* front me some walking-around pesos?

Just before I left, Solomon called from New York. He said, "If you've got seven or eight more songs like these, Vanguard would like to do an album."

No way, as in "far out."

Without the *Life* assignment, I don't see how I would ever have gotten to Cuba. The ticket might have been paid for some other way, but I could never have navigated the appalling pit of Mexican customs without the help of *Life*'s Mexico City man.

There I stood alone in this high-domed building at the pier, the place abuzz with anxious-looking people like me, all of us hoping to make it onto a boat that was about to leave for Cuba. The border official had just told me that my visa was invalid. I had no idea what to do.

Then at my side I heard a deep voice say, "You Oglesby?"

I turned and saw a tall, broad-shouldered fortyish man in a creamy tropical suit, neat white collar and tie, white Panama hat, and trim mustache. He had a square, tan, rugged face.

"Yeah," I said.

"I'm Jenkins from *Life*. Let me see what help I can be."

He led me back through the crowd to the customs gate, said something to the official, then led me through the gate to the dockside crowd waiting for the on-ramp to lower.

"Have a good trip," he said, and was gone. I had to admire him.

THE FIVE OTHER SDSers making up the delegation that I was or was not a part of had left days ahead of time from Yugoslavia on a Czech ship bound for Havana and therefore never needed such arcane services. I rendezvoused with them in Havana. Despite my not being part of the SDS delegation, I never felt excluded. The six of us hung out together and had a good Havana holiday.

We had ritzy, somewhat run-down rooms (frayed satin sheets, a cracked mirror in a silver case) at the Havana Libre, with a balcony overlooking Havana Harbor and the world's most perfect beach. After a room-service breakfast with a pot of liquid speed called Cuban coffee, we would meet in the gold-chandeliered lobby with several dozen delegates from other countries, then pile into yellow school buses to ride maybe an hour out of the city to the first spot of interest for the day. This might be a stud farm, a citrus plantation, a new health clinic in the countryside. We would get back to Havana, still Cuba's *La Parásita,* in time for some great food and an evening free for circulating.

The Cubans' fierce concentration on the tangible details of economic development was the theme of the whole celebration. This reflected the worldview of the Cuban government as of year ten of the revolution. The key shared belief of the Cubans we talked with was that they would be able to consolidate their military victory economically within two or three more years.

Our guides were constantly checking to make sure we saw the miracle of revolutionary Cuba's having, for example, already adopted the basic principles of modern agronomy. Or industrially: a little spark-plug factory had been set up by the Cuban hero Che Guevara deep in the sierra, far from highways, far from a trained workforce, in anticipation of the day when Cuba would build its own automobiles and be economically self-sufficient.

We rebels of the First World soon became, frankly, a little bored by the Cubans' preoccupation with work and industrial development. We tried not to be rude about it, but finally a few of us couldn't help showing a little exasperation with the Cuban agenda. Was meeting production targets all they cared about? Was the romance out of the revolution now for good? Why didn't they show us their great battlefields? The July 26 Movement's secret guerrilla bases in the sierra?

But then a new thought started to form. Maybe the story here was not really production so much as the *failure* of production. The official line was that revolutionary Cuba had taken hold of its economic destiny in a mere decade of power. And without question, the Fidelistas had achieved much in a short time and against enormous odds. They had overthrown the corrupt and brutal regime of Batista, despite its American support. They had formed a government despite constant sabotage, military harassment, and economic quarantine.

Yet the more urgent story here seemed to be that after all this time and despite major support from the Soviet Union, Castro's government still faced so much basic, even emergency repair work on the economy.

We began to see through our boredom with stud farms and spark-plug factories. What the Cuban revolution was really about, we began to realize, was the hurried inculcation of a national work ethic suited to the demands of modern production. We saw how much depended on the Cuban people's willingness to work hard individually in the pursuit of nearly impossible national objectives. We saw that everything uptight and anxious about the Cuban spirit traced back not only to the American embargo and the blockade that would stay in place for decades to come, but to Cuba's fears of underproductivity as well. If revolutionary Cuba could modernize its workforce and develop anything approaching an independent economic life, then it could resist being Sovietized. If it also could resist the return of American colonization, then maybe it could declare its national independence secure and its revolution a success. Only then could the Cubans settle down to the more relaxed sort of national life they all wanted.

One of our day tours in the school bus illustrated the immensity of the tasks facing revolutionary Cuba, I thought, with almost comic clarity.

We were taken to a small hydroelectric station with a dam not more than fifty feet across. Down the river at intervals of two hundred yards or so, we could see the remains of two other dams.

"No one knew how to build a dam," said Jaime Sonpoda, our affable young guide. "All our engineers had fled to Florida. But we had to generate power and irrigate our fields. To do these things, we had to have dams. So we built the first one, the one you can see farthest down the river. Since we didn't know how to build a dam, we just did it. We picked out what seemed to be a good place. We dug a canal to divert the stream. We installed some wooden forms. We mixed up some concrete, poured it into the forms, waited for it to set, then released the stream. For a while, it worked.

"But then one day the dam stopped holding water. The river had dug beneath it. So we found another good spot and built another dam, the second one you see down the river. We gave this one a deeper base. It held water longer than the first one, but then it cracked. But both times we learned something more about how to build a dam. Finally, the third one, the one you see here, worked okay. At least, it has worked so far."

Lightbulb.

Most Americans saw Cuba as little more than a bit of territory lost to the Soviets and maybe, secretly, still a base for Soviet military forces, possibly including missiles. BD and her hypermilitant comrades saw Cuba much the same way, the difference being that they liked it. The story of the revolution, as they saw it, was about battles and ideologies and the defeat of American imperialism.

Maybe, once upon a time, this had been true, but now things had moved on. As of year ten of the revolution, the story of revolutionary Cuba that needed to be told to Americans of the left, right, and center alike was about those three little dams thrown together in the sierra by people who didn't know how to build dams, and the one that finally seemed to work. It was about Che's useless but shrinelike spark-plug factory built deep in the mountains, far from any city. It was about Castro's grimly realistic attempts to revive Cuba's export trade. It was about Cuba's sweaty efforts to re-create itself economically, in fact from the ground up, in hopes of re-creating itself politically. If its effort to accomplish this failed, Cuba would become somebody's sugar bowl and fun house again.

To be sure, SDS's small-d democrats had no trouble seeing serious flaws in Castroite socialism. The revolution was supposed to be organized from the bottom up, not from the top down. And any way you cut it, Castro was a dictator.

But as serious as were Castro's flaws, they paled in comparison to Batista's, a brutal dictator whom the United States government had not had the least trouble getting along with. As long as the roulette wheels of *La Parásita* had kept turning and the cheap sugar and rum had kept coming, no one in Washington had had much to say about Batista's tyranny.

Moreover, the best possible arguments the United States government could make for democratic reforms in revolutionary Cuba would be to stop parachuting its CIA-trained teams of saboteurs into the Sierra Maestra, cease its cruel and counterproductive naval blockade, lift its absurd travel ban, normalize relations, and give these people a little time to learn how to build dams.

Our group of SDSers began to see good strategic reasons for a major SDS program focusing on Cuba. A speculative reason but still probably the most important one was that Nixon seemed highly likely to revive the old Bay of Pigs crowd and order a serious invasion.

Another reason was that SDS was growing a bit Vietnam-weary. We needed the lift of a new theme to remind everyone, including ourselves, that we were not a single-issue organization. The need to think about Cuba's plight might help us think more freshly about our own.

So how, we started wondering, might we gringos create a project focused on Cuba's production problems without getting abstract and obscure?

A way occurred.

IN HONOR OF the tenth anniversary of its revolution, Cuba had launched an all-out national campaign to produce 10 million tons of refined sugar in 1969, about 25 percent better than its record harvest. Cuba's slogan for this effort was *Los diez miliónes van!* ("The 10 million are coming!") This slogan was plastered everywhere, as though seeing it a lot might help people believe it could happen.

The chief reward of such a harvest would be that Cuba would grow somewhat less dependent on Soviet aid. Was this not what the United States kept saying it wanted?

And the Cubans had a realistic chance of achieving their goal. They easily had 10 million tons in the fields. They had enough trucks to carry them to the refineries. They had enough refineries to turn the cane into sugar. They had enough small ships to carry this much refined sugar to the big ships waiting in the harbor to be loaded. They had buyers.

The only problem was a simple shortage of manpower. The cane had to be cut by people wielding machetes. There were lots of machetes, but not enough people. If the campaign failed, it would be with uncut cane still standing in the fields, empty trucks, and idle refineries. *Sí, gracias,* they knew about the superiority of mechanical over manual harvesting, and they had begun a program to develop a sugar combine. But as things stood in 1969, the Cubans' only way to harvest enough cane was to pour themselves into the fields en masse. Carpenters, lawyers, plumbers, whatever, all would have to cut cane. Most of them would be swinging their first machetes.

This seemed to locate the center of the Cuban revolutionary experience in a way that went beyond bands of brave rebels in the mountains. As our guide, Jaime, said to me, "Do you know how to cut cane or build dams?"

Those three dams were a perfect microcosm of the struggle against underdevelopment, *subdesarrollo,* which was the Cubans' constant preoccupation. Batista, they said, had warped the Cuban economy into a monoculture around sugar for the benefit of American sugar companies. Cuba needed to bring more of its assets into production and therefore had to build new infrastructure. To do this, as with those dams that failed, ordinary Cubans had to do work they had never done before and didn't know how to do. They had to learn on the job. They couldn't delay the reckoning.

Our little SDS group gradually warmed to our guides' preoccupation with this. We were happy just to be in Cuba, of course, happy to enjoy the glorious beaches, the incredible cooking, the endless sunshine, the jazzy nightclubs. Yet we were all political nuts, too. That's why we were there. We started to wonder if SDS could help the Cubans make their goal.

Reflecting on this one morning toward the end of our stay, standing on a balcony of the Havana Libre to watch the sun rise over Papa Hemingway's sparkling sea ten stories below us, one of our SDS group, Janet Simon, said, "It's too bad there's no way we can help these people."

An idea had been buzzing. It popped out. I said, "What if a bunch of SDSers just came to Cuba and started chopping sugarcane?"

Janet laughed. "What do we know about cutting cane? We'd chop our legs off!"

"Right," I said, and then I watched her get it.

WE PITCHED THE IDEA to the larger SDS group, which quickly became enthusiastic about it. It would give SDS access to a larger world and a strategic focus besides the Vietnam War. We decided that I should bring up the idea with our guide, Jaime, being careful to make it clear to him that any SDS project would have to be formally approved by our National Council, which would meet next in March, just two months away. Jaime said he would bring it up with his boss right away.

The next afternoon Jaime asked me to come with him to our hotel's front door. "We are treating this idea seriously," he said.

A military driver arrived in a staff car to take me to the seaside home of Carlos Rafael Rodriguez, Cuba's ambassador to the United Nations and its second in command behind Castro.

He met me warmly at the curb, a balding, grandfatherly man with a small, compact form, a white goatee, and an understated elegance. He invited me to admire the view—mountains on one side, beach, surf, and sea on the other—then led me to his shadowy, book-lined office and offered me lemonade. He congratulated me on the American movement and asked me to present the concept of an SDS sugar brigade that I had outlined to Jaime.

I made sure he knew that this was not a formal SDS proposal but rather an inquiry to see how Cuba might feel about such a project.

"Cuba certainly understands," he said with a wry chuckle, "the need for caution on both sides." He reminded me that Cuba's bad experience with the Progressive Labor Party a few years before had made it especially sensitive about contact with the American student movement. Yet Cuba also recognized that SDS was itself at odds with PL for much the same reasons that disturbed Cuba. "The Progressive Labor Party is a dangerous organization," he said sadly. "It expertly uses radical rhetoric to attack radical forces." Cuba had not invited PL to the current celebration.

Then he asked if SDS would be able to organize such a large project so quickly. I agreed it would tax us but said I was sure we could do it. We could enlist a brigade large enough to have an impact in both Cuba and the United States.

"Your proposal is most intriguing," he said. "Of course, we will have to consider it carefully because of its many political and security ramifications. I will try to have an answer for you soon."

"Excellent." I reminded him that I was leaving shortly.

"Está bien," he said. "I'll see what I can do."

Early afternoon two days later, I was on a Spanish airliner at José Martí International Airport. I still had heard nothing. The deal must have fizzled.

Then from my window seat halfway back in the cabin, I saw a motorcycle with a sidecar speeding across the tarmac toward the plane. I saw the flight steward go down the boarding steps to meet it. The motorcyclist and his passenger were in military uniforms. The passenger was clearly an officer. He wore a beret and a snug military jacket with a necktie. He got out of the sidecar and spoke briefly with the steward. The steward came back aboard the airplane and called my name over the PA. "Señor Oh-gles-bee, please come to the front of the aircraft."

I squirmed out of my seat and walked up the aisle, with everyone turning to get a look. The steward said, "Sir, you have a message. Please come with me." He led me down the boarding steps.

The messenger was a tall, erect, middle-aged man. He said, "Mr. Oglesby?"

"Yes?"

"I am Colonel Domingo," he said in barely accented English. "Ambassador Rafael Rodriguez has asked me to tell you that a proposal from your organization would be welcomed by the Cuban government. The ambassador will contact you soon for further discussions at our United Nations embassy in New York. Do you have any questions?"

"Thank you, sir," I said, trying to return his formal manner. "I have no questions. Please tell the ambassador that I am gratified to receive this information. I look forward to seeing him in New York."

He nodded. "I will convey this message promptly. Thank you, sir." We shook hands briefly. He got back into the sidecar and sped off. I went back to my seat, thinking what a wonder I had seen.

I had a long trip home through Madrid because that's how the travel ban worked. You could go from the United States through Mexico to Cuba, but you couldn't go from Cuba through Mexico to the United States. Finally I was back in New York with the notes for my *Life* article in one pocket and my notes for the sugar-brigade project in the other, and in the back of my mind thinking about the album I was about to record for Vanguard. And there was the move to San Francisco to start thinking about.

Things were happening.

16 | Skipping Sugar
New York, Chicago, and San Francisco, 1969

As soon as I got back to New York, I called our Chicago office to get the cane-cutting idea into the pipeline. I was lucky to get Bernardine. She was our "interorganizational secretary" and therefore the proposal's logical start-up guy.

"Yes, Carl," she said warmly. "How was your trip to the revolution?"

"Great. I'll tell you all about it when I get to Chicago," I said. "But listen, I've got a great proposal for a major new SDS project."

She laughed. "Do I really want to hear this?"

"Yes, you'll like it. The Cubans like it. I just want you to get the gist of it, okay? Okay?"

"Well, go ahead."

I had used the flight to lay out the main talking points, and I ran through them quickly: Cuba's effort to reap a 10-million-ton harvest. The need for manual labor to bring in the crop. Many machetes but too few people. So SDS should organize a brigade of volunteers to defy the travel ban and go to Cuba to cut cane. This would be symbolically potent in its defiance of the travel ban, but also of concrete use in the harvest. Even the inexperienced can help. Castro himself has approved the project in principle.

Time is short. We should get this to the NIC and the NIC should get it to the chapters. SDS people will like it because they like Cuba and detest the travel ban. A brigade of American students will confront

Nixon with political difficulties should he be inclined to invade Cuba. We should set up a project office to start working on recruiting, publicity, fund-raising, legal advice, transportation, and security details. We'll coordinate with Cuba's UN guy.

"So what do you say?"

I had thought she would be immediately excited because I knew she admired Cuba.

There was a pause. Then she said, "Well, I don't know. It sounds like a big job."

"Yeah, but we can handle it. It'll be good for us."

"What role do you see for yourself in this?" she said.

"Well, you know, I could get on the stump for it. I should probably be the liaison guy with Rafael Rodriguez at the UN. Whatever."

"So you see yourself playing a major role?"

I thought she was wondering how committed I would be.

"Well, you know. It's my proposal. I'd be the logical person to pitch it to the NC in March, help draft something formal, write it up for *New Left Notes,* maybe help with recruiting, do some PR work. The Austin NC would be the perfect time to get things rolling."

She said, "You're assuming that we'll decide to do this?"

Her comment seemed to raise an uncertainty about it, and that was my first surprise. "Well, why wouldn't we jump at it, BD? I mean, Castro himself has said he wants it. I thought you were one of his big fans."

"Castro is a great hero of the Cuban people, but he's not running SDS."

"BD, I can't imagine that SDS wouldn't want to do this. You know we could use another focus besides Vietnam."

"Do you think SDS could bring it off?"

"Without question. It's made for us. Obviously we'd have to keep PL out. We'd have to set it up outside SDS anyway, so that shouldn't be impossible. All we need is a little strong direction."

"And you see yourself supplying this strong direction?"

My first sense of trouble. "Do I hear a note of comrade Klonsky in that? Will he say I'm just trying to build a power base?"

"Well, suppose he did. What would your answer be?"

"You're telling me you don't know? You think I suddenly want a power base? Whatever that is?" Pause again. I waited for her to say something like, "Of course not," but it didn't come.

So I said, "Bernardine, as you well know, our organization does not lack for talented people. There must be twenty or thirty SDSers who could help organize a program like this. Good leadership won't be a problem. We could rev up Todd Gitlin or Helen Garvy, maybe Casey Hayden or Paul Booth. You know. Lots."

"Okay. Stop."

"Hey, you put the question. Forgive me for answering it. Think of Paul Potter, Greg Calvert, Carl Davidson, Karen Jeffreys, Lee Webb, Jeff Shero, Karen Ashley. Our great orator, Steve Max, could really fire people up. You'd do a beautiful job yourself. You're not going to be a national secretary forever. I'm not trying to build a power base. Who needs a damn power base? I just want to see this happen. We could set up recruiting offices in Boston, Atlanta, Austin, Chicago, Ames, Berkeley. No problem, BD. This thing could explode. People have been needing another big focus to go with Vietnam. You know that. All we need—"

"All right, Carl!" she said sharply. "You've made your point. Give me some time to think about it."

"Sure, but time is short. We should let the Cubans know that we're ready to propose it to SDS."

"Don't try to steamroller me, okay? I said I'll think about it. I'll talk to some people. I'll get back to you."

"Are you going to be in Chicago soon?"

"Probably in a week."

"I'll see you in a week then."

"I'll look forward," she said.

BD's cool—well, cold—reaction surprised and disappointed me, of course. But at least the proposal was in her shop. Enthusiasm might come from elsewhere. And anyway, the big decision would lie with our next National Council meeting, scheduled for March at the University of Texas in Austin.

So I unrolled a sleeping bag at a friend's place in New York and began spending my days with a *Life* editor to get my Cuba notes worked up into an article and my evenings at the Vanguard studio with a four-man backup band that Maynard Solomon had booked. When the article and the taping were done, I split for Chicago to start mapping out the Cuba project with Bernardine.

I called her from O'Hare. She sounded busy and distracted. She didn't want me to come to the office because our corresponding secretary, Fred Gordon, was there. Not well known at our last convention, Gordon had nominated himself for the job on an antielitism platform, always a winner in SDS, and had then turned out to be close to PL, our enemy. So BD asked me to meet her at a dingy luncheonette near our office on East Sixty-third Street, in a student ghetto near the University of Chicago. I splurged for a cab to make sure I got there on time, sat down in a booth facing the window, and started getting my mind on Cuba.

She came puffing in only twenty minutes late in a parka and the standard SDS uniform of worn jeans and a red T-shirt with the black "fist of the revolution" that had become our logo. She gave me a pro-forma hug and we sat. We ordered coffee, my second refill, and got down to it.

"So what's happening?" I said, eager to hear all the feedback she must have been getting on the cane-cutting idea.

"We're extremely busy with plans for the March NC."

"I assume you've talked my proposal over with a few people."

"A few. We have to keep it from PL, as you know."

"Well, like, whom have you discussed it with?"

"A few people," she said, as though to assure me that she wasn't going to drop any names.

"Okay. What have they said?"

"They've raised some questions."

"Yeah? Such as?"

"We have lots of things to think about. There's going to be a big trial here stemming from the DNC actions. We have to be sure to be ready for that."

"Well, have you talked to the NIC people yet?"

"I'm not sure it's time. I have a lot to do. How did your recording sessions go?"

"Fun, but we've got serious stuff to talk about."

"When's your flight to San Francisco?"

"A few hours. So just update me and I'll get out of here."

She seemed to level herself. She sipped her coffee black, no sugar, not taking her eyes off mine. She said, "So when's your *Life* article coming out?"

"Probably next week."

"Are the Cubans going to like it?"

"They won't be crazy about it," I said, "but neither will the State Department."

"How about your comrades? Will we be crazy about it?"

"You'll read it. We'll see. But whether you all like it or not, this proposal is still a good idea."

"Please, Carl. I told you we're thinking about it."

Big breath. "Come on. Who do you mean by 'we?'"

"Some people I know and trust on the NIC," she said, "and two or three others."

"Not including me, right?"

She shrugged slightly and looked at her watch.

"Bernardine, I don't get it. You seemed negative about this on the phone. Now you want to close me out of your discussions of it. Since I'm the guy who raised the idea with the Cubans and am the logical guy to propose it to SDS, and since I'm an elected member of the NIC, why shouldn't you want me in on your talks?"

"You've had your input. The rest of us know what you want."

"Really? And what do I want?"

She looked out the window at the gray, cold day. The Chicago sidewalk was piled with grimy snow. Then she looked back to me, her mouth turned down, almost sadly.

She said, "Some of us think you want something a little too much like the Peace Corps."

I didn't get it. "Wouldn't setting up an illegal Peace Corps to revolutionary Cuba be terrific?"

"You make my point."

"Snap out of it, comrade. If we ran this thing right, we could leave

Peace Corps recruiters eating our dust. We could pop the Peace Corps in two like an apple! Don't you think that would be an amusing scene? Wouldn't it be great to stroll in masses around D.C. with signs saying, like, 'Peace Corps to Cuba'? Or, 'Cuba loves the Peace Corps'? The right-wingers would start bitching that SDS was in the Peace Corps' pants, but that would be cool, too, don't you think?"

She turned to gape at me with what looked like terminal incredulity.

"*You* snap out of it, Carl!" she whispered intensely, stabbing her fore-finger into my arm, not gently.

I hung tough. "Damn it, BD, I'm buying the coffee, all right?"

She looked away.

"You've got to listen," I said. "Maybe you'll hear something you haven't rejected yet. We can get PTA and church groups into this," I said. "You know, good, old-fashioned regular Americans as well as stu-dents. We could pitch it to unions, to trade groups, to Rotarians and Elks. Don't you see? We could be like the Cubans. We could reach out to all parts of society, like the Cubans have to do. To the very kind of ordi-nary people we always say we're trying to reach."

"This comes from no solid political theory, Carl," she said softly. "You're just improvising."

No political theory? That was novel. Yes, the idea had come unbidden out of the Cuban blue. But once it had struck, the arguments for it were, I thought, obvious.

I said, "All right, how about this? The basic aim of this proposal— you're right about this—is *not* to make the revolution. I admit it. It's to make the revolution *less necessary.*"

"This is foolish." She looked over her shoulder for a clock, but there was none. "Why am I sitting here?"

She was sitting there at least partly because I was holding her arm on the table, and I was doing that partly to keep from getting stabbed with her finger again and partly to keep her from leaving.

"And it's doable, Bernardine," I implored. "We don't have to send a thousand cane-cutters to make a difference, or even a hundred. One good solid group of thirty or forty reasonably able-bodied Americans? Then maybe some kind of spin-off? Listen, BD, as long as a group of

Americans was on the island, and behind the right kind of publicity support, try to imagine it: It would be politically next to impossible for Nixon to start a new invasion. Yes, and listen!"

"Carl, you're getting a bit wild-eyed," she said, moving her hand slightly.

"No, dig it," I persisted. "Just think of the political situation we could create here around a group of more or less normal American citizens who had dared to break the travel ban for the explicit purpose of helping Cuba make itself less dependent on the Soviet Union. Giving Cuba better ties to real people in the U.S.? Tell me about it! And what if other countries picked up on it? Wouldn't it be cool to help Cuba coordinate an international effort? We'd spread our name, make some solid international contacts. And you know what? We might even help the Cubans cut down a little more sugarcane. BD, tell me what's not to like."

She had taken a long blink and started shaking her head slowly at my mention of "normal Americans." Now she faced me with a look of blank resignation and a little exasperated sigh.

"May I have my hand back?"

"If you don't listen, I'll put it in my pocket."

She scoffed and brought up her other hand quickly and pushed my hand away. I didn't struggle. Later I decided I should have, somehow, for many reasons. As it was, I leaned back in my seat with both hands in my lap. She leaned back, too, sitting erect, her head tilted back, looking at me down her nose.

"The only real justification for the project you've proposed," she said quietly, "would be to build American support for the revolution."

"Well, how could we possibly support the Cubans better than by recruiting ordinary Americans to cut cane?"

"I'm not talking about Cuba, Carl."

I didn't have a glimmer what she meant. I said, "Okay, what are you talking about?"

"Let me try again," she said wearily. "The only important benefit of such a program—all right so far?"

"Go on."

"Would be to bring back more committed revolutionaries."

"Bring back to where? You mean back to the United States?"

With a mirthless chuckle, she said, "Are you being obtuse to amuse me?"

Finally I got a glimpse of it, but I couldn't believe she was serious. I said, "So you're saying Castro should help create evidence to prove what the U.S. government has been panting to prove all along? That Cuba is a cauldron of hemispheric subversion? That the Cuban government is training Americans for acts of revolutionary violence in American cities?"

"Keep trying to remember, Carl, that our side favors the revolution, okay? And we don't expect it to be nonviolent."

My turn to shake my head slowly and look weary. "I can hear the old B-26s warming up already."

She shrugged and said, "Then maybe this project isn't worth the effort."

Incredible. I burst out, "As a friend and former comrade, BD, allow me to suggest a shrink."

"Keep your shrink. I'll go with Marx."

She gathered her parka and started to leave. I said, "Please listen just a little more. I don't think you're seeing this right." She stopped. I said, "Just be clear. We've got a chance here to confront the bad guys on an important, volatile issue, and all the good arguments are on our side. I can't believe you think it's not worth the effort."

"Arguments." She sighed. "Carl, why do people have to keep reminding you that the revolution is not a debating society?"

"Better a debating society than fantasyland."

She laughed. "So you really do think the revolution is a fantasy?"

"I really do think your sense of what's happening in this country is like something from the Red Baron. I mean, talk about infantile leftism! You read two or three pages of a Marxist comic book, and presto, you think you can, like, foretell the Apocalypse."

That seemed to stir her. Pulling her long, dirty, dark hair away from her face, she leaned toward me, her brown eyes small and sharp, her voice held low but molten.

She said, "You want the Apocalypse, Carl? You'd see it right in front of you if you'd just open your eyes. Young people everywhere are demanding fundamental change. They are more and more militant. They are bolder and bolder. They are moving all across the United States, throughout Western Europe, in Japan. Third World colonies are in revolt in Latin America, Africa, Asia. In the inner cities our black comrades are starting—you may have noticed this, Carl?—our black comrades are starting to pick up the gun. Our task is to prepare for struggle in a mother country that is already well into the process of falling apart. Okay? And as for infantile leftism, you might look to yourself."

I always admired BD's stormy side, the rap she could lay down when she was pissed. But this moment fell beyond good sportsmanship, so I just let my gloomy face speak for itself.

In a moment she said, a bit sadly, I thought, "We used to see the same world, Carl. That seems to have changed. But now, really, I have work to do. I have to go. I hope you have a good trip home."

She put down a buck for her coffee and left without looking back.

Ah, Bernardine. She made me think of what Gunther says of Brunhilde, "Lo! now, not the Devil in hell could escape her." And certainly she was backed by an increasingly strong elite in the supposedly antielitist SDS. Her group called itself at this point the Revolutionary Youth Movement, which would evolve into the Weather Underground, the cadre that followed BD into terrorism and in the process blew up three of their loveliest people.

"When you pick up the saber," Emma Goldman said early in the nineteenth century, "you hand it to your enemies."

Unfortunately, the nascent Weathermen had no time to ponder the experience of others. They were young and angry and lived in a separate reality of their own. Many of them had been comfortably raised with a middle-class sense of entitlement, which they brought too easily to their politics. They believed that SDS was passé and that it was their right and their moral duty to take the step beyond nonviolence to terrorism. They were not personally violent. Even as terrorists, they confined themselves to symbolic targets and never killed anyone but three of their own, by accident.

But their vanity was boundless. They believed they were right simply because they were who they were. And after they had picked up a few deadly phrases from Marx, they went from knowing what was right to knowing what was "correct," as though politics were like arithmetic.

I flew back to San Francisco feeling like an incorrect liberal lost among manglers of the dialectic and wondering if I should simply write a note of apology to Rafael Rodriguez, something like, "Dear Ambassador: SDS's officers find the cane-cutting project too tame."

WHEN I AT LAST got home to San Francisco, I poured out my feelings to Beth. She was sympathetic, but she said, "Why persist when you know you can't win?"

"Because I'm not sure I can't win."

She laughed and said, "I only know what you tell me, Carl, but if I'm hearing you right, it's already over."

Beth was a smart, grown-up woman with a warm heart and a cool mind, a petite, strong build that three childbearings had left intact, quick, gray-blue eyes that could see through nonsense, and a perky nose that she knew how to turn up. She was proud of me for my SDS venture and had given me indispensable support, especially in keeping our kids sane through some crazy circumstances. But she was never a true believer.

She said, "You know, it's hardly as if you don't have alternatives. You could look into pitching this Cuba thing to SANE. You could go back to school, try to get another teaching job. You could write another play, maybe some more songs, bring that side of you out for a while." Then gently she added, "You might even take some time to hang out with our kids."

Touché. It was as though my play *The Peacemaker* had descended on my life, as if the role of the play's hero, Dyke Garrett, had taken me over. I was behaving just as he does when his wife, Sally, tells him what he very well knows: "Why try to reason with people whom you know to be unreasonable?"

But I couldn't accept it. I couldn't stop believing that we SDSers still had a chance to surmount our internal differences. We could maintain an aggressive but nonviolent opposition to the war without falling into an ultraleftist fever. We could find ways to relate to the suicidal Black Panthers and the mysterious Business International group alike without cracking at the spine. We could cope with continuing penetration by PL and the FBI by clinging to our commitment to democracy. We could bring SDS out of all this, through the general crisis of the Vietnam War and the civil-rights struggle, as a significant force in American education. By establishing an influence in academia, we could influence brain trusts. By influencing brain trusts, we could influence the national agenda.

And if we accepted the sugar-brigade proposal and carried the project out with energy, I believed, it could make a big, positive difference for SDS as well as for Cuba. So how could I just stand aside and watch our hotbloods try their best to blow the project and SDS to smithereens?

So I kept begging the people I knew on the NIC for a meeting on the Cuba proposal.

It was not until the last night of our March National Council meeting in Austin that this meeting finally convened.

Once it did, of course, the main agenda item turned out to be me.

PART III | Crashing

17 | Star-Chambered in Texas
Austin, 1969

A GROUP OF college presidents began the 1969–70 academic year with a special summit meeting in Denver devoted to the question of how to handle "restless youth." They agreed that it was time to get tough.[1] They left Denver resolved to strengthen campus security forces and to seek close ties to municipal police, especially to Red Squads. They would give the FBI access to their students' files. They would help army intelligence identify their draft-card burners. They would arm their campus police with real bullets. So how did the new policy work?

The period from the fall of '68 through the winter of '69 was probably SDS's busiest period. The House Internal Security Committee that investigated us in 1970 found our hand in twenty major acts of campus protest at schools large and small and from one coast to the other, all of which were met by repressive police measures. The House Internal Security Committee pointed out, not without some admiration, that SDS only grew stronger and bolder with every arrest.

AUSTIN IN MARCH was green and warm. The University of Texas rescinded its agreement to let us hold our spring National Council there, perhaps in view of the school presidents' summit, but we found other halls near the campus. We were even able to hold an antiwar rally at the state capitol without getting in trouble with the locals.

I was in the grip, of course, of a growing anxiety about my proposal to go cut cane in Cuba. Bernardine and her friends in the national office collective were certainly taking their time, insisting that the decision was too big for the national office to make. Well, now we were at a National Council meeting. It was decision time.

There would certainly still be a problem with PL, which had been attacking Cuba and Castro at every chance for having—no laughter—betrayed the revolution. They had also been attacking North Vietnam and Ho Chi Minh for much the same reason, as well as the Black Panther Party and its popular Breakfast for Children program. PL's attitude toward Cuba seemed unconnected to anything in particular Castro was doing. As Carlos Rafael Rodriguez had said to me in Havana, PL was expert in using radical rhetoric to attack radical causes.

PL phonies were among us that March in Austin in greater numbers than ever in the form of a well-organized "Worker Student Alliance," PL's name for its student wing. But regular SDSers were there in greater numbers, too. There were several hundred of us to maybe fifty of them. So if ever there was a time for us true SDSers to confront PL and reassert control of our own organization by kicking them out, this NC would seem to have been it.

I made yet another plea to Bernardine that we put the PL problem on the agenda and then move on to my proposal on Cuba.

"Maybe," she said. "It's a tough one. Let me talk to some other people."

"We can't let PL drive us out of our own house," I said. "And listen, we really do have to make a decision about the sugar brigade."

"Later," she said, and started striding away.

I followed her. "Bernardine, you've been telling me 'later' for two months."

"I'm setting up a special meeting of the NIC to discuss some other questions," she said, "so maybe we can talk about PL tonight."

"If we talk about PL tonight," I persisted, "when are we going to talk about the Cuba project?"

"Maybe tomorrow."

"And tomorrow and tomorrow."

"Carl, obviously the NC's got a lot to think about. I'll try to get it on the agenda."

"What do you mean, *try*?" I asked.

"Look it up."

"The NIC's only got a very short time to form a policy."

"Correct."

"Then we've got to present it to the NC."

"Correct."

"Then the NC's got to debate it and make a decision." She kept turning her shoulder and striding away. I kept stepping in front of her. It was for the circus.

If we were going to do this thing, then we had to decide to do it there in Austin; otherwise our window of opportunity would close. The cane was ripening on its own time. We couldn't go ahead with a project of this magnitude without the blessing of the NC, and the NC wouldn't meet again until the annual summer convention. Making no decision in Austin would be the same as voting it down.

"If we want this to happen," I said, "we've got to act *now*!"

"All *right*!" she snapped, shooting me what was not a loving look. "I'll see what I can do!"

At about noon of the next day, with our ranks already thinning, the dozen or so NIC members still present at the convention finally got together to talk, I thought, about the sugar project.

We met in a classroom down the hall from the auditorium where the NC sat trying to conduct last-day nuts-and-bolts business in an atmosphere dominated by PL's open hostility. The atmosphere was ugly. I'd seen some shoving. I'd heard that a few punches had been thrown.

School chairs lined the walls of our classroom, which was painted in two shades of bilious academic green.

With the turmoil of the larger meeting seething in the background, our smaller group got to work. At last the NIC would move on the Cuba proposal.

"We're all starting to worry about our rides home," said Bernardine, "so we should get down to business. Consider that the meeting is in order," she said, slapping her thigh.

"As I'm sure everyone here has been informed," she said, "we need to make some big decisions, and quickly." She looked around the room as though to see if anyone questioned this.

She nodded. "Okay. Carl has proposed that SDS take on a big new program around Cuba. He wants us to organize a large group of Americans, at least several dozen and maybe several hundred, to go to Cuba in violation of the travel ban to help the Cubans harvest their goal of 10 million tons of sugar. Castro has staked his government on achieving this goal, even though 10 million tons would be a lot better than Cuba's best harvest so far. Which was what, Carl?"

"About eight million tons," I said.

"So this harvest is a big deal for Cuba. And it would also be a big deal for SDS to take part in it. It would involve a national campaign with lots of international implications. Okay?" She made a palms-down gesture and raised her brow and looked around the room. All of us were still.

She went on. "Carl presented the concept of such a project to the Cuban government on his recent trip there, and—"

"Correction?" I said, holding up my hand like a good schoolboy.

She looked at her watch and said, "Yes, Carl, quickly."

"Actually, I presented the concept first to the other people in the SDS delegation. We talked about it for a day. Then we all agreed that I should present the idea to the Cubans. I spoke for the whole SDS delegation."

"Okay," said Bernardine. "The Cubans' reaction was positive. They told Carl they would like to see a firm SDS proposal. So the next step is for the NIC to decide whether or not to present this idea to the NC. Okay? If we report it out to the NC in time for it to make a decision, and if the NC decides to go with this, then there are many practical and political questions that we will have to start working on right away. Okay?"

She gave the room a long look. When she was satisfied that she had everyone's attention, she looked down at her notes and said, "Okay, Carl, you have the floor. Please be brief."

Judging by the fragment of a document released to me decades later through a long-drawn-out suit under the Freedom of Information and

Privacy acts, I have to credit the FBI for an excellent transcript of what I said. Without question the feds had a state-of-the-art recording system in that room. Either one of our NIC members was miked or there was a bug on the wall.

The FBI report is stamped CG 100–40903 and dated May 8, 1969, about four months after the event. It notes that the Justice Department was considering a grand-jury complaint against "SDS leaders" for sedition (no such complaint was ever filed), so maybe it was prepared in that connection. The part released to me reads as follows:

> OGLESBY after describing his trip to Cuba states: Cuba's economy will begin to take off if she harvests 10 million tons of sugar in 1970, and the revolution has staked its honor on reaching that goal. If Cuba gets the 10, the revolution is stronger than ever. And this show of strength would almost exactly coincide with the failure and virtual breakdown of the Alliance for Progress. This is a key political fact. Couple it with the U.S. defeat in Vietnam, which asks for vengeance, and Czechoslovakia, where the USSR explicitly affirmed and the U.S. military implicitly accepted the politics of spheres of influence, and you have a world situation that puts Cuba once again at the hot spot. What will Nixon do? This is a question which Nixon may not immediately answer. But Cuba is nevertheless going to be with us for a long time.

Everything above and below that is censored out.

When I was done with this display of my timid-liberal politics, BD said, "I think most of us find the idea generally appealing, and we thank Carl for the proposal. But such a project would have many chances to go astray. Its result can only be positive if it's based on correct politics. Its politics can only be correct, of course, if it's organized within a Marxist-Leninist framework. Otherwise, it would just be like a Peace Corps kind of thing with slightly more radical slogans. Okay? And we obviously don't want that."

This Peace Corps rap was apparently becoming a theme, but it was more surprising to me that Bernardine might actually try to base an important political decision on her understanding of Marx and Lenin.

She took a breath, looked at her notes again, then looked around the room at everyone but me.

"So therefore," she said, "we have to talk about Carl's politics."

"Excuse me?" I said. "My politics?"

"We have to look at the assumptions that he would bring to a project like this," she said. "This will be difficult for us all, but it has to be done before we can move ahead. Okay? I believe Arlene has prepared a list of specific points that we have to take up. Arlene, you have the floor."

This was Arlene Eisen Bergman, a pale, smart, dark-eyed woman from the Bay Area, maybe in her late twenties, someone I hardly knew. The smoothness with which BD changed the subject from my proposal to my politics and gave the floor to Arlene made it clear that my comrades were not improvising.

Arlene stood up by the desk and began by raising a question that I would never have thought of putting first, or even at all.

"What is the basis," she said to the room in a strong, teacherly voice, "of Carl's right to propose such a project to SDS? The SDS leadership's view is that Carl has made a point of rejecting Marxism-Leninism, and, therefore, that he has no right to propose such a project, not to SDS and especially not to the Cubans in the name of SDS."

I immediately blew my cool. "Hey, friends," I blurted, "I didn't propose anything to the Cubans. I only made an inquiry. And where's this ideological test coming from? Since when is SDS a Marxist-Leninist organization?"

"Carl, please!" snapped Bernardine.

"Please, my ass, BD!" I snapped back. "I mean, you guys are welcome to your own private fantasies, but listen, SDS is a democratic organization! You want me to read you the 'Port Huron Statement'?"

"You're out of order, Carl!" said Bernardine. "Arlene, please continue."

"You want order?" I said. "Okay, I call personal privilege. Before we take one more step, I want you to explain to me why an elected officer of SDS has to be a Marxist-Leninist, whatever you mean by that, before he can propose a project to SDS."

"Carl is clearly trapped in our early, bourgeois stage," Arlene said, addressing her words to the group and, like BD, not looking at me. "We were younger when Carl joined us," she said, "and more naive. We had not yet realized the need for a Marxist-Leninist perspective."

"So SDS is Marxist-Leninist now?" I said, stupefied.

Arlene said, "No one in this room but Carl would have to ask such a question."

I saw a friend of mine from San Francisco, Neil Buckley, squirm in his chair and start to raise his hand, a small gesture that I took some heart from.

"When the hell did this happen?" I said.

"The fact that Carl needs to ask such a question proves in itself how badly he has lost touch," said Arlene, still avoiding my eyes. "SDS has evolved. Carl has fallen behind."

"Arlene," I flared, "I'm more in touch with the SDS membership than anybody in this room. Who travels to more campuses than I do? Who got more votes to be on this council?"

Bernardine stared at her notes and said, "Carl, you're badly out of order. But to answer your question, be assured that we know what you say to your audiences. You might as well be recruiting for the Peace Corps."

"The Peace Corps again! What the hell is this really about, Bernardine?"

"We intend to tell you," she said coldly. "Arlene, please continue."

Arlene cleared her throat and looked at her notes. "Since the subject of the Peace Corps has come up," she said, "let's start with that. Many of us are aware of Carl's relationship with one Warren Wiggins. Carl, please tell us who Wiggins is."

"As you very well know, he's the director of the Peace Corps training camp in Puerto Rico."

"And how do you know him?"

"He called me up one day.'

"Very good. And why?"

"To say that he thought highly of SDS. To say that we had supporters in the government."

"Certainly he seems to think highly of you," said Arlene. "We know that Wiggins paid you to go to Arecibo several times to address his trainees."

"Several? I went there twice."

"Oh. Only twice. We know you were sympathetic to Wiggins' suggestion that SDS send teams of organizers to Puerto Rico and the Peace Corps office in Washington to help develop a new training program for the Peace Corps. We know this because you have talked about it with several members of SDS. Surely you don't deny this?"

"On the contrary, Arlene," I said, "I think it would be a great shot for us."

"A shot at what?"

"Why, at greater influence, greater prestige, a wider audience. What else do you want?"

"We take note of Carl's attitude," said Arlene with satisfaction, as though I'd handed her a damning confession.

"In the next place," she said, looking at her notes, "we have Carl's continuing friendship with groups in the neoimperialist camp. For example, a little over a year ago, he presented a paper in Washington D.C., to the American Institute of Planners, at what they called their Fiftieth Anniversary Consultation. While there, he sat on a panel with the fascist pig Herman Kahn. This is a documented fact which Carl cannot deny."

"Yes, and on that same panel were antiwar liberals like Max Lerner and Robert Theobald and Claude Brown. What are you trying to make out of this?"

"The NIC takes note of your apparent pride in consorting with liberals," said Arlene with a sneer.

"If you guys yourselves would consort with a few more liberals," I said, "maybe this half-assed Leninist crap—"

Bernardine looked at her watch and said, "Carl! You will have a chance to respond later. We know this is hard for you. It is hard for all of us. But if you can't control yourself, we'll have to ask you to leave the room."

"Leave the room? At my own trial? And what if I decline?"

Bernardine said, "Arlene, we're running really short on time. You still have the floor."

Arlene looked up from her papers. "Even more questionable," she said, "is Carl's insistence on encouraging an SDS relationship with a man named Eldredge Haynes of a group called Business International. It has been pointed out to Carl that this is very likely a front for the CIA. Yet he has persisted in organizing meetings between it and SDS groups."

Rules of procedure be damned, I couldn't restrain myself. "Arlene, I'm trying to get our message out to anyone who will hear it. Do you want to know why?"

"Actually, no."

"If these Business International guys are CIA, I say all the better! Let them all hear directly what we're trying to say! Let them all spread out and tell their brothers."

Arlene gave the room a long, incredulous glare. "You are either stupid or treacherous, Carl," she said. "You open lines to the very groups that most passionately want to destroy us, and then you expect us to believe that this is good."

"The more clearly they see us," I said, "the less they'll feel compelled to destroy us!"

"This is incomparable bullshit," she said. "The more clearly they see us, the better they'll know how to destroy us."

"Arlene, face facts. The feds don't have the least difficulty penetrating SDS."

"Oh?" said Arlene, turning for the first time to look me squarely in the face. "What can you tell us about that, Carl?"

Bernardine said quickly, "Arlene, let's move along."

Arlene said, "I do not want Carl to be confused about this. The fact that the FBI takes an interest in what we do is not a reason for us to make their work easier."

"But it is a reason," I said in a tightening knot of consternation, "to hold on for dear life to our basic democratic message, Arlene. We've got to protect the idea of participatory democracy because that's the only thing that can protect us. And we have to take this message to anyone who will listen to us, including spies and big businessmen."

"So our enemies can always be certain of our plans?"

"Grow up, Arlene. Or wait. Are you telling me that SDS has secret plans now?"

"I ask the committee to take note of Carl's judgment."

What did she mean? I could only stumble ahead through a gathering miasma. Maybe get another few swings out of my trusty SDS populism. So I let the old rhetoric fly, searching the room for a slight nod of the head or the like.

I said, "The better the spooks and the suits and the ordinary nine-to-five liberals know what SDS has to say about the Vietnam War and racism and democracy—come on, you guys, please listen!—then all the better will they see that SDS is totally homegrown and that we really do have something to say. Some of these guys may already be turning around, like Joe O'Neal, the CIA man in Vietnam that I told people about. And you know why? Because some of us sat down next to Herman Kahn and nuked him!"

With a growing disbelief, Arlene said, "This is more amazing than I'd expected. Carl, do you actually think you can reason with the ruling class?"

With a growing disbelief of my own, I said, "Arlene, do you actually think you can win a war with the ruling class?"

"Not if people like you think we can all be friends."

"And otherwise? If people like you think we're condemned to be enemies?"

She leaned toward me across the desk and gave me the current mantra: "We're only saying, 'Dare to struggle! Dare to win!'"

I elegantly riposted, "You're actually saying, 'Dare to fuck up! Dare to piss on victory.'"

But she barely blinked. "It appears to us that you're seeking an SDS alliance with the very forces responsible for the napalming of Vietnamese villages."

"No, I don't want an alliance, Arlene, as I've made clear in what I've written about this. I want a dialogue."

"Oh, *dialogue,* " Arlene said with a laugh. "How fresh!"

"I want a chance to make these guys face what this war is doing to real people. I want them to understand how barbaric and pointless it is."

"Oh," she said, rolling her eyes, "and then they'll stop?"

"You've got a better plan, Arlene?"

"Yes," she said. "It's called the revolution. You may have heard of it?"

"I think I have," I said.

"Yes? And? Tell us what you think the revolution is."

"You've got to be kidding me."

"What *is* the revolution, Carl?"

I'd heard variants of this question a lot in my circuit riding and so had an answer at hand. And like the fool I should have played, I flew into it.

"The revolution is anguish and chaos, Arlene. It's anger and catastrophe. The revolution is no drinking water. It's raw sewage in the streets. No hospitals, no doctors, no schools, no teachers, no food in the stores, blasted houses, little kids with no parents."

Arlene wasn't hearing what she wanted. "All right, Carl, enough rhetoric."

I plunged ahead. "Violent revolution is what people turn to when they have no alternative."

"Stop!" Arlene commanded.

Bernardine said, "Carl, we get your point."

"No, you don't. You've never even tried to get it."

"This is nothing but liberal phrase-mongering," Arlene said smartly.

"Okay, comrades, you tell me. What is the revolution?"

Speaking precisely, pointing each syllable, Arlene said, "The revolution is what happens when revolutionaries act."

"Act? As in putting on makeup and costumes?"

"Act as in picking up the gun."

This was really happening. This was not a stage play. I said, "What if the cops have more guns to pick up?"

"If the idea of class conflict frightens you," she said, "you should stay out of it. Maybe you could get a job with the Peace Corps, or with Business International. Do whatever you want, Carl. But don't try to make SDS an arm of the government."

I took a big breath and tried to compose myself. "Are you telling me, Arlene," I said, "that SDS is now formally a revolutionary Marxist-Leninist organization?"

She looked up from her notes. "What SDS is or may become remains to be seen. But we are telling you most emphatically that the purpose of SDS is *not* to organize college kids for the Democratic Party."

Bernardine spoke up. "Arlene," she said, "let's move on."

Arlene picked up a different page of notes. "This article you wrote for *Life* on your trip to Cuba, Carl. I believe we've all read it. It is just filled with liberal criticisms of the Castro government. The Cubans can't vote. The economy is stagnant. Everything depends on Soviet aid. You barely mention the U.S. quarantine, the embargo, the constant CIA raids."

"Top Cuban officials who knew I was writing that piece talked candidly to me about the serious problems they face because of the mistakes they've made. Yes, they admit it, even if you won't."

"All right, Carl," said Bernardine.

"They tried to industrialize their economy before they had a good plan and enough capital."

"Later for this," said Arlene.

"Their haste made them too dependent on Soviet aid."

"We understand what you're saying," said Arlene. "We must move on now."

"And the promise of democratic reform—do you remember democracy, Arlene, BD, everybody else? The crowning jewel of the July 26 Movement? This has been postponed so long it looks like a lost cause. The Cubans themselves concede this."

"Are you through?" said Arlene dryly.

"No."

"Who are you to criticize the Cuban revolution?" she asked.

"Who am I? Must I have a license?"

"You must have a commitment to the struggle."

"Arlene, struggle to remember, please, that I'm the guy who conceived and proposed the cane-cutting project in the first place, which is what I thought we were here to talk about. I'm the guy who pitched it to the Cubans and convinced them that SDS could bring it off. Do you deny this, Arlene?"

Arlene shared a look with BD, then said quietly, "We have no need to deny or affirm a thing. We are only here to ascertain your political perspective. Your own words condemn you."

"Condemn me? Of what?"

"If there were the least remaining doubt that you are a hopeless bourgeois liberal, Carl, there stands the appalling fact that you dared to publish this article in *Life* magazine. You surely are aware that *Life* has been a mouthpiece for imperialist anticommunism since Henry Luce founded it."

"Yeah, Bernardine told me."

"How can you possibly apologize for that?"

"Apologize? No, I boast of it!"

"Boast of joining hands with reactionaries?"

"You can call them what you want, kid, but we have no better way to reach the wider audience that we've always been trying to reach."

Bernardine stepped in. "Carl, we know you needed someone to buy your ticket, but it's beyond reason that you take pride in becoming a mouthpiece for the Luce empire."

"BD, listen here to me. Castro and Rafael Rodriguez were delighted that the piece was going to be in *Life*. That's exactly the audience they want access to."

"Carl, please!" said Bernardine, speaking harshly for the first time. "We cannot be responsible for the false consciousness of a few Cuban bureaucrats."

Even a few of her supporters in the room dropped their jaws at that one. It was the Grand Canyon of BD's arrogance. "You dare to put yourself in judgment of people who actually fought a revolution."

"You're out of order!" BD said, her anger rising to mine. "But once and for all, Carl, whatever the Cubans may think, SDS is not trying to reach the readers of *Life* magazine."

"Then who the hell are we trying to reach?"

She stopped for a moment, seeming to compose herself. In a lowered voice she said, "Carl, the revolution is not going to be made by big businessmen and the middle-class readers of *Life*. "

"The revolution?"

BD was smart, but as Dr. Johnson first noticed, some ideas are so absurd that only the very brilliant can espouse them.

"Comrade, have you totally flipped out? We can't even stop the war in Vietnam, can't even roll back poverty, racism, and sexism, and you're talking about making the revolution?"

"Correct," she said coldly. "We cannot stop the war machine and deal with social problems by the nonviolent methods you seem committed to. We've tried that approach. We've reached its limits. What don't you understand?"

I must have looked as crazy to her as she to me, but I still couldn't believe this was happening. What is that, a state of shock? "Bernardine, our enemies will drool to hear this!"

She said, "Carl, listen. This question of strategy has been discussed and decided at previous meetings. We have no time to go over it all again."

"What previous meetings?"

"Do you remember our discussion of this in my room?"

"That was a meeting?"

"Do you remember our meeting at the airport?"

"You're kidding me."

"And there were several meetings of the NIC."

"Where was I?"

Bernardine said, "Perhaps you were busy playing your macho games with impressionable coeds."

This was getting really dirty. "Macho games with coeds?" I gasped.

"Impressionable coeds," she corrected. "We all know what you do."

"Really? My, my, Bernardine! So you consider yourself an impressionable coed?"

A little snicker went around the room. Even Arlene had to turn her face aside.

But BD kept her cool. "Arlene, please go on. We're wasting time with all this. We still have to return to the plenary."

Arlene arranged her notes and looked around the room. When she saw that all were attentive, she looked directly at me, her face more solemn than before.

"As I've told you today, Carl," she said, "many of us are puzzled by your failure to adopt the revolutionary stance that our situation requires of us. We've cited your obstinate rejection of Marxism-Leninism, your clinging to an outmoded liberal philosophy, your ties to *Life,* your flirtation with the Peace Corps, with the American Institute of Planners, with Business International. We might also have mentioned your call for a common cause with liberals in your speech at the SANE march. Or that bizarre last chapter in your book *Containment and Change,* where you actually propose an alliance with what you call, let's see, 'principled conservatives.'

"But time is short," she said, "and there's a final, bigger problem to talk about." She looked at Bernardine, who nodded.

"Like what?" I said.

"We are all aware that you came into SDS from a job in the defense industry, where you held a secret clearance. For a time, most of us were willing to overlook this. We did so because your former ties to the defense industry gave you added credibility in your talks against the war. But lately some of us have felt a need to rethink this. We feel you have a right to hear our concerns."

Arlene looked at BD again and then, for the first time, at the heavy-jawed Klonsky, who sat silently exuding gloom through the entire meeting.

"And please don't misunderstand us, Carl. We're not making an accusation here. But you deserve to know that some of us have begun to wonder, frankly, where your loyalties really lie. In view of your liberal philosophy, your background in the defense industry, your government and business contacts, and your continuing efforts to lead SDS into alliances with liberal and even conservative groups, we are compelled to wonder if you might have been, all along, a federal agent."

Arlene handled her role well, I thought. Her voice was firm but not harsh. She didn't take her eyes from mine.

"Let us stress," Bernardine said, "that we are not presenting this as a final conclusion, Carl. Our point is, rather, that we can find no way to dismiss the possibility."

"No way," I said.

"We're extremely sorry to have to tell you this," BD said, "but there it is. We thought you deserved to know our thinking."

My friend Neil Buckley tried to speak up for me. "Wait a minute," he said, "aren't you guys being a little rough? I mean, Carl's a brother. He's given to the cause."

Bernardine cut him off. "Neil, please save it. Arlene has a final point to make. Arlene, continue."

"In view of the above," Arlene said, "the NIC is hereby advising you, Carl, that SDS will have nothing to do with this proposed Cuba project, much as it appeals to many of us, if you insist on playing any kind of role in it. If you agree to step aside, the NIC will propose that SDS adopt it and will put all its efforts into making it succeed. But if you refuse to step aside, SDS will reject the project. If you try to organize it outside of SDS, we'll do everything we can to ensure that it never gets started. If you compel us to, we'll denounce the project to the Cubans as a probable CIA penetration ruse."

She let the moment hang, then said softly, "Do you understand what we're telling you?"

"You've made yourself very clear, Arlene," I said.

I remember that I didn't flinch. There was an odd buzzing sensation in my head, but my breath stayed even. I recall marveling at my own strange calm as I scanned the circle where everyone was looking at me expectantly. I even paused a moment at the grim Klonsky. Except for him, these were all friends with whom I had shared some good times in the past few years.

My eyes came back to beautiful, straight-faced Bernardine, who made no effort to avoid my look.

"It's up to you, Carl," she said. "If you agree to back off and let us organize it, the project will go ahead. If you insist on playing a role in it, we'll kill it."

It was up to me to say something, but I didn't know what to say. So like Huckleberry Finn, trusting to Providence to put the right words in my mouth, I just started talking.

I said, "You know, Bernardine, you guys are good, I admit. But you missed a couple points."

Eagerly, as though she really wanted me to talk my way out of this, she said, "Of course, Carl, you have a right to say anything you want. We promise to listen with open minds."

"Well, good then," I said. "Your research was good, but I would fault it for not picking up a few key points."

"Please tell us," said Bernardine.

"For one, I gave a talk about a year ago to the Political Club at the U.S. Naval Academy in Annapolis. Got a standing O, in fact. Can you dig it? A standing O at the Naval Academy for a speech against the Vietnam War? I even got invited back. Man, that was a kick."

Bernardine looked at Arlene and shook her head.

"Then a little after that," I said, "I had a gig at the U.S. Army General Staff and Command College at Fort Leavenworth. That was cool, too. I gave my usual antiwar rap in a big lecture hall, then had dinner with some faculty types, a bunch of officers. They actually wanted to know how I thought the U.S. might get out of Vietnam. Then I talked to an air force group in Denver. Talked a lot there about cluster bomb units. To go from there to Union Theological Seminary, man, that was a first-class mind blow! I'm going, like, hey, this is what SDS is all about!

"And I'm all the more surprised that Arlene didn't pick up these other, well, errors of mine because, you know, I bragged about them. Gee, Arlene, you really could've used these things. I mean, navy? Air force? Army? At least half of those guys must have been intelligence officers, right?"

Neither Bernardine nor Arlene wanted to say anything, and that was fine by me, so I got up and walked to the door.

Neil followed me. He was a curly-haired, skinny guy from Detroit whose revolutionary hero was Miles Davis. He was soon to leave SDS, move to the Bay Area, and organize a jazz octet. He turned at the door and said, "You know something? You guys are full of it."

Out in the hall, we could hear one of the PL guys in the big meeting room bombarding SDS for its incorrect analysis. Neil and I left the building and found a bench in a little park nearby.

I said, "I don't think I know what just happened."

Neil chuckled and said, "Oh, sure you do, man."

"Yeah? What?"

"You just got your ass kicked."

Naturally I was sore, but it was a fatiguing kind of anger, not the energizing kind.

"I've got to say something about this to the main group, don't I?" I said to Neil.

"Like what?"

I thought it over for a moment and said, "Good point." Still, we started assembling some thoughts and boiled them all down to four main conclusions.

The first was that SDS had three enemies, which were PL, the FBI, and SDS itself. The second conclusion was that the most dangerous of these enemies was SDS. The third was that it would be fatal for SDS not to take action against PL. The fourth and final one was that any conceivable action that SDS might take would be fatal.

"Neil, don't these things need to be said?"

"You're out of it, man," said Neil gently, but he got up and led me back to the main meeting room, a large lecture hall not nearly full, with no more than three hundred people in it. We sat in the back. The PL-driven debate about who was a true revolutionary and who a running-dog capitalist pig still wailed and moaned around us. When a moment came to make a move, I could see no use in it. Shock and anger dissolved into despair at the depth and complexity of the crisis that had taken hold of SDS. And me.

"So in the words of the master, what is to be done?" I asked, turning to Neil. He said, "Well, I'm gonna go watch the game."

"What game?"

He shrugged. "It's Sunday. There's got to be a game."

———

IF I HAD FOUGHT, how would I have done it? What would have happened?

I would have to have gotten the floor somehow in the main meeting room. There might have been a tussle for the microphone. A minion of BD's would have hurried out to tell her what was happening. She and Arlene and probably Klonsky would have come storming into the room, the rest of the NIC people streaming behind, perhaps shouting that I had no right to speak. There would have been glorious pandemonium, a scene worth painting on a wall.

And there would have been no cane-cutting project. The Cubans would have gotten spooked out.

On the other hand, if I didn't fight but just surrendered quietly, there would at least be a Cuba project.

And an SDS. It would be battered and bloody but still breathing.

So that's what I did. That is, I did nothing.

And most of the time I'm glad.

BD put together a strong organizing committee under Julie Nichamin and Brian Murphy and gave the project a snappy new name, the Venceremos Brigade, *venceremos* ("we will conquer") being the motto of Cuba's July 26 Movement. The cane-cutting project became, as SDS historian Kirkpatrick Sale puts it, "one of the most imaginative enterprises ever undertaken by the American left."[2] There were 216 recruits in the first contingent, which left for Havana by way of Czechoslovakia in November 1969, with several hundred more to follow in three contingents over the next four years.

Once in Cuba, the brigadiers were welcomed and oriented, bused to a plantation, given machetes and a quick course in how to use them, and put to work. The Venceremos Brigade did not make the difference. The 1969 harvest fell about a million tons short of Castro's promised 10 million. It was Cuba's biggest harvest ever but still not big enough to pay for its enormous cost. Castro admitted failure and offered to resign but was told it was okay, his countrymen still loved him.

Cuba's revolution continued to founder. But it did not collapse.

And even though Nixon was now president, there was no new Bay of Pigs.

MY RELATIONSHIP WITH the Venceremos Brigade did not end in Austin.

Shortly after the Austin NC, the Venceremos Brigade people contacted the Cuban UN mission in New York. This confused the Cubans.

A secretary at the Cuban mission called me in San Francisco to say that the ambassador would be in New York soon and would be pleased if I would be available for a meeting. ASAP.

So one evening a few days later, I found myself in a quiet little Irish pub on Third Avenue not far from the UN building with Ambassador Carlos Rafael Rodriguez.

"My government is somewhat bewildered," he said. "Why are you no longer involved in this project?"

I tried to put the best face on the situation but thought he should know what had happened in Austin.

He listened carefully with a heavy face. Then he said, "I am sorry, my friend. Cuba cannot afford to get involved in the internal conflicts of the SDS. I am sure you can see this. I am afraid we must cancel the project."

I summoned myself. "Carlos, please, may I beg you to reconsider?"

"*Como no.* Please tell me what you think."

So I did my best. The program's strength, I said, would lie less in the politics of its organizers than in the numbers of committed Americans who would experience the Cuban revolution face-to-face. Julie Nichamen had been part of the project from the start. And the Venceremos Brigade would be a strong, dedicated crew. They would work hard in Cuba and would return to spread the story of the Cuban cause in the United States.

A day later, after another discussion with Havana, Rafael Rodriguez called for another meeting at the same place.

I got there first and waited for him in a booth at the back. I was working on my second Sam when he bustled in about half an hour late but with a warm smile.

He ordered a straight Chivas Regal and water, his taste in liquor, I noted, the same as that of my Bendix bosses on 11/22 five years earlier.

Our amenities were cordial but brief. "In view of our last conversation, it pleases me to tell you, *mi amigo*, that Cuba will proceed with this project."

I started to tell him how glad I was to hear this, but he raised a forefinger and added quickly, "But there is one condition we must ask you to meet. You must promise to be available for frequent private consultations with me on the management and the progress of the project. We will ask you to review the list of volunteers that the new organizers have agreed to send us."

I gladly promised to do that. Then we spent the rest of that meeting talking about Bernardine. She worried him. Since I wanted the project to go ahead, I touted her strengths. I don't know how he had formed his impression of her, but I thought it was pretty accurate.

"*Muy impetuosa,*" he said.

"But she's energetic and honest, Carlos, I promise you. And she's willful enough to get the job done."

I could hardly not have felt a little tickle of irony at defending to him the woman who had pushed me off the project, and whose group was now claiming to have conceived it. There was no one to share this delicacy with but him, but he appeared to have a cultivated taste for such things. He said with a chuckle, "What laws of history speak to us here?"

He insisted that our meetings be private and that I was to keep them secret. He assumed the FBI and the CIA were watching us, but he was adamant that our meetings not become a subject of SDS gossip.

So we set up a communications channel. From then on through the first year of the project, we met about once a month for a status review. We always met in that same Irish pub on Third Avenue, doubtless well observed by the feds but a secret from *la impetuosa*.

18 | Things Fall Apart
San Francisco and New York, 1969

I DIDN'T TAKE my expulsion from SDS well. I could neither get over it nor think of anything practical to do about it. I spent some time with my kids, and it was healing to do that, but the kids didn't know me well and seemed to stiffen. "Daddy" was a role that I had forgotten the words for. Aron tried, I thought, to love this man who was suddenly there every day but with an invisible Do-Not-Disturb badge where his blue badge used to be, a man whom her mother assured her was famous afar if a stranger at home, the man who was her father and whom she was therefore supposed to love. I would read her some stories; then she would want to go back outside to play. My guitar brought some solace and I tried to make up some new songs, but the lyrics were as inscrutable to me as to anyone who heard them.

I escaped to my boyhood pleasure of building model airplanes, the kind you make of a framework of long, thin balsa stringers glued into formers. These make a structure you then cover with damp tissue paper. The paper stretches tight as it dries and you then give it a coat of clear dope to stiffen it, then paint it. Maybe it was the fumes of the dope and the glue, but making these things took me beyond the world of Marx, Nixon, and the Weathermen.

Our family took day trips to a friend's place on windy Muir Beach, where Aron, then twelve, long-haired and radiant, kept her pony, a half-Arabian, silver-dappled beauty named Tamar. While Aron rode Tamar bareback around the meadow and the beach, Shay and Caleb and a few little kids would gather to watch me fly my airplanes. They would yell with delight when one of them got airborne. Then Shay would tell me not to feel bad when one of them crashed.

The crash was probably what I was looking for. One minute, this beautiful feather-light structure was flying on its propeller, driven by a wound-up rubber band, then it would spin its power out and come gliding down to crash on the rocks and be instantly transformed into a tangle of torn paper and broken sticks. I would hold the wreckage lovingly, trying to imagine what a little pilot might have felt as he watched the rocks coming up at him and realized there was nothing he could do.

But such mystical moments couldn't keep me from brooding on what had happened to me and SDS. And the more I brooded, the more puzzling BD's motives came to seem. She knew me too well, I believed, to think I might be a cop.

Or did she?

The truth was that no one could be above suspicion in the brave new world that our very success had propelled us into. Maybe the feds were playing smoke-and-mirrors games to disrupt the movement's leadership. Might the rumor that I was a secret agent have been a cointelpro op?

I dismissed this thought at the time, but federal documents released decades later and some good books on the subject have taught us that this is a classic cointelpro technique. The feds call it "bad-jacketing" or "black-jacketing," you tell me why. Maybe BD was already dealing with FBI-planted doubts of my loyalty to the movement when she put me on the SDS Cuba delegation. Maybe that's what she meant when she said she hoped that a taste of revolutionary Cuba would "radicalize" me again. She was living, after all, with the certainty that bad guys were prowling among us, and she was quicker than I to guess that their mission was to destroy us, not just to see what we ate for breakfast.

All that being said, the more I stepped back from that scary, bewildering session in Austin, the more certain I became that I had to say something about what was happening to SDS

I was scheduled to deliver some lectures at Dartmouth that fall courtesy of a grant from the Tucker Foundation. My original plan had been to talk about the origins of the war, but in view of the Chicago DNC police assault and what had happened in Austin, I thought it more to the point to talk about SDS's crippling leadership crisis. I turned those talks into what amounted to a farewell address to SDS and published it in the August–September '69 issue of the New Left's best magazine, *Liberation,* under the title, "Notes on a Decade Ready for the Dustbin." A sample:

"On every quarter of the white Left, high and low, the attempt to reduce the New Left's inchoate vision to the Old Left's perfected remembrance has produced a layer of bewilderment and demoralization which no cop with his club or senator with his committee could ever have induced."

The irony of it was obscene. Even as BD and her cohorts in comic-book Marxism were scrapping national SDS as a used-up relic, SDS chapters were at cruise speed. There was no more creative or effective opposition group on stage, nor had SDSers ever been in higher form. Our chapters at American University, Georgetown, Boston University, and Kent State, for example, had led nonviolent actions that spring supporting black ethnic studies and attacking war-related research, ROTC and police-officer training programs. All these actions succeeded.

So I'm sorry I let myself become demoralized instead of enraged by Austin. After the *Liberation* piece, I just opted out. I had no energy, no vision, no agenda.

And no help. The SDS old guard had been matriculating to other lives, and my assumption that they would help hold us together had not been sound. When my session in Austin that March at last brought this home to me, national SDS had already crashed. The mixture of PL intrusion, FBI black ops, and our new leadership's view that SDS was history had already proved fatal. The best I could do for SDS after Austin was to crash my little airplanes into rocks and watch my daughter Aron ride her pony on the beach.

IT DIDN'T HELP that Beth and I were finally losing it. We had left the navel-gazing Yellow Springs for San Francisco to try to get a grip on our marriage.

It didn't work. One day Beth came to me at my desk and said, "Carl, have you got a minute? I think we should talk."

"Sure. Talk about what?"

"I think it's time for us to go separate ways."

"What makes you say that?"

She chuckled. "Oh, the way we get along."

As Yeats had put it in 1921, "Things fall apart; the center cannot hold."

THE WAR GOT worse than ever as President Nixon and his national-security adviser, Henry Kissinger, implemented Nixon's 1968 campaign promise of a "secret plan" to end the war, a plan he called "Vietnamization." This turned out to mean pulling American troops back, turning ground combat responsibility over to the disinterested South Vietnamese Army, and unleashing the Strategic Air Command, which could now load up the huge, ungainly B-52s with racks and racks of five-thousand-pound demolition bombs and fifteen-hundred-pound daisy cutters and send them over targets in Laos, Cambodia, and Vietnam, sometimes blasting the same target with squadrons of bombers for days on end.

Nixon appears to have reasoned that bombing 'em back to the Stone Age would take the urgency out of widening American unhappiness with the war by cutting our own casualties and untying the hand formerly tied behind our back. At last we were going all out to win this accursed nonwar of a war and get it over.

At the same time, Nixon took all remaining constraints off the government's widening operations against the movement. According to Kirkpatrick Sale, the White House was soon coordinating an armada of "no fewer than twenty federal agencies . . . geared to maximum surveillance, disruption and harassment of the New Left."[1]

The flagship of this armada was the FBI's "Cointelpro: New Left," which was manned by more than two thousand full-time FBI agents. These agents were supported by more than two thousand informers, each of whom was paid three hundred dollars a month.

And besides the FBI and its hirelings, there were the other agencies for which we have no manpower or budget estimates, although we may fairly suppose that the black-ops pros of the National Security Agency, the CIA, army intelligence, the Civil Service Commission, and the Department of Health, Education, and Welfare did not work for free.

On top of the federal programs were the municipal police Red Squads that were operating in every major city in the country, and these were not mom-and-pop deals. The Chicago Red Squad was running 500 agents, New York 143, Los Angeles 84, and Boston 40.[2] And under the terms of Cointelpro, all of the agencies, federal and municipal, were supposed to be coordinating their work with the FBI. Everything the other agencies had, the FBI should have had.

With what I learned about government costing practices in my defense job, I would confidently bet that the overall price tag for the Nixon era's secret and illegal attacks on the New Left, attacks that centered on SDS, must have been upwards of $50 million a year, with a total over Nixon's time in office of more than $250 million. What kind of deranged cost-benefit analysis could justify such an expense?

And what did the police state get for all its money? As to its basic intelligence take, the result doesn't seem to have been at all impressive.

For example, the personal file the FBI finally released to me after a decades-long court fight runs to about four thousand pages. When I first got the boxes and saw how many pages there were, I thought, *Great, I'm about to see myself as others see me.* But despite its bulk, the file turned out to be thin. Most of these reports were generated between 1968 and 1971, exactly the period of "Cointelpro: New Left," but not a single page bears on the Cointelpro ops themselves. Many pages, of course, are heavily redacted and several hundred withheld altogether to protect "sources and methods," though sources and methods are the heart of this story. Even so, I find it odd that there is nothing in these papers on my leaving a secret job in the defense industry and instantly becoming SDS's president at the very moment at which SDS was threatening to violate the National Security Act. This threat was a clownish act meant more to prick the media than to draw real federal blood. But high-level Bendix people were worried about it, as I have recounted earlier here (see chapter 1). They knew that I knew some highly embarrassing military secrets, such as the air force program to "weaponize" Agent Orange and to stockpile illegal pathogen warheads. I cannot imagine that Bendix people failed to tell the FBI what I had learned in my job. But the FBI seems not have been warned.

Moreover, there is nothing on my trip to South Vietnam in 1965, nothing on my illegal trip to Cuba in 1969, nothing on my several New York meetings with Cuba's UN ambassador, nothing on my role in the illegal Venceremos Brigade, nothing on my several speaking trips to Europe, just one page, originated by the State Department, on my two trips to Japan, and just one page, also originated by the State Department, on my involvement with Sartre's war-crimes tribunal.

Apart from feeling screwed as a citizen by the fact of this surveillance, I also feel screwed as a taxpayer in that it was so sloppy. In any case, firm conclusions about "Cointelpro: New Left" and the government's several other SDS-penetration programs are impossible to draw from such a meager database. But suspicions are unavoidable with so many dots to connect.

- J. Edgar Hoover told the House Internal Security Committee on April 17, 1969, that the New Left was "a firmly established subversive force dedicated to the complete destruction of our democratic values" and that "at the core of the New Left is Students for a Democratic Society."
- We have certain knowledge that secret agents from several parts of government infiltrated SDS.
- We know that by 1968 at the latest, the FBI's mission went beyond intelligence-gathering to destruction.
- We know that the classic guise of the counterintelligence agent is that of the radical firebrand; that is, provocateurism is a basic weapon of the militant right wing.
- As soon as SDS crashed, "Cointelpro: New Left" was terminated.

No less a connoisseur of such arcane matters than Daniel Ellsberg of Pentagon Papers fame told an interviewer for *Rolling Stone* in 1973:

> Someday we should reopen the question of how it really came about that SDS was shattered in the way that it was, and who might have been involved in the disputes between PL, Weathermen and SDS. The antiwar movement was shattered during that period; there were disputes over the issue of violence. And I would be very curious at this point to know just who was paying some of those people who were so hot on violence.

Ellsberg does not raise this question to say that SDS lacked in tragic flaws. He knows that it was rich in them. But the events of SDS's final days conform so closely to the classic provocateur scenario that Ellsberg's question cannot be dismissed.

Soon after the breakup of my marriage, I left San Francisco in the middle of the night with whatever I could pack in a duffel bag, headed east because I was already as far west as I could get without a boat and because there was a place to crash for a while in Denver, then another in Ames, then one in Pittsburgh, and then it was time to go to Hanover to give my talks at Dartmouth on the apparent self-destruction of SDS.

Sometime about then my Vanguard record came out and got some nice notices in a few small papers and a long but sneeringly dismissive review in *The New York Times*. More interesting than my music, as the reviewer saw it, was the question of whether it was ethical of Vanguard to use my name as a speaker to market me as a singer. Sigh.

Then the *Evergreen Review* was suddenly rocked by one of the first militant actions of the emerging women's liberation movement.

Evergreen was a cutting-edge New York literary magazine published by Grove Press and edited by Fred Jordan, an erudite, suave, impeccable man of about fifty with a European polish. Fred had flattered me by asking if I had anything to show him, and I'd responded with an essay, "The Idea of the New Left," in which I argued that the key to progressive politics in the advanced countries was no longer Marxism's industrial workers but the technical professionals of the white-collared middle class. *Evergreen* published it in its February 1969 issue; then Grove Press republished it later that year as the introduction to an anthology I edited titled *The New Left Reader*. Fred and I had become friends.

One day when I was in New York he took me to lunch in Greenwich Village and asked if he could put my name on the *Evergreen Review*'s masthead as an associate editor. He also asked if I had any fiction to show him.

I tried to avoid falling at his knees. With a savvy literary pro like Fred to guide me, a masthead position with *Evergreen,* and a sophisticated house such as Grove Press to publish me, maybe I would have a literary life after all. I still wanted to come out of this strange tour of duty in the movement somewhere near where I'd started it, as a writer of plays and fiction and maybe a little high-speed lit crit instead of polemics all the time. And I assured Fred that I did indeed have the draft of an angry young man's first novel in the cage. So a solid connection to Grove Press would give me a great shot at making a move back into real life.

But then big trouble exploded at *Evergreen*.

A group of young women staff members had grown angry at the way Fred and other men at the magazine were treating them. They complained of being relegated to goferhood. They saw Fred as routinely preferring male contributors to female contributors. They were tired of it and they weren't going to take it anymore.

Fred said he might discuss the workday issues, but as to being made in effect coeditors, the women could just forget it.

So, led by staff writer Robin Morgan, a group of about ten women walked into Fred's office one day, sat down, and announced that they wouldn't leave until their demands were met.

Fred told them he would not negotiate with them until they left his office, and that under no circumstances would he concede editorial control. The women stayed where they were.

After two days of unheeded warnings, Fred called the police.

They came promptly. They grabbed the women by the hair, pulled them out of Fred's office, deposited them on the sidewalk, and told them not to reenter the building on pain of arrest.

Fred fired them. The women met in Robin's apartment and decided to send a letter to the magazine's associate editors asking them to resign in support.

I got a copy of this letter. I looked through the back issues I had on hand and saw that the women's basic complaint was correct: the editors and contributors were all men. And I knew from our talks that Fred tended to dismiss the feminist cause as a distraction. Most troubling was Fred's appeal to the police to remove the women by force. Perhaps this was all he could do, but that did not seem a gallant way to handle disputes between comrades. In no way did I leap at the opportunity to throw myself on the sword of women's lib, but these women were movement sisters. How could I not support them? So I sent *Evergreen* a resignation letter with a copy to Robin. I never heard back from her.

SDS itself had a mixed record with sexism, as had the movement generally. All five of SDS's presidents were men. Bernadine was the only woman among our three national secretaries. Only one woman spoke at SDS's antiwar rally of 1965. Sometimes a streak of blatant sexism surfaced in our allies, as when one of SNCC's field secretaries joked that "the only position for women in the movement is prone." But SNCC women seemed to find this less insulting than silly. One observed drily that the "prone" bit "implied an unusual sexual taste."

I met with Fred at a coffee shop near his office in the Village. He wanted me to reconsider.

"I think there may be something a bit precipitous in your decision to leave us," he said.

"Me, too. But how did you let things get so badly out of control?"

Fred said gently, "In view of what seems to be happening to SDS, you must be asking yourself the same question."

"Point taken, but still."

A rich elegance in his voice, he said, "Carl, surely you can see. It was unthinkable that I allow the magazine to be captured by force."

"But why did you call the cops?"

"Grove Press is sympathetic," he said, "to the causes of the New Left, as you well know, including that of the new feminism. But I am responsible to our publisher and to our readers. I am *not* responsible to the gang of female thugs who took control of my office through sheer force of numbers."

"Did you try to talk it through with them?"

"Picture, if you will, an office filled with angry, excited women, their arms interlocked, chanting as though schooled in choral discipline, 'No more coffee runs!' As I trust you may well imagine, this does not conduce to creative dialogue."

"Come on, Fred, that scene couldn't have come out of nowhere. Robin says *Evergreen*'s office culture has always trivialized women. These complaints weren't new, were they?"

"Trivialized women have always been free to seek other office cultures," he said with his lofty disdain.

I said, "Some of these women were really good writers. Isn't that why they were on the staff? Yet they're bitching that you send them out for the coffee."

"Carl, my good friend," he said, his elegance at its snottiest, "I know you haven't spent much time in New York lately and may easily have failed to notice, but here, I must tell you, *someone* goes out for the coffee."

"As I'm sure you know, Fred, when troubles come, they come not one by one."

Fred gave me a long, warm look. "Carl," he said gently, "do you really hope to be crowned the king of women's lib?"

NOT LONG AFTER my lunch with Fred, another little chunk of my life fell off. It was another forced resignation, or forced at least as I saw it.

I had accepted a terrific offer of a two-month-long fellowship at the California Institute of the Arts in Los Angeles. The institute had extended a similar invitation to the philosopher-king of the German New Left, Herbert Marcuse. After Marcuse accepted, the Walt Disney family, an important sponsor of the institute, had looked more closely into Marcuse's political views and found them distasteful. His invitation was withdrawn. I don't know why the family didn't find my own views also distasteful, but there had been no talk of their withdrawing my invitation. The gig would have been supercool, but I felt I had to do something to support Marcuse, so I wrote another letter of resignation. Such letters were becoming an art form for me. From its close:

> Sometime last winter, the Institute advertised itself prominently in *The New York Times,* giving a list of faculty names and scheduled guests, including my own. If this ad was written before Marcuse was dismissed, why was his name not there? If it was written afterward, on the other hand, how could you have been so presumptuous as to use my name as if nothing had happened?

A little over the top? Get a load of the next one.

The editor of *The Paris Review,* Peter Moscoso-Gongora, had written to ask if I had some fiction he might look at. Travel back in time and tell the eighteen-year-old kid in sooty Akron that one day he will get a request like that from a classy avant-garde literary journal like *The Paris Review.* Tell that kid that he will respond as follows:

> The world we face is too bizarre for fiction. Fiction itself is threatened, the stance of the artist is threatened, by the forces we have to confront *now.* This is not a time for withdrawing into an imaginary world but for acting in the real one.

Maybe I was trying to put a comforting political mask on a fear that I couldn't do it anymore, that I had burned out whatever I'd had of an artist's spirit and just couldn't start making up stories and plays again.

Nor was that the end of my resignations, although in the summer of 1971 I actually managed to get through one of these proffered forays into the world of the well funded without getting my conscience bent out of shape. This one was at the Aspen Institute for Humanistic Studies, where I spent two delicious months hanging out with Gonzo journalist Hunter Thompson and Jan Wenner, the publisher of *Rolling Stone,* participating in panel discussions on the state of the American soul and presenting a well-received paper on my Big-Bang Theory of

American history, "The Yankee and Cowboy War" (which I later expanded into a book with the same title, published in 1976). I'd even given a talk on SDS at the army base in nearby Fort Collins.

My time at Aspen seemed like a dream, filled with great people, great talk, great parties, great mountains. I spoke my pieces, dropped a little something with Hunter, and got along fine.

19 | To the Chicken Coop
Putney and Chicago, 1970

LANKY, RED-HAIRED John Douglas was thirty-something, independently wealthy, and an iron sculptor with a bushy mustache. He lived near Putney, Vermont, in a classic, foursquare farmhouse he had lavishly remodeled and added a wing to. His father was a director of General Foods and had been an undersecretary of the air force in the JFK administration, but John had not needed the Vietnam War to send him on a different path. He called himself "cradle-stoned" and had a gift for non sequitur. He was soft-spoken and wore a constant half smile of disbelief.

His artistic style was, as he once called it, "doodleism," meaning that he welded pieces of junkyard scrap together however they seemed to fit. He worked in a large studio he had set up in his big red barn, filled with heavy-duty ironworking tools and tanks of propane. Whether welding or not, he was always in bib overalls and a heavy-duty brown work shirt, the shirt always buttoned at the neck and the wrists, always with some Band-Aids and a tube of ointment in one bib pocket and a pack of Camels in the other. Maybe because he spent so much time looking at the tip of his welding torch, he always seemed to be gazing away from you, as though he didn't quite see what you were saying. But his air of incredulity was warm and amused, whether optical or doctrinal. John was good-hearted. I felt welcome in his doodled household, as though I were a new piece of scrap.

On one side of the original house, John had added a large hall with a grand stone fireplace at one end and a projection booth and a well-equipped film-editing room at the other. This was used by movement filmmakers from New York and Boston Newsreel groups who would come up for days at a time to put their films together and give them their first public screenings. Stack the benches to the side, and the screening room became a dance hall.

After my month at Dartmouth and then another at MIT, I'd gone to John's place with the Boston Newsreel people for a screening of one of their films. I'd struck up a friendship with John. He saw I was at loose ends and invited me to stay at his place for a while.

The one building on the property that needed finishing when I moved in was the chicken coop. This was a solid building about a dozen feet square out beyond the barn, maybe 300 feet from the main house. It hadn't seen a live chicken in decades. The coop had been steam-cleaned and had the sweet smell of the grassy meadow where it sat. John and I put in some insulation, a new floor, inside walls, and a ceiling. We ran some power out to it and put in a little potbellied stove that John happened to have in the barn. I built a high bunk and under it set up a long desk, finding a soothing relief from the tortuous ambiguities of movement politics in working with wood and tools, a replay of my model-airplane therapy in San Francisco. The one window in the coop looked out on a long, broad, grassy hillside sloping off into other hillsides that rolled into a distance of forests and farm fields and a far-off range of mountains, a church steeple rising clear of tall pines down in the village of Putney maybe two miles away.

And there in this new Eden—an Eden, say, for pieces of sixties scrap—I sat down to doodle some notes for my Big Book. This Big Book would revolutionize the revolution. It would show what had gone wrong with SDS and the New Left.

But all it ever came to were several hundred single-spaced pages of Vermont scrap to be moved in the ensuing years from the back of one closet to another in a loose-leaf notebook marked "The Chicken Coop

Book." It didn't get opened up again until I sat down decades later to write the book in hand.

On reading it, I found myself looking for reminders of the actualities of my time in Putney and was disappointed to find that it consisted mostly of high-minded theorizing on theories. My desire then, it seems, was not to try making sense of my life but to show that the New Left was *new,* not a replastering of Marxism but a new way to think about politics. So my notes have little to say about my time in the chicken coop but instead are riffs on the work of those who made up my pantheon in those days, notably Gramsci, Ruffiero, Merleau-Ponty, Auerbach, Cromwell, the Levellers of 1648, Locke, Jefferson, Adam Smith, de Tocqueville, Aristotle, Sartre, Camus, Hannah Arendt, Pericles, Freud, Nietzsche, and a "dialogue" I'd had with one Alan King at the "Club of Rome." I'd toyed with a lot of titles (how about "Through a Class Darkly"?), but lacking a final choice had started calling it simply "The Chicken Coop Book," partly because of where I'd written it but also because it suggested how I felt about my performance in the movement and the awful symbolism of living in a house that had been built for chickens.

There are a few existential nuggets in it, like the line spoken apropos of nothing by laid-back John in his kitchen at supper one night: "Games should never be played by more than one."

Or a snippet of dialogue from the same table:

Harry, in a sigh of chemically assisted reverie: "Oh, man, I'm back about nine centuries."

Fay: "You can call home from there, you know."

Harry: "We don't have phones yet."

Fay: "So call collect."

Or an observation by Jenny, a visiting filmmaker from New York: "After a certain age, sailors run out of water."

Or Nancy, a filmmaker from Boston: "Irony is like salt and should not be eaten by the spoonful."

Or one evening coming back from a grocery run to Putney when Mike and I got pulled over by a friendly officer of the law who said his name was Al and said, "Okay, my friends, what're you carrying?"

Mike said, "Groceries."

Al said, "Look, I wouldn't bust you for a few numbers. I'm looking for weight."

He shined his light quickly around our backseat and looked in the trunk, then said, "All right. When you get some poundage, let me know."

Then a few days after that, the faraway non sequitur of the Chicago conspiracy trial suddenly moved to my foreground.

IT WAS A MORNING early in 1970. John came crunching out the snow path to the chicken coop to tell me I had a call. He didn't know who it was. I followed him back to the main house and went to the phone in the kitchen.

"Hello?"

"Carl, my friend! This is Tom Hayden."

We hadn't talked since August '68 in Chicago.

Now he was in Chicago again, standing trial with the other Chicago Seven on charges of conspiring to cross state lines to foment a riot.[1]

That he greeted me as his friend put me on guard right away. We were both Ann Arbor guys, but we had never been friends. Only in the loosest sense of the term had we even been comrades. He'd been against making the war the focus of SDS organizing in 1965 when I'd been for it. When he changed his mind at the end of that year, the first thing he did was make a trek to North Vietnam, which I saw as thoughtless. He had used his clout as a father of SDS to call for the demonstrations at the Chicago DNC, which I had tried to talk him out of. He had supported the Weathermen's "Days of Rage" and had even advised movement people to start taking target practice, which I thought was suicidal. Now he'd gotten his nuts in a vice with this costly and useless conspiracy trial. Why was this man calling me? And calling me his friend?

"Carl, listen," he said, "I can't talk long, but you've got to help us out here. We're in a serious situation." His voice had some urgency in it.

"Why? What's up?"

"We were planning on presenting some witnesses tomorrow who

suddenly can't make it. If we don't have a witness to put on the stand, Judge Hoffman can rule that our defense is over. He's pig enough to do that. We can't let that happen because we've still got some major witnesses to present, so we've got to find people to put on the stand tomorrow. I'm counting on you to say you'll come and testify for us."

"Wait a minute, Tom. Slow down."

"No, I can't wait a minute. Just tell me you'll be in Chicago by ten in the morning."

"You mean, like, tomorrow morning?"

"Right. We might have to put you on tomorrow afternoon."

"Hey, Tom, I'm out in the country here. How would I get to Chicago? I don't even know if I could get a reservation. And besides—"

"Carl, I know you can find a way. We're really screwed if you don't do this. Call here when you know your flight and we'll have somebody at the airport to pick you up."

"Tom, shut up. I don't want to do this."

"Nobody's asking you to want to do it. Just do it. We need you. Okay?"

"Look, I'll think about it."

"Hey, thanks, man! I knew we could count on you!"

"I have not said I'll do it."

"Look, I really gotta run. Call with your flight plans. I'll see you tomorrow."

Click.

Thanks to capitalism's amazing airline system, and once again against my firm resolve to have nothing to do with the Chicago action, I was in Chicago that night, ready to take the witness stand the next day to say supportive things about the guys whose hubris had led the antiwar movement into a disastrously useless conflict it had no way to win.

The Chicago Seven's attorneys had found some more last-minute witnesses while I was in transit, so it was two days before I got put on the stand to testify for about an hour. I went on right after Chicago mayor Richard J. Daley, so the Federal Court Building was packed with policemen and journalists that morning.

The Seven's defense attorneys had put Daley on the stand to make him admit that he'd told the police to attack the demonstrators, and at all costs, including heavy physical intimidation, to keep us away from the Coliseum, the Democrats' convention site.

The federal grand jury had indicted the defendants on charges of crossing state lines "to conspire to incite, organize, promote and encourage riots" and "create a situation in Chicago where these people [the demonstrators] would riot."[2]

It was a crazy charge and a crazy trial, and the craziness started with the courtroom itself, a two-stories-high statement of a federal bureaucracy's vision of grandeur. Defendant Abbie Hoffman called it "a neon oven." That was apt enough except that ovens, even cold ones, imply at least some memory of warmth, and it was hard to imagine there ever having been any warmth at all in that place. The fluorescent lights that lit it from behind a lacework inner ceiling pulled all sense of warmth out of it, even from the huge dark-wood panels that lined the walls, so that the wood itself seem melted and poured into a mold, something prefabricated of cold, thin plastic. No doubt because of my memories of the Chicago streets of that past August, it seemed lit by electrified tear gas, just the kind of colorless, chemical light one imagines suited to the taste of Big Brother, a light without shadows and with a scent of electricity.

And even more Big Brotherly was the prosecution's idea that the demonstrators' panicked efforts to escape the unprovoked police assault I had seen unfold at the Grant Park band shell was in any sense a *riot*. Even defense counsel William Kunstler's widely accepted correction that the band shell melee was a "police riot" seemed wrong. "Riot" conveys a sense of spontaneity, and there was nothing in the least spontaneous about what I saw the police do that day. I know this for a fact. I had watched the beginning of it all from the best seat in the house, center stage at the band shell. I had seen a squad of police, evidently on some command and acting as one, detach from the larger group that encircled us, form up into two orderly columns, and then march two abreast through an opening in the police cordon straight into the crowd, beating people to their left and right, making no effort to arrest anyone, and with all the spontaneity of a regimental drill.

The same eagerness to be violent was in the air the morning of the day I testified, when Mayor Daley was on the stand. I saw a young SDSer, Howie Machtinger, stand up in court to remind His Honor that he was a pig. Two burly marshals hefted him by his arms, dragged him out to the waiting room, threw him against a wall and roughed him up, then carried him off under arrest.

The riotousness of the DNC story, its qualities of helter-skelter improvisation and absurdity, lay less in the events of convention week than in the conspiracy trial, and more in the defense than in the prosecution.

The prosecution was in fact all too rational. Yes, there was something goofy about putting a clown such as Abbie Hoffman on trial. But of the seven defendants who were tried together, at least four of them—Jerry Rubin, Dave Dellinger, Rennie Davis, and Tom Hayden—were skilled captains of the movement. The very act of bringing charges against them in itself tied up a vast part of the movement's all-too-limited resources, and this at a time when Nixon's escalation of the air war should have had the movement's undivided attention.

Moreover, Nixon's request that federal prosecutor Tom Foran, a Democrat, stay on the case when Nixon might have appointed a Republican to take it over was a piece of tactical shrewdness from the same bag. It lent the prosecution a patina of bipartisanship it did not deserve.

As to the defense: gallows humor has its place, but not to put too fine a point on it, that place is the gallows, and the Seven went into their trial not yet condemned. So why did the Seven play—and play so clumsily—to the cheap seats? Why did they seem to need so badly to show what scorn they felt for the judge and, even worse, for the jury?

In the juror-screening process, for example, of what strategic or tactical or PR use was the merry-pranksterism of the defendants in having an uptight and proper man such as Judge Julius Hoffman ask prospective jurors: "Do your daughters wear bras most of the time?" The given justification was that such an "untraditional" question was meant "to flush out cultural issues."[3] But what could this mean to the straight-seeming but presumptively honest and fair-minded middle-American juror prospects? That only those with braless daughters need apply? That you couldn't understand the Chicago Seven unless your daughters had fled to the counterculture?

The swagger in showing such contempt for the judge and the jury might have played well in Berkeley and Cambridge and two or three college towns in between, but it was utterly at odds with the more prosaic but also more tenable strategy proposed by defendant John Froines when he told a pretrial press conference, "We want the jury to become part of the antiwar movement. We want to turn the courtroom into a schoolhouse. . . . If the government is going to try us for 'intent,' then we are going to show why we came to the Democratic convention in the first place, why we're against imperialism, racism, against the war."[4]

This is actually what I tried to do in my little hour upon that stage. Notwithstanding what writer John Schultz called my "monkishly thinning long hair and the manner of an aggressive scholar."[5] I took the stand to say in a polite, even voice that the movement did not rally in Chicago to get into a street fight with the police but to state the case against the war. If some of us had prepared for violence, as by bringing motorcycle helmets, it was not because we wanted violence but because we had good reason to fear that violence would be visited upon us.

Schultz says Hayden was shaking his head often during my account of the several phone conversations I'd had with him and his co-organizers in the months before Chicago "as if he did not want anyone to believe that he had ever been so naive about possible police violence in Chicago as Oglesby made him sound." But whatever Hayden wanted people to believe once the trial was under way, the whole argument between him and me before the DNC demonstrations revolved around the question of violence. I had said that violence was unavoidable whatever we did, and Hayden had countered that the demonstrations would be peaceful. I didn't believe him and I didn't believe he believed it himself, and that's why I had argued that the movement should not go to Chicago. Whether or not Hayden was jiving me during the run-up to the DNC is a separate question that I can't pretend to answer. He and I never spoke to each other again after the trial.

Schultz says prosecutor Foran cross-examined me "as if he were standing in a reptile house looking through a glass at a cobra."

As often as I could in my testimony, I tried to address the jurors in language I thought they might understand. My aim was to make it clear that nobody on our side had wanted the physical confrontation that developed, that this confrontation happened because of Daley and the police.

But it was also true that the organizers had known for a virtual certainty that they were leading the movement into a street fight with the Chicago police. Yes, I believed the organizers had wanted a peaceful assembly, and especially that they had wanted a peaceful assembly before the murder of Robert Kennedy. They had recognized the threat of an illegal police assault, however, and had simply resolved not to be intimidated.

In my cross-examination, prosecutor Foran used my presence in Grant Park to ask if I had heard certain speakers say things that might remotely be construed as inciting to riot. For example, Foran asked me if I had heard the speech of one Tom Neumann, who was not one of the defendants.

"No, sir," I said. "He spoke after I left Grant Park."

Nonetheless, Foran pressed on. "Did you hear Mr. Neumann tell the crowd, 'We are no longer waiting for them to make moves. We have decided, some of us, to move out of this park in any way that we can, to move into their space in any way that we can, and to defend ourselves in any way that we can'?"

"No, Mr. Foran. As I told you, I left the park before Neumann spoke."

Then Foran would read another passage from Neumann's speech and ask me if I had heard that one. Why did Foran keep asking me about such utterances after I'd already told him that I had not heard Neumann speak? Why were the defense attorneys not objecting? Foran's purpose must have been simply to get this sort of angry language (hardly conspiratorial, in any case) into the record, thereby hoping to put some beef on the claim he would make in his summary: For the defendants, he would say, "Law is viewed as merely a collection of casual suggestions that they can obey or not as they see fit."[6]

This was nicely turned. You could see why the guy was a big leaguer. But it was cheating to use my testimony this way. So I thought this should at least give me a chance to say what I thought such out-of-context quotations meant. I wanted to tell the jury that the Seven in fact did not disdain the law. On the contrary, they believed in it deeply and had the courage to insist that it applied to all citizens, including the police, who broke the law in assaulting the protesters without cause; the mayor of Chicago, who broke the law in ordering the police to shoot rioters to maim and looters to kill; and the president of the United States, who broke the law in waging an undeclared war in Vietnam.

So I kept trying to explain in this way what might have provoked this guy Neumann's angry statements, but Judge Hoffman kept telling me to answer Foran's loaded questions with a yes or a no. I thought it was a blatant display of the court's bias and it irritated me.

So I finally tried to strike back. I looked up directly at Judge Hoffman and asked, "May I address the court, Your Honor?"

I thought he seemed surprised that I spoke politely to him. "Why, yes, you may," he said.

"Why is it impossible for this court to tolerate an explanation of reality that goes beyond yea or nay?"[7]

Hoffman looked at me as though I were, well, a cobra behind glass. There was a brief moment when I thought he might actually try to answer me. I was eager for a colloquy. But then he looked away and told Foran to continue and to give me a chance to answer his questions fully. But then Foran said he had no further questions, and that was that.

I left the courtroom with a pro-forma fist salute to the defendants, and I got out of Chicago as quickly as I could, very glad to get back to quiet Putney, glad that my little foray from the coop to the Loop was over.

The debate within the movement about the Chicago Seven trial—what it meant and how to relate to it—remained intense.

Should it be the antiwar movement's main organizing focus? Or, as I believed, was that a political cliché that would only distract us?

I said to anyone who would listen that the trial should be left to the jury, that there was nothing that the shards of SDS and the newly leaderless student movement could do or say about it that would not make our situation worse, that our strategy should be to make sure that the war itself rather than the movement against it remain the subject of the national Vietnam debate.

But the Weathermen saw things otherwise. They had called for a "national action" to "kick ass," as Mark Rudd put it, to mark the opening of the trial. Weatherpeople had blown up the statue of the policeman in Chicago's Haymarket Square to open their "Days of Rage," a campaign in which they were joined by virtually no one.[8]

The Weathermen's most notable statement during this period wasn't even about the war. It was Bernardine's rhapsody on the Charles Manson gang's then-recent murders of eight Hollywood people, including the pregnant Sharon Tate.

"Dig it!" she was reliably reported to have said to her audience of Weathermen at Flint that winter. "First they killed those pigs, then they ate dinner in the same room with them, then they even shoved a fork into pig Tate's stomach! Wild!"

I wish I were making that up, but I'm not. After BD's salute to the Manson gang, the Weathermen's sign of greeting was no longer the fist. It became four outstretched fingers, symbolizing the tines of a fork.[9] (BD later said that her statement was a joke mocking violence in America.)

I got back to my chicken coop from Chicago as to an island of sanity in a stormy sea of madness. The whole country seemed to have gone nuts. At the Douglas farm there was maybe a little too much singing and dancing and funny stuff to smoke. But in Chicago, in the aftermath of major student risings in Paris and Prague, it was not only movement people who came to sense what an American police state might feel like. The ambience of the Chicago Seven trial made the Douglas farm seem like a kind of Eden. I returned to Vermont with an eagerness to get back to my coop for chickens and the Big Book I was trying to write.

After the Chicago Seven were found guilty in February (their convictions would be appealed and overturned on a technicality), militant, often violent street actions broke out in many cities, as, for example, in Isla Vista, California, where someone burned down the Bank of America building.[10] But it seemed far off, and I was glad I could turn away from it.

Then another character entered my sequestered little Eden, stage left. And things changed still again.

ROBERT KRAMER was a movement filmmaker of about thirty when he arrived at the Douglas farm that winter, a handsome, rather aloof guy who had been active with the New York Newsreel collective. He had a bit of a rep as the writer-director of a highly political black-and-white feature film titled *Ice,* which was then playing to a strong response in Paris.

In *Ice* he had set out to show what an armed revolution might look like in the setting of a contemporary American city. He was especially interested in the security aspects of an urban guerrilla group's life. His vision was of a nightmarish encounter in which the would-be revolutionaries were obliterated as much by their chosen roles as by the political police who delivered the coup de grâce.

Kramer had come to stay at the Douglas farm to work on a new film, a Newsreel documentary. It was a moment in his life as well as in the life of the movement as a whole in which the dominant questions at hand were: Who were we? What was this "revolution" that so many of us were now saying was about to happen? And of greatest practical importance, what resources could we marshal against the newly elected Nixon, this shallow, cynical, ruthless, bleak-spirited man who had come from the heart of American darkness to put the screws on the movement's leadership while intensifying the air war in Vietnam almost beyond comprehension?

Kramer at that point believed with Bernardine and the other Weathermen that the "correct" next step for the movement was "to raise the level of the contradictions"—indeed, that it was "time to pick up the gun," a slogan borrowed from Malcolm X by the more militant Black

Panthers. In this respect Kramer was an implicit Weathermen, though he was never a part of the Weatherman collective, nor to my knowledge did he ever do anything violent to anyone.

But Kramer did bring firearms to the Douglas farm, a twenty-gauge shotgun and a thirty-eight-caliber pistol.

"Things are going to come to guns at last," he told several of us matter-of-factly over the kitchen table one evening, "so we should accept them into our lives and familiarize ourselves with them."

Naturally, I thought it was beyond bizarre to think that a few shots at a paper target on a tree would get us ready to wage the revolution. But Robert was a persuasive guy, and I was still preoccupied with my deep bruises from the Austin NC. I was surprised that laid-back, peaceful John Douglas seemed to think that Robert made sense. So I didn't try to stop what was happening. I just spent more time scribbling in my chicken coop.

Two ridges or so away from the main house, in a meadow on the most secluded part of his property, John let Robert set up a firing range. Robert encouraged the variety of people who lived for a while at John's farm or passed through it to take a hike over there and show that they were not afraid to pick up a gun.

John thought that this would not create a problem for the local folks, since many of them were hunters. By standing custom, many of them actually hunted on John's property. Many New Englanders, in fact, were contentiously proud of the people's right to bear arms. The New Hampshire motto, "Live free or die," was hardly a call to pacifism. The Vermonters around us in Putney were as blasé about hearing guns go off as were New Yorkers.

I might have argued with Robert about this a little more vigorously, but I guess I'd come to believe by then that you couldn't win arguments with fundamentalists, whether the right-wing sort, who thought America could win in Vietnam if it dropped more bombs on more targets, or the left-wing sort, who thought the movement could stop Nixon if it started shooting people. Robert was among those who took it as a given that class warfare was brewing and that target practice in John's meadow was a way to start getting ready for it. It didn't seem to occur to anyone but me that this was nonsense.

When I said to Robert that, no matter how angry and how desperate we were about Nixon and the course of the war, this idea that it was "time to pick up the gun" was just romantic posturing.

"Look what happened in the last presidential campaign," Robert said. "The peace Democrats were able to nominate a man like McGovern on a strong antiwar platform, and this just drove the whole American center to the right. We got Nixon, and the war's worse than ever. What's so rational, Carl, about sticking with a strategy that loses even when it wins?"

I made the point, of course, that things would have been different if King and Bobby Kennedy had not been slain, but Robert simply said with a calm little smile, "Ah, but they were, weren't they?"

And when I said, all right, but the strategy of armed violence was simply playing to the other side's strength, he answered, "Were your beloved Sons of Liberty playing to the British Empire's strength? Is the PLO playing to Israel's strength?"

So I just stopped trying.

I think otherwise rational people such as Robert and the Weathermen looked to violence seriously because all of us had grown so infuriated with the war's continuing escalation and so frustrated with the limits of nonviolent protest, limits that seemed built into the political system. Chagrined liberals might dismiss them as "revolutionary wannabes," but the Weathermen were born in a reaction to the exhausted, impotent quality of the period's liberal dissent.

The hike out to Kramer's firing range became a kind of movement hajj, the way to prove that one was serious about one's politics. Others around the country were coming to be of the same mind. When unknown militants commandeered an ROTC plane and dropped three homemade dud bombs on an army munitions dump outside of Madison in January 1970, the University of Wisconsin's student newspaper supported the bombing attempt on the grounds that legal protests were getting nowhere.[11]

Then, on March 6, 1970, two weeks after the Weathermen had exploded three bombs outside the Manhattan home of the judge presiding at pretrial hearings of Black Panthers,[12] there came word of a huge explosion, shortly before noon, in the Greenwich Village town house of James P. Wilkerson. His daughter Cathy had let her comrades use the place as a bomb factory while her father was vacationing in the Caribbean. Three good, young people had killed themselves. Diana Oughten had babysat my kids. Terry Robbins had helped me figure out what my songs were about. Teddy Gold and I had talked about existentialism during the Columbia sit-in two years before.

The blast drove the other Weathermen underground.

Bernardine was later to claim that the Weathermen struck only symbolic targets and had not meant to hurt anyone, yet the town house bomb was packed with roofing nails, clearly making it an antipersonnel weapon.[13] This point was not lost on Nixon adviser Daniel Patrick Moynihan, who sent a memo to his White House colleague H. R. Haldeman on March 12 perceptively observing: "We have to assume, for example, that the Mad Dog faction of the Weathermen will in time learn to make anti-personnel bombs, as they evidently were trying to do in Miss Wilkerson's house. . . . Political violence is not new to the nation. . . . But I do believe the present situation is different. What we are facing is the onset of nihilism in the United States." I wonder if Moynihan knew he was echoing Nietzsche's late-nineteenth-century prophecy, "The rise of nihilism is the story of the next two centuries." Said Moynihan to Haldeman, "Dealing with the old Stalinist Communist Party was child's play compared to dealing with the Weathermen."[14] The Weathermen in Greenwich Village had crossed some wires, it seems, while trying to assemble a bomb they had meant to plant in the headquarters of a bank not far from there.[15] They had already blown up a statue of a policeman in Chicago and set off a small bomb in the men's room of a Chicago police station. Even after the town house, they bombed as many as a dozen other targets.

I should have kept my mouth shut at John's dinner table soon after March 6 but blurted out, after all of us had shed another round of tears, that this was where the violent road would always lead.

Robert answered, courageously enough, "The town house people were right to have been making that bomb. This is how the revolution must develop now. Naturally, at the beginning, we'll make mistakes, sometimes painful ones. But committed revolutionaries learn from such mistakes and go on."

"Obviously you're not going to learn from the town house mistake," I said with a snarl, "since whoever made it is dead."

Robert answered mildly, "Carl, we have to realize that the rulers of the American empire are not going to roll over and play dead in the face of the kind of moralistic entreaties that you seem to go for. The radical changes we want in this society can only be achieved if we're willing to fight for them."

"What radical changes are you talking about?"

"We're all socialists here, aren't we?" he said.

"I think we all oppose the war, racism, sexism, poverty," I said. "Does that make us socialists?"

"Do you think we can achieve these goals under a system of capitalist imperialism?"

"As a quick and dirty first estimate, Robert, I would say that's at least ten orders of magnitude more plausible than your pipe-bomb dreams."

"Not to a true revolutionary," said Robert with a slightly condescending smile.

"So you're a true revolutionary?"

"Carl, look. At least I'm getting ready."

"Getting ready for what?"

"Ready for whatever it will take to change this country's leadership."

"And this is guns?"

"My gun is a hell of a lot better bet than your pencil."

"Robert, all your gun is going to do is give the cops an open season." I had tried the same argument with Bernardine. Her answer was that I should wake up, meaning, I had guessed, that it was open season already.

Daily events kept the question of violence in our faces.

On March 9, three days after the town house explosion, word came that two SNCC field secretaries, Ralph Featherstone and Che Payne, had been killed in the explosion of a bomb in their car. Some rightists likened this to the Weathermen explosion and theorized that Feather-stone and Payne had inexpertly made the bomb with the intention of planting it in a courtroom. A few conspiracy mavins on the left theorized that SNCC's adversaries had planted the bomb, intending to kill the more influential H. Rap Brown. Brown gave this theory credence and immediately went into hiding.

Then, on March 11, in the early morning hours, a large bomb blew out the side of a Maryland courthouse. Twenty-four hours later, within a half-hour span, bombs exploded in three Manhattan skyscrapers housing the offices of Socony Mobil, IBM, and General Telephone and Electronics. A group calling itself "Revolutionary Force 9" had given the police a half hour's notice of these blasts so they could clear the buildings of janitors and night watchmen. Three hundred false threats were phoned in that day.[16]

VIOLENCE IN THE MOVEMENT angered the public, but between January and April, public approval of Nixon's handling of the war dropped from 64 to 46 percent.[17]

Robert was gratified that the town house disaster didn't stop the movement's plunge into violence. I wondered if this might be because the new taste for violence bore out the premise of his film *Ice*.

"This is where things are going," he said calmly, "whether we like it or not. If you can't get with it, you might as well just let Nixon have his way."

"Picking up the gun, Robert," I said, fuming, "is hardly going to stop the war."

"Really?" he chuckled. "So tell me, Carl, what has nonviolence gained us so far? Have we stopped the war?"

"We started from nowhere five years ago," I said, "and now almost half the American people are against the war."

"And this is going to stop Nixon? Nixon needs a majority? Nixon cares what people think? Refusing to pick up the gun," he said, "is the best possible way to make everything we've won so far meaningless."

"Okay. Suppose I grant your point. There needs to be an organized group committed to armed struggle. So why don't you and your com-

rades just go off to the sierra and form a new group to do tl
screw around with SDS?"

"No cigar," he chuckled. "SDS is an important organization
to be rescued from liberal stagnation."

I shook my head in wonder at this guy. "Robert, you're sucl
man," I said. "How can you fail to see that the path of violence
to the grave?"

"Carl, you're also a bright man," he said with a cheerful sm;
can you fail to see that a social movement progresses by stage:
violence achieves its objectives, fine. If it doesn't, the moven
a choice. It either becomes more militant or it accepts defeat a

Then in his dreamy way, John said, "Ah, there's truth on b(
Let's go get some beer and play some poker."

So Robert's shotgun and pistol stayed. A few hanger:
passersby at the farm occasionally trudged over to Robert's fir:
to try them out. I could hear the shots from my chicken coop,
crack of the pistol, the deeper *pow* of the shotgun.

The winter before the firing range got going, after a snov
neighborly Putney man with a snowplow fitted to his pickup l
out to clear John's driveway. He did this purely as a favor, with(
asked to do it or expecting anything in return. It might have
same guy—a neighbor half a mile up the road said he thou
glimpsed the snowplow truck—who drove by at dawn one
Robert's firing range had been especially busy, and put a round
John's big front window. Not to hurt anyone, it seemed. Just t
point.

John and Robert and I cleaned up the spray of glass and cı
square of wood to tape over the hole, which was fairly neat. 1
had splintered but not shattered. We tried to dig the slug oı
opposite wall, but it was buried in wood and John decided to !

"Ah, let it stay," he said, stepping back and lighting up ;
"Every house needs some memories." He mixed up a little plast
compound and filled up the hole.

John didn't think this had anything to do with Robert's tarξ
tice. "Some kid probably thought he saw a deer," he said with

"and just fired off a wild shot." It didn't ruffle him. He said, "You know, I've been thinking about putting a new window in there anyway." And later that day Robert went back to the meadow to get a few rounds in, as though to make a point.

So push had come to shoot. There was nothing to do about my conflict with Robert except to leave. I had been planning to go back to Boston a little later anyway. So I cleared out of the chicken coop, packed my few things into the soupy pale-blue Plymouth I'd bought from a local kid for a few hundred bucks, said a few cordial good-byes, even to Robert, and headed south out of Eden.

20 | From an Abandoned Weathermen Crash Pad

Cambridge, 1970

BY SOME MASTERSTROKE of coincidence, the mother of us all, what awaited me in Boston was another production of the same play, *The Peacemaker,* that had caught SDSer Roger Manela's eye back in 1964 in Ann Arbor and had opened the door on this long, strange trip.

The Boston Theater Company was doing the play this time, under the direction of a good old pro, David Wheeler, and with another old pro, Ralph Waite (star of the TV serial *The Waltons*), in one of the lead roles. It isn't as though I'm so proud of this play as a work of art, but productions of it bracketed my time with SDS. And given the story of the play, the irony of this seems inescapable. Just as Kramer was in a sense living out the story of his film *Ice,* so had I been living out the story of *The Peacemaker.*

The play's hero, Dyke Garrett, was based on a country preacher who shows up in a minor role in the histories of the well-known but ill-understood conflict between the McCoys of Kentucky and the Hatfields of West Virginia. This was one of several such family rivalries that became violent in the Civil War, then worsened in the 1870s and '80s when coal was found in the Blue Ridge Mountains and the railroads came to get it. Dyke was close to both families and was agonized as their conflict moved toward violence. He thought he should do what he could to stop it, even when both patriarchs warned him to stay out of it.

His wife, Sally, also wanted him to stay out of it. There was nothing he could do. Intervening, she said, was far less likely to make peace than to arouse the wrath of both families against him. She wanted them to sell their land to the railroad and follow their sons to Kansas. "These old men are beyond reason," she said to Dyke, "and if you keep thinking you can reason with them, so are you."

So the play's central conflict is not between the rival clans, whose clash is a historical given, but between Dyke's idealism and Sally's realism. The question the play tries to confront is not whether peace is better than war, but rather: If you can see in advance that war is a virtually foregone conclusion, and if attempting to intervene against it is certainly dangerous and all but certainly futile, are you still under a moral obligation to intervene? Is the moral imperative contingent on the possibility of success?

Dyke hears Sally out but still feels compelled to intervene. The audience, being of the future, knows that Sally is right about the feud and that Dyke will fail to stop it. Was he a fool, or did he do the right thing?

From my lofty perch as the playwright, I had no idea that a choice very like the choice I'd confronted my peacemaker with was about to arise in my own life. When it did, I hadn't the heart to be a hypocrite or the courage to be a coward.

THE CAMBRIDGE APARTMENT I fell into had been the crash pad of the local Weathermen until the town house explosion of March 6. It was a third-floor, two-bedroom walk-up in a comfortably run-down, student-infested, racially mixed, politically active part of Cambridgeport, a neighborhood of old wooden three-deckers a short stroll from the Charles River and five minutes by bike from Angell Hall on the Massachusetts Institute of Technology campus, where my class would meet. On a normal prerevolutionary night before the town house disaster, you might have found a dozen or so Weathermen gathered there to do some weed, listen to some Stones, and ponder the question of how to make the revolution. Then after the town house, Weathermen everywhere went running for cover, so this place had become available. I learned of it through the movement grapevine just as my argument with Kramer was getting hard to live with. It was perfect for me, a few blocks from the Massachusetts Avenue bus line that crosses the Charles and runs right to the Boston theater where *The Peacemaker* was going into rehearsals.

At first the Weathermen angle didn't reach me because I'd hurriedly thrown my things there one night with my car double-parked, then spent the next week in Boston at the home of director Wheeler, going over his plans for the production.

Waite was to play old tough-minded Devil Anse Hatfield, but other commitments kept him out of Boston until about two weeks before we were to open. So until then, I would read Hatfield's lines and walk through his blocking with the other actors.

Always before, I had seen the story through the peacemaker's eyes, so it was new for me to play through it as one of the warriors. Yes, I know, I'd written the part, but I'd written it looking at Hatfield through the eyes of Dyke Garrett, seeing him as an antagonist. But actors know that if you say a character's lines as if you mean them, then pretty soon you do. Here I was declaiming "Kill all the McCoys! Kill all their friends! Just get rid of the damned things! Stomp 'em back to the Stone Age!" And in Hatfield's scenes with the would-be peacemaker: "You're a fool, my old friend. Mankind's eternal lot is war. You don't like it and I don't like it, but there it is. Now, just get the hell out of the way if you don't want to get hurt."

When I finally came back to Cambridgeport to settle into my new place, it was the middle of the day. There was lots of light because there was a vacant lot on one side. The apartment took up the whole third floor. The windows all gaped without a shade or a curtain. Weedy ailanthus trees climbed past the windows on the side, the new leaves just starting to come out. The trees swayed against the house in a spanking spring breeze.

There was not a stick of furniture there. The apartment was bare right down to the brown wooden floor, which had been swept clean.

But what grabbed you were the walls and the doors.

The dirty white walls were thickly covered in Weatherman graffiti, all painted with a broad paintbrush in huge, slashing black and red letters:

OFF THE PIG!
SMASH CAPITALISM!
CHANGE OR DIE!
SMASH THE MILITARY-INDUSTRIAL STATE!
SMASH MONOGAMY!
HO! HO! HO CHI MINH! THE NLF IS GONNA WIN!

One slogan lipsticked on the bathroom mirror was in praise of the little boy said to have derailed a freight train in California:

MARION DELGADO! LIVE LIKE HIM!
My favorite was the elegantly simple:
DO IT!

All the interior doors had been taken off and stacked in the back landing. Neither bedroom had a door. There was no door on the bathroom. Weathermen didn't believe in the things doors stand for. The desire for privacy embodied, in the Weathermen cosmos, the worst side of bourgeois individualism. It was born in the same reflex that denied the body, abstracted the person, and thus prepared a kill target. Besides, private intimacies might lead to private agendas. To avoid this, everyone must go to bed and the bathroom with everyone else. Private pissing was counterrevolutionary.

REHEARSALS WERE IN full stride on April 30, 1970, the actors just getting off book, when Nixon announced the bombing and invasion of Cambodia.

Half a dozen or so political friends and several cast members and I made up an affinity group in the crowd of several thousand that collected on Mass Ave from MIT to Harvard Square that night as though by instinct.

No one had called for a protest rally. No one had organized a demonstration. There were no bullhorns, no new speeches by angry young professors, no hot new protest tunes from local rock bands with names like Enemies of the State or ContraBand. There were oceans of students around us and the usual flow of hippies, townies, and street people, but overwhelmingly the crowd was made up of regular-looking, forty-something grown-ups, no one saying much. Most of us looked more dazed than angry. Certainly it was a quiet crowd. No one chanted slogans. The spring night was warm enough for a light jacket.

We all moved choppily to no battle plan, a smell of urgency in the air, a feeling that all we could do was improvise, but no one knew what. Where was this going? How far was Nixon ready to go? And what were we going to do tonight?

"Are we a mob?" said Patti Collinge, the wonderful actress who was playing the peacemaker's wife. "Or just a crowd? Or maybe a *milling* crowd?"

Then scores of mounted police suddenly appeared and formed into a containment line along the southern side of Mass Ave.

They might have come from Mars. The huge horses as well as their riders wore visored helmets and gas masks. How had they arrived so suddenly? The spring air was soon sharp with the smell of the tear-gas grenades they sent whirling and sparkling toward us, our provocation being that we were parading without a permit.

For hours there were great surges up and down Mass Ave through blue clouds of tear gas, the cops charging, then falling back. Teams of medical-school students on our side appeared, wearing white jackets and carrying buckets of water, so that soon almost everyone had the minimal protection of breathing through a dampened handkerchief. We would break up and retreat into the side streets when the mounted police charged, then regroup behind them when they fell back.

Then the police reassembled in two groups, one toward Harvard Square half a mile to the west and the other toward Central Square half a mile to the east, probably to encircle us. Many of us also divided spontaneously into two groups moving slowly in opposite directions behind the horsemen. Most headed east toward Central Square to try to join another big group we had heard was coming up from MIT. My little group happened to be in Putnam Circle more or less between Harvard Square and Central Square. Suddenly all went quiet.

We found ourselves wondering what was next, whether we should go east or west or just stay where we were. We noticed that the window of Design Research, an upscale home-furnishings store we were in front of, had been smashed.

The items displayed inside the broken window were oddly undisturbed. A porcelain bowl had apparently been knocked off a shelf and had broken neatly in two, but that was about it. A service of elegant dinner crystal still stood intact on shelves draped in white satin and strewn with pink and white rose petals.

Then Patti pulled herself tall. Quietly, more to herself than to anyone around her, she said, "Well, I guess someone's got to do it."

She gracefully stepped through the broken window onto the display case and without hesitating picked up one of the wineglasses from the set. She stepped back out of the window frame and turned to our little group.

"There!" she said proudly, holding the glass up to be admired. "We've looted!"

STUDENT REACTION TO Nixon's April 30, 1970, invasion of Cambodia—Operation Rock Crusher—was immediate and massive across the country's campuses,[1] nowhere more so than at Kent State, my first school. Ohio governor James Rhodes ordered a brigade of the National Guard onto the campus to restore order. He warned the Guardsmen that the students were "scum."

The situation at KSU had been tense for a while. In April, having crashed a trustees meeting to demand that a war-related research project be ended, the SDS chapter had lost its charter.

Then on the night of May 2, two days after Cambodia, either an angry student or a provocateur had torched the ROTC building.

The Guard were summoned to restore order but only brought more disorder. Student-Guard confrontations immediately became violent. On May 3, Guardsmen bayoneted several students.

At 12:30 P.M. the next day, May 4, without warning, Guardsmen fired sixty-one shots in thirteen seconds point-blank into a group of about two hundred students, murdering Allison Krause, Sandra Scheuer, Jeffrey Miller, and William Schroeder and wounding nine others. The Guardsmen claimed to have fired in self-defense. The Scranton Commission, later mandated to determine the facts, found that the Guardsmen had been in no danger when they fired into the crowd. The students had been 200 feet away and withdrawing. After watching a video of the event, a former Marine officer exclaimed, "That was a salvo!" That is, the shots were fired on command.[2] But the Guardsmen's claim of having fired individually in self-defense was supported and broadcast by the media. Sixty percent of Americans believed that the students had deserved what they had gotten.

Ten days after the KSU murders, at Jackson State College in Mississippi, two more students were murdered and 12 wounded when police fired a 28-second barrage into a group of demonstrators.[3]

Students across the nation rose up in outrage. In the weeks after the Kent State and Jackson State murders, more than 4 million students clashed with police or the National Guard or in some other way disrupted campus life. There was violence at seventy-three schools. Students went on strike at 350 schools, including all of the elite universities. Classes were suspended at 1,350 schools, more than half the country's total number. More than 500 schools were forced to cancel classes. Fifty-one closed for the rest of the spring semester. Thirty ROTC buildings were burned or bombed. Heavily-armed National Guardsmen were called onto twenty-one campuses.[4]

Journalist Kirkpatrick Sale was not being melodramatic in observing that May 1970 was "without doubt one of the most explosive periods in the nation's history and easily the most cataclysmic period in the history of higher education since the founding of the Republic."[5]

The Weathermen must have been on air. I wondered if Kramer was ready to move past shooting at paper targets on trees.

OFFICIAL ATTEMPTS TO suppress the movement during this period were not limited to campus murders. Only after the 1972 scandal of

Watergate and the resulting exposure of the Nixon administration's "Family Jewels" did we learn of the "Huston Plan," a counterintelligence program created by Nixon aide Tom Huston to coordinate all federal resources against us.

As an old Cold Warrior myself from my years in the defense industry, I can understand why the government thought it needed intelligence data on the movement. But I'd had no idea how extensive the government's penetration efforts were, until writer John Schultz's research discovered one almost amusing case in the Chicago Police intelligence files. "Of six people present in one antiwar meeting in the summer of 1968," Schultz writes, "at least five were agents, unbeknownst to each other, reporting on each other, the meeting even chaired by an agent."[6]

But if spying on us was one thing, quite another was an aggressive undercover campaign to destroy us. And there is strong evidence that this is what the FBI tried to do.

Consider what is on the public record:

For a 1971 Public Broadcasting Service film, journalist Paul Jacobs interviewed three former FBI informers who said that their FBI handlers had urged them to join the movement not only to spy on it but also to urge people to commit criminal acts, including burning buildings. Might this have been the case at Kent State and the several other schools where ROTC buildings were torched in 1970? Whether the ROTC burnings were the work of protesters or the police, the provocateurs were there. Their purpose was to motivate violent police attacks. As one of them told Jacobs, "The FBI agent . . . told me to burn the buildings . . . so that the state troopers could have an excuse to come on campus . . . and crush the rebellion on campus."[7]

Nor was the FBI the only player of secret games. Though its charter prohibits domestic operations, the CIA had targeted the movement with a program it called MH Chaos at about the turn of the decade. Its outcome, however, had a twist.

The purpose of MH Chaos, as a former CIA consultant put it to a well-placed mutual acquaintance in navy intelligence, was "to see if the American antiwar movement was being funded by foreign powers."

According to this source, the CIA discovered the awful truth that we were hardly funded at all, that we SDSers ran our national mayhem machine on chump change and fried peanut butter, and that we were nobody's creature.

The CIA, bless its ornate heart, reported this to Nixon in its "Restless Youth" reports. Nixon was dissatisfied with this finding and directed his own team to investigate us. The White House Secret Team was put to the task.

We still have no idea what the members of the Secret Team did. All we know is that Nixon ordered them to attack the antiwar movement at the moment when our creative energy was going into breaking up.

SDS's main antiwar slogan in 1964, when I was just getting interested, was "Part of the way with LBJ!" But things changed quickly. By 1965 the slogan was "Bring the troops home!" By the time of the Chicago DNC confrontation, this had become "Bring the war home!" As the black movement had gone from King's "Freedom now!" to Cleaver's "Off the pig!," so had SDSers gone from "Make love, not war!" to "Ho! Ho! Ho Chi Minh! The Viet Cong is gonna win!"

But at the beginning of 1972, Nixon's fourth year in office, it was far from clear that the VC were even going to survive. VC "liberated zones" in South Vietnam and supply lines in Laos and Cambodia were the targets of daily attacks by low-altitude aircraft dropping canisters of napalm and herbicides such as the infamous poison Agent Orange. The Vietnamese claimed to the Russell-Sartre tribunal that phosphor bombs, pellet bombs, and bombs armed with nonlethal pathogens also were used, the aim of these weapons apparently being to overload Vietnamese medical facilities and thus demoralize the civilian population. In both the South and the North, the lumbering B-52s, flying high above Vietnamese defenses, saturated their targets day after day with tons and tons of high-explosive bombs. The navy's cruisers stood offshore and hurled artillery shells at any target within forty miles of the coast.

This was Nixon's "secret plan" to "Vietnamize" the war. He had pulled our troops out of active engagement to cut the losses that he thought were fueling antiwar sentiment at home, then turned our airpower loose, the strategy proposed years earlier by air force general Curtis LeMay. Cynical as many of us in the antiwar movement had grown by then about American politicians, we still found it frightening that Congress would let Nixon get away with such extreme measures without a declaration of war, despite the facts that a majority of Americans had turned against the war; our NATO allies were noisily appalled by what we were doing; and our national aims, beyond simply wanting not to lose, remained so unclear.

So Vietnam was being attacked with a violence unprecedented in history. Nixon seemed to be saying, "Nothing you do will make a difference. The more you try to demonize me, the fiercer a demon I will become."

BERNARDINE AND I had our final crossing that winter in Madison, less than a year after my star-chambering in Austin.

The Wisconsin SDS chapter was always strong and active. Ignorant of the events of Austin, it had asked BD and me to speak for the antiwar side in a debate about the war. Maybe it was the nice honorarium that softened her disdain for debates. We were up against two law-school profs.

The question of antiwar violence was in front of the Madison audience because on New Year's Day there someone had tried to blow up the ROTC ammo dump. I figured that the other side would challenge us about this, so I brought it up with BD before we went to the platform, thinking to get on the same page.

She brushed me off. "Carl, you still don't accept what the NIC decided in Austin, do you? You can say whatever you want. You don't speak for SDS."

I tried to be friendly. "You know where you can put that, BD. It's you guys who don't speak for SDS, not me." But she saw no need to discuss it.

The attempted bombing came up right away. In introducing us, the moderator asked us all to address this question. The first prowar speaker hardly spoke of anything else. The applause was perfunctory.

Then it was my turn. Such actions were understandable because people were frustrated and angry, I said. The most recent poll showed that 73 percent of Americans now opposed the war, yet Nixon had made the war more violent than ever. Understandable as it was, however, the attempted bombing at Madison was counterproductive because, as our discussion demonstrated, it made us talk about the antiwar movement's tactics instead of the war itself. Perfunctory applause.

The second law prof said he was gratified to hear me oppose the attempted bombing and he hoped antiwar activists would listen. He restated his partner's argument that it was to be deplored. Perfunctory applause.

Then Bernardine stood up. "The only thing deplorable about this attempted bombing," she said in her matter-of-fact way, "is that it failed."

From the stage you could see the audience gasp, hear the sharp intake of breath throughout the hall.

The moderator looked aghast. Then he jumped out of his chair and strode across the stage toward Bernardine, wagging his finger as though he were addressing an unruly child.

"Now, now, Miss Dohrn! We'll have none of that here!"

But Miss Dohrn was not an unruly child. She was an angry young woman. She turned on him sharply and slapped his hand out of her face.

"How many ROTC ammo dumps get dropped on Vietnam every day?" she demanded, glaring straight at him.

He recoiled, his eyes bulging, his mouth agape.

"How many starving Vietnamese kids could you feed for the cost of one useless ROTC ammo dump?"

The audience seemed at first as stunned as the moderator. Then everyone burst into fortissimo applause, without smiles, with a strange solemnity throughout the hall. The applause went on and on, easily for half a minute, then stopped cleanly, as abruptly as it had begun.

By the end of the evening she had virtually the whole house with her.

We were alone briefly afterward in a classroom waiting for rides that would take us in different directions.

"That was one of your great performances," I said.

"I was not performing," she said sternly, shaking her head and pulling her coat on with rough jabs. Before I could answer, she said, "Listen, Carl, that was not one of your more compelling ideas."

"What?"

"I can't believe you want us to make a statement against this attempted bombing." She looked me up and down. "What are you thinking when you say such a thing?"

So she wasn't going to take any prisoners.

"You know damned well what I'm thinking, BD, and you know I'm right."

"Bullshit," she said quietly.

It was the same old argument I'd had with her in Austin. I was a hapless liberal who took heart from the fact that the antiwar side was winning the debate. BD was a revolutionary who believed that mere public opinion would never stop the hawks and that the pigs were coming after us no matter what we did, so we should just get ready.

Bernardine buttoned her coat and grabbed her briefcase. She said, "Look, maybe I'll see you later."

She went out the door to meet her ride. That was our last chat.

IN APRIL MY DAD was operated on for lung cancer. I went to South Carolina to be with him.

When he came to in the hospital in Spartanburg, he said, "What the hell did they do to me?" His whole upper torso was wrapped and he was in restraints.

I went back to Cambridge to put my things in order so I could move to Cowpens and take care of him. As soon as I got home, Uncle Jim called.

"Buddy," he said, "your daddy's dead."

Back home for the funeral, all my aunts and uncles were careful to avoid political subjects, sticking to the heat, children, health, what a fine man my father had been, and why wasn't I eating better. My cousins Rita and Judy acted proud of me for getting on TV.

But when I went back to Cowpens again that summer to deal with legal matters, Uncle Jim found time at a family potluck at Pop and Granny's place to say, "There's something I want to talk to you about, Buddy. I wonder if you'd come down to the river with me for a little bit." He nodded for me to follow him.

We went down through what had been Pop's lower cotton field, Jim loping on ahead without looking back, me wondering what was up. He had been my favorite uncle when I was a kid. I got to know him when he returned from the paratroops after World War II and stayed with my family for a while in Akron. I was ten years old, and Uncle Jim was my hero. His body was lithe and muscular from paratroop training. He had bright, alert brown eyes, short black hair, a challenging manner, and a devilish grin set off by a gold cap on one of his front teeth.

Sometime between that time in Akron and this time in Cowpens, Jim had been ordained as a minister of the Southern Baptist Church. He preached at the new, redbrick, white-steepled Green Valley Baptist Church in the nearby town of Chesnee. He was still lithe, muscular, and intense, but with salvation his grin had become a permanent frown.

I had assumed from his first invitation for a walk to the river that this was going to be serious, but I wasn't sure if it would be about a land squabble that had been simmering between us or his sense that I had left the church. Or maybe he thought it was time we reconciled and that the river would be a good place to do it.

I followed him down the long hill through the cotton field to the woods that ran by the river, then along a twisting path through the woods out to Big Rock.

Big Rock was where the men of the family went when they wanted to be boys. It was their base camp when they went to phone up some cats.

When I emerged from the woods, Jim was out on Big Rock with his hands on his hips, glaring at the river. The narrow Pacolet was running clear.

I could tell right away that Uncle Jim didn't have tender memories on his mind. His fierce, penetrating eyes were in full glare. He was not Uncle Jim now. He was the Reverend James S. Oglesby, bringer of the Word. Was he going to ask me if I'd left the church? Did he want to baptize me?

Big Rock was a forty-foot-wide boulder of pale gray stone that jutted halfway across the little river. Big Rock was broad and flat on top, perfect for fishing from, with plenty of room for half a dozen people to hang out on.

"All right, Buddy, I'm gonna put it to you point-blank."

"Sure, Jim. What is it?"

"What is this here SDS thing we hear people talking about, and you in it? Are you in that thing?"

I was still trying to cope with what had happened in Texas. I wasn't sure that SDS still existed, or that I was in it if it did. How could I explain that scene in Austin to him? From his standpoint, SDS existed and I was in it.

So I said, "Absolutely, Jim. Proud of it."

"We hear people saying you all are a bunch of pinkos and some kind of Commie front and you believe in throwing out our way of life, blowing things up, burning things down."

"Some SDS people have started to favor violence, Jim. I've got to admit it. But most of us don't. I sure don't."

"Do you favor the Commie side in this here war, Buddy?"

Try drawing a distinction between Commies and nationalists at a place like Big Rock to a man like Jim.

"I don't call them Commies, Jim."

"Everybody else does. All the preachers and the other learned men that I talk to around here sure do. Do you think you know something nobody else knows?"

"The other side in this war is just fighting to be free to run their own lives."

"Free from what?"

"A while ago, the French. Today it's us."

"In the name of the Lord God Almighty, Buddy, you talk just like a damn Communist!"

"Jim, if you want to talk about this in a levelheaded way, I'll be glad to sit down with you. But—"

"Is that what Boop and me and your cousin Charles and his boy Eddie all been fighting for? And all them other boys? Fighting and dying for you to come along and take up for the Commies?"

The light reflected brightly off the swirling river and crystals of quartz in Big Rock. Just above us the water raced through a narrows and splashed over a little waterfall.

"Uncle Jim, please try to hear what I'm saying." I leaned toward him. "It doesn't make you a Commie or a pinko just because you don't like the Vietnam War."

"Buddy, who are *you* to think somebody asked you to open your mouth about this here war?"

It stopped me for a second. Plenty of people had challenged my views, but no one had ever told me I had no right to say what I thought. "Well, damn it, I'm somebody who cares enough about this country to expect its leaders to obey the law."

But Jim had no patience with that. He said, "Let me just ask you this one question, Buddy, and you might as well tell me the truth right now because sooner or later I guarantee the truth will be known. Do you mean to do harm to this country?"

His fervor pissed me off. "Who the hell are you to ask me a question like that? 'Do *you* mean to do harm to this country?'"

"You know where I stand."

"Do I? Do you support the Civil Rights Act?"

"We're talking about the Vietnam War here, Buddy. What are you up to?"

"Uncle Jim, along with most of the people in this country, I'm against the war. I'm trying to get this country's elected officials to listen to the people and obey the law."

"Buddy, your cousin Charles was damn near killed in Vietnam! His boy, Eddie, he was a Ranger there! How in the name of all that's good and holy can you show such disrespect against them like that?"

"The only disrespect I've shown, Jim, is for the politicians that let this happen. The only way to support our troops like Charles and Eddie is to get them out of that place."

"What do you want us to do?" said Jim. "Just hand it over to the Communists?"

"No, just hand it over to the Vietnamese people."

"Oh," said Jim, glaring at me. "Who are *they* shooting at?"

"All right, then," I said, "tell me this. If we can't trust the Vietnamese people, then who are we fighting for?"

"Buddy, how in the world can ordinary people like me and you claim to know better than our elected government officials which side is right over yonder?"

"That's not so hard, Jim. Just read a few books. Read the newspapers."

"Ain't none of us got the time nor the education to study it. We wouldn't know which end to start at. You and me, we can't even talk that language. Can you? Can you talk in Vietnamese?"

"No. So what?"

"And here you are, trying to sound like you know something about it!"

"At least I've been there."

"Buddy, you listen here to me." He held his forefinger in my face. The ruby of a membership ring glistened. "If the president says we've got to do this thing, all right, then, by the Lord God Almighty, we've got to do it!"

"To hell with that, Uncle Jim," I said, no longer trying to be polite. "Only the Congress can declare a war. Didn't they teach you the Constitution at that Bible college?"

Jim turned abruptly away with a disgusted sound and took two or three steps farther out on the rock.

"Jim, you're not even going to listen to what I have to say, are you?"

He turned back to face me. "I've done heard what you all have to say, Buddy, and it ain't a damn thing but Commie propaganda!"

"You're telling me that the Constitution of the United States is Commie propaganda?"

"The president knows better than anybody else what this country needs, and if he says we need to win this here war in Vietnam, then we need to win it. You hear me? When you all up yonder tie his hands to where we can't win it flat out and get it over and done with, it just means more of our boys are going to get killed and hurt."

"We could never win it flat out."

"This country can do whatever it puts its mind to do if people like you start pulling your part of the load."

"Jim, what would you do if you thought this war was wrong?"

He said with a growl, "Ain't nobody asked you what you thought about it, you hear me? You let them hotshot college professors start leading you around thataway, there ain't no telling what you believe anymore."

"If you'd shut up and listen a minute, I'd be glad to tell you."

"Somebody has led you astray, Buddy. You were baptized a Christian. You were raised in a good Christian home. Carl and Alma, they had their troubles, but I can't believe how far you have fallen."

Me, neither, but that was another story.

He stood taller and in his pulpit voice said, "The prophet Isaiah hath told us: 'Woe to the rebellious children, saith the Lord, that take counsel, but not of me.'"

"Uncle Jim, try to listen for a minute," I said. "I appreciate your concern for me, but—"

"You have chosen to run with the rebellious children," he said, "and I can only pray for your soul if you promise on this here rock to change your ways." He was pointing to the rock between us.

Was he telling me to kneel? "Jim, I don't care what you pray for. Let's just try to get along in the family. I don't plan to move to South Carolina, so that shouldn't be too hard."

The brown river ran white through the rapids. The afternoon sun shone with its hard South Carolina bluntness. Some blackbirds flew up the river. Jim and I stared at each other. I didn't know what else to do, so I said, "All right?" and held out my hand.

He didn't take it. He said, "The Lord God knows I hate to say it, Buddy, but you are one lost soul if I ever saw one. You hear me? A lost soul! You are locked in Satan's clutches! Sure enough, you are bound for hell!"

What if I had just sworn Jim to secrecy somehow and then given him a summary of Arlene's brief against me in Austin? Yes, my secret-clearance job, my lectures to business and military groups, all of it. And the fact that

SDS was now in ruins. It would all have fit together neatly. I wouldn't even have needed to tell Jim an out-and-out lie. I could just have said, "Please realize, Jim, and go tell your learned friends, that things are not always what they seem." I'd have watched his eyes as what I was implying registered, then said, "Here's my hand again. Let's shake. If you love this country, you have no problem with me."

I'm glad this occurred to me only later, when I read of Abbie Hoffman's admission in the Chicago trial, "I don't know whether I'm innocent or guilty."[8] Otherwise I might have been tempted to say this sort of thing to Uncle Jim on Big Rock. Certainly several of my SDS comrades—or former comrades—would have found it only all too credible.

Instead I said, "Uncle Jim, you're an ignorant, self-righteous bully. If men like you are headed for heaven, you know what? I think I'd rather go to hell."

He glared at me a moment more, then shook his head and strode past me off Big Rock and disappeared back into the woods.

I took a minute to stare at the Pacolet, then followed him back up the hill, wondering if he had spoken just now for the family. Had everyone known his purpose in taking me down to Big Rock? Did I still have a place among my Cowpens people? Maybe Jim would only have to shake his head and frown and everyone would know that I was a lost soul.

As soon as I got back up the hill to the farmyard, sweaty and feeling more estranged than I had since Austin, I heard one of Jim's daughters, my bright-eyed cousin Rita, sing out my name.

"Hey, Buddy!" Rita called. "I've been a-looking for you all over! Where in the heck have you been?"

"Well, your daddy wanted to go down on the river for a little talk."

"Oh, phooey on him!" she said with a laugh. She took me by the hand and led me back to the picnic table. "You've got to taste my strawberry-cream pie," she said, "because I know how you love it, and I made it especially for you!"

And everybody but Jim wanted to know how I liked it. I grinned like crazy. I got whipped cream all over my whiskers. I said, "Rita, it's the best thing I ever tasted!"

21 | The Miracle of Watergate
Washington, D.C., 1972

IN APRIL 1971, the FBI abruptly claimed to be canceling "Cointelpro: New Left." If it actually did this, I can't help but wonder if it was less because of embarrassment at public exposure than because the program had accomplished what seems to have been its main purpose, the destruction of SDS.

In that same month, April 24, 1971, six years after SDS had brought twenty-five thousand people to Washington in the first big antiwar demonstration, an antiwar march drew ten times that many, among them several hundred members of Vietnam Veterans Against the War, who threw their medals away at the White House gate in an astounding display of disgust. But the troop level in Vietnam was also an order of magnitude greater than the 21,000 of 1965, drawn down from a peak of more than 500,000 but still at 270,000. And the B-52s were pounding targets in North Vietnam, Cambodia, and Laos with unprecedented fury.

BERNARDINE AND HER group concluded that SDS could not protect itself from penetration, whether the overt penetration of PL or the covert penetration of the FBI and the other secret police and military arms that we correctly assumed had targeted us.

So national SDS could no longer exist. SDS chapters around the country would have to reorganize into small, closed cadres of mutually trusted people. A more secure communications network would have to replace the mail and the phone lines of the national office. The national office would have to be closed.

The Weathermen had some great moments, as in September 1970, when they organized the escape of acid guru Timothy Leary from a California prison, where he was doing ten years on a marijuana charge, then helped him get away to Algeria. His punishment was flagrantly excessive, so this action won sympathy. And the skill the Weathermen showed in breaking Leary out of prison and getting him out of the country bespoke a serious ability to concentrate.

On the other hand, there was their "Days of Rage" offensive of October '69, when they blew up the statue of the policeman in Haymarket Square in Chicago for the second time and simultaneously bombed eight courthouses across the country where movement-related cases were being heard. They were careful not to hurt anyone, but their bombing campaign failed to ignite the general uprising that their rhetoric had convinced them to expect.

They really believed that the revolution was on its way. They believed that blowing things up was the way to hasten it along.

They produced a theater of the absurd and called it the revolution.

Their crowning act, a duet with the FBI, was the destruction of SDS.

Certainly the Weathermen did not end the war, nor did the broader movement whose nonviolence the Weathermen had scorned.

What ended the war, or began to end it, was the arrest of five burglars in the Democratic National Committee headquarters in the Watergate complex in Washington on June 17, 1972.

These burglars, the White House "plumbers," had broken into the DNC to rescue the so-called Pentagon Papers, purloined by Daniel Ellsberg, a civilian analyst who worked for the Pentagon and consulted with the Democrats. These documents, showing that important military analysts had grave doubts about the war, could have been politically useful to the Democrats.

So Nixon organized a small group of CIA vets, the "plumbers," to fix the Ellsberg leak. They broke into the DNC offices at Watergate to retrieve the documents that Ellsberg had stored there. Because of a clumsy mistake in the break-in, they got caught. Nixon tried to fob the plumbers off on the CIA. This should have been easy because they all had CIA backgrounds. But one of them, James McCord, sang to the judge. The burglary was not a CIA job, McCord said; it was a White House job.

With this, Nixon was finished. The House Judiciary Committee opened hearings against him on May 9, 1974, and on July 30 recommended impeachment. To avoid impeachment, Nixon resigned. The moderate Republican congressman Gerald Ford had meanwhile replaced the corrupt Spiro Agnew as vice president, Agnew having been cashiered on routine tax-evasion charges.

It was not until April 23, 1975, that President Ford, speaking in New Orleans, declared the Vietnam War finished. On April 29, the U.S. military implemented a plan known as Option IV for the last-minute evacuation of Americans still in Saigon. Option IV gave rise to scenes of frantic Vietnamese hands grasping for space on the landing skids of the last chopper to leave Saigon.

SDS no doubt helped set the stage for this final act, but by that time it had already long since been carried from the field in a body bag, dead for as long as it had been alive.

SO THE WAR was finished. We didn't exactly lose it, but we certainly didn't win it. And except for the enormous suffering and waste, it didn't seem to make much difference.

It took Vietnam about a decade, until 1986, to start opening its doors to foreign products and foreign capital. American businessmen were soon being welcomed.

In about another decade, in 1995, the United States and Vietnam normalized diplomatic relations.

In another five years, on July 13, 2000, Washington and Hanoi signed a broad trade agreement granting American companies access to many sectors of Vietnam's market.[1] A week later, the U.S. House voted to extend Vietnam's eligibility for U.S. exports. Vietnam opened its doors still wider in hopes of luring American tourists.[2]

Yes, American tourists. Maybe they would want to see VC caves and tunnels. The villages of Son My and My Lai. The staging areas for the Tet Offensive. Maybe some tiger cages. The old American bases at Cam Ranh Bay and Danang.

And, yes, maybe the tourism could be reciprocated. What Vietnamese would not want to see the University of Michigan, where the teach-in movement had begun? Or the Watergate complex, where Nixon's Secret Team had been busted? Or Grant Park, where the Chicago police had stormed the antiwar demonstrators? Or the town house in Greenwich Village, where three Weathermen had blown themselves up? Or the Kent State campus, where the Ohio National Guard had murdered four students?

AND WHAT OF those who had destroyed SDS from the inside out?

Once the war was over, the Weathermen were out of work, their shared fantasy in ruins. If I could have been a fly on the wall at any single private rap session from this period, it would be the one in which the Weathermen gathered to confess to one another that the revolution was not going to take place.

SDS, too, of course, had long since been done for, or as Ford said of the Vietnam War itself, "finished."

In a 1960s world without the Vietnam War, the intellectual task of SDS would have been to reimagine the democratic left.

Its political task would have been to redefine the interests of what traditional radical thought dismissed as the "middle class" even as an increasingly high-tech economy was turning this class into a new proletariat and making its brainpower central to production. The original SDS had seen its natural constituency as this "new working class" and had been far from thinking of itself as revolutionary. Following the lead of the black civil-rights movement, it had advocated direct action but had remained explicitly democratic, reformist, and nonviolent. As the House Committee on Internal Security put it in its surprisingly objective, almost admiring report on SDS in 1970, "As long as it was self-disciplined and dedicated to the peaceful pursuit of sincere social concerns, as long as it encouraged orderly dissent, it held the potential for making a useful contribution to American life."

But Vietnam imposed its own imperative, and SDS became in effect a single-issue antiwar organization, finally to be driven by the Weathermen to a self-destructive espousal of violence, an adventurism born of an almost willful ignorance of history.

I cannot say we had much freedom of choice. There was no way that SDS could have avoided the war. Like everyone else, we came upon the war as a terrible accident burning in the road, an event without logic but inescapably right there in front of us. We just had to jump in and do what we could.

And I was among those who most insistently pushed SDS into antiwar politics. Up until my turn, every SDS president had encouraged community organizing focused on the urban poor. It was I who interrupted a conversation on strategy of which I was largely ignorant to argue that the Vietnam War was the main issue before us and that students and teachers, and through them the middle class, were the main elements of the opposition.

SDS's rapid growth came about because of the war. In 1960, when it still called itself the Student League for Industrial Democracy, it had chapters only at Columbia, Yale, and Michigan and fewer than 100 members. By the decade's end, a Senate investigating committee found 317 SDS chapters across the country, and our membership ranged from the same committee's estimate of 30,000 to the Associated Press's estimate of 70,000 or to our National Office's claim of 100,000.

But we failed to develop adequate ways to control or even to monitor our internal affairs in the vastly larger organization that we had become by 1968. Weeks of chapter mail piled up at our chronically understaffed pigsty of a national office. As much as true political differences among us and our debilitating fight with PL, and perhaps even as much as the government's still-secret operations against us, it was our lack of a functional center that led us first to factionalism and schism, then to a total inability to protect ourselves from penetration, and finally to smithereens.

At the same time, we were not a total loss. *Life* said of SDS: "Never in the history of this country has a small group, standing outside the pale of conventional power, made such an impact or created such havoc."[3]

And truth to tell, there is comfort in knowing that we counted. As Admiral Thomas Moorer, chairman of the JCS during the Nixon administration, told historian Tom Wells, "The reaction of the noisy radical groups was considered all the time. And it served to inhibit and restrain the decision-makers. . . . [SDS] had a major impact . . . both in the executive and legislative branches of the government."[4]

Cool.

I TOOK A short vacation in 1975 and rented a place on Martha's Vineyard for the month of September. The war had been over for no more than half a year by then, and it was still reaching a lot of us that at last the killing had ended. The toll: more than fifty-eight thousand Americans, an estimated two million Vietnamese and another million Cambodians and Laotians.[5] More than three million people shot or bombed or burned to death.

My Martha's Vineyard place was a new, modernistic two-story house built into the side of a sandy, bushy hill maybe three hundred yards from the beach. Its roof was raked sharply upward from back to front. It faced the beach with a wall of floor-to-ceiling windows maybe thirty feet high, giving the place the look of a great abstract sailing ship. In front of it, a rutted, sandy driveway wandered down to a little road, and beyond the road, a footpath led through low bushes to a sandy beach strewn with boulders. The beach was on the southwestern corner of the island near Gay Head, a brilliant rocky promontory.

One day the radio said a hurricane was coming. I called the young Boston architect who had built the place to see if there was anything I should do. He said he had built the house to withstand a force-twelve wind, so I settled down to enjoy the ride.

All day the skies darkened. By nightfall the wind was howling. The hurricane seemed headed straight up the driveway. By midnight the whole of outdoors was one great black shriek.

I don't know if I saw the highest winds. By morning, the spinning anemometer on the porch was reading well over forty miles an hour, with gusts to fifty. The sea was boiling white all the way to the horizon. A wild, foamy surf was pounding the beach. But the sky was cloudless and brilliant. A fine wind-driven mist made the air itself sparkle in the sunshine.

So I leaned into the wind and ventured down to the beach. The storm waves had washed the sand away. All that was left was gravel and shale. Huge boulders had been tossed about and turned over.

Then around Gay Head away to the east came a flock of black birds. They were awesome creatures, powerful fliers. They seemed to relish the wind. They made me think of Noah's raven, the first creature out of the ark, because of the way they took to the storm. They would fly low for a while and let the wind fling them down the beach, then turn and tack sideways, beating upwind for a while before spreading their wings to soar upward, then dive and swoop and do it all again.

I watched them until they were gone from sight, then stood transfixed on the windy beach. At that moment I fell in love with these strong black birds. I could see why Noah just put the raven out of the ark and let it go. He must have known it was built for this kind of weather.

I decided at that windblown moment on the beach in the sparkling air and before that frothy, pounding surf and that totally new shoreline that if I could ever choose my own symbol for the movement at its best in the bad time that had just ended, it would be these birds—I will always think of them as Noah's ravens—because of the way they took to the wind.

Ours was a movement of ravens, say I, a great flocking and soaring to and fro in the big storm of the American sixties. Sometimes we could really fly.

When we crashed, it was from an enormous height.

Notes

2 Stumbling on Vietnam

1. Karnow, *Vietnam*.

3 The Joy of Movement

1. Sale, *SDS*, 193.
2. Klatch, *A Generation Divided*, 190.

4 The Bourgeois Gentlemen of Vietnam

1. Sale, *SDS*, 136–42.
2. Dougan, et al., *Nineteen Sixty-Eight*.
3. Wells, *The War Within*, 14.
4. Ibid.
5. Ibid.
6. Ibid.
7. Karnow, *Vietnam*, 680.
8. Wells, *The War Within*, 15.
9. Ibid.
10. Gitlin, *The Sixties*, 168.
11. Ibid., 163.
12. Zaroulis and Sullivan, *Who Spoke Up?*, 3.
13. Ellsberg, *Papers on the War*, 114.
14. Dougan, et al., *Nineteen Sixty-Eight*, 81.
15. Wells, *The War Within*, 31.
16. Ibid.
17. Sheehan, *A Bright Shining Lie*, 512.
18. *The Pentagon Papers*, 363; Sheehan, *A Bright Shining Lie*, 580.
19. McNamara, *In Retrospect*, 174.
20. Ibid., 217.
21. Kaiser, *American Tragedy*.

5 Build, Not Burn!

1. Sheehan, *A Bright Shining Lie*, 689.

6 Build Not! Burn!

1. Sale, *SDS*, 10.
2. *The New York Times,* December 10, 2003.
3. Ibid., 249.
4. Ibid., 249–59.
5. Ibid., 250.
6. Wells, *The War Within*, 64–65.
7. Sale, *SDS*, 250.
8. Karnow, *Vietnam*, 24–46.

7 Great Debates and Petty Spats

1. Ungar, *FBI*, 111–157.
2. *The Pentagon Papers*, 16.
3. Karnow, *Vietnam*, 503.
4. Ibid.
5. Ibid., 504.
6. Ibid., 503–4.
7. Ibid., 505

8 Running with Sartre

1. *The New York Times,* January 25, 1982.

9 One Way to Skin a Cat

1. Wells, *The War Within*, 136.

10 Banned

1. U.S. House Committee on Internal Security, *Investigation of Students for a Democratic Society*, 55.
2. Ibid., 55–57.
3. Sale, *SDS*, 383.
4. U.S. House Committee on Internal Security, *Investigation of Students for a Democratic Society*, 57–59.
5. Ibid., 89–93.

11 Cointelpro, Anyone?

1. Karnow, *Vietnam*, 523.
2. Clifford, *Counsel to the President*, 473.
3. Bamford, *Body of Secrets*, 282.
4. Dougan, et al., *Nineteen Sixty-Eight*, 10.
5. Clifford, *Counsel to the President*, 468.
6. Ibid., 468–9.
7. Ibid., 474.
8. Ibid., 476.
9. Ibid., 478–9.
10. Ibid., 485.
11. Ibid., 613–4.
12. Karnow, *Vietnam*.

13. Jensen, *Army Surveillance in America, 1775–1980*; Churchill and Vander Wall, *The COINTELPRO Papers*.
14. Clifford, *Counsel to the President*, 613–4.
15. Wells, *The War Within*, 255.
16. Jensen, *Army Surveillance in America, 1775–1980*, 245.
17. Ibid., 246–7.
18. Wells, *The War Within*.
19. Ungar, *FBI*, 143.
20. Sale, *SDS*, 456.

12 Finding the Radical Center

1. Karnow, *Vietnam*, 292.
2. Goodwin, *Remembering America*, 465.
3. Wells, *The War Within*, 127; McNamara, *In Retrospect*, 233; Halberstam, *The Best and the Brightest*, 768.
4. Ungar, *FBI*, 306.
5. Karnow, *Vietnam*, 557; Clifford, *Counsel to the President*, 267.
6. Zaroulis and Sullivan, *Who Spoke Up?*, 152.
7. Wells, *The War Within*, 242.
8. Karnow, *Vietnam*, 547.

13 The Whole World Is Watching

1. Farber, *Chicago '68*, 130.
2. Karnow, *Vietnam*.

17 Star-Chambered in Texas

1. Sale, *SDS*, 500.
2. Ibid., 571.

18 Things Fall Apart

1. Sale, *SDS*, 544.
2. Ibid.; Jensen, *Army Surveillance in America, 1775–1980*.

19 To the Chicken Coop

1. The Chicago Seven were originally the Chicago Eight: Rennie Davis, Dave Dellinger, John Froines, Tom Hayden, Abbie Hoffman, Jerry Rubin, Bobby Seale, and Lee Weiner. Black Panther leader Bobby Seale was the only black member of the group, and he was the only one of the Eight who demanded that he be permitted to defend himself. He was entirely within his rights to do so, but for his own opaque reasons, Judge Julius Hoffman not only refused him this right but also began citing him for contempt of court every time Seale restated it. As John Schultz reports this struggle (in *The Chicago Conspiracy Trial*), Seale, deferentially enough, even asked Hoffman to tell him the applicable rules of procedure so he could conduct his self-defense properly. Hoffman cited Seale with a contempt-of-court charge each time he did this, then told him to shut up about it. When Seale refused to do so, Hoffman ordered him gagged and bound to a chair. When Seale continued to vocalize even through the gag, Hoffman had him removed from the courtroom. His case was separated from that of the seven white "conspirators." Seale was sentenced to four years and three months

each for sixteen counts of contempt. The white defendants and their lawyers were cited with seven counts of contempt. These were overturned two years later. None of the whites served time.

2. Schultz, *The Chicago Conspiracy Trial*, 9.
3. Ibid., 383.
4. Ibid., 29.
5. Ibid., 221.
6. Ibid., 301.
7. Ibid., 221.
8. Wells, *The War Within*, 366.
9. Ibid., 401–2.
10. Ibid., 406.
11. Ibid.
12. Ibid., 407.
13. Ibid.
14. Ibid., 414.
15. Several Weathermen escaped through the rock garden at the town house's rear. The half-clad Cathy Wilkerson and the naked Kathy Boudin ran into the street and were aided by neighbors. They escaped. Boudin's address book contained the number of a minuteman munitions expert who was advising the Weathermen on how to build bombs. Had they misunderstood his instructions? Or had he misled his students?
16. Wells, *The War Within*, 407–9.
17. Ibid.

20 From an Abandoned Weathermen Crash Pad

1. Wells, *The War Within*, 420.
2. *The New York Times*, October 9, 1986.
3. Zaroulis and Sullivan, *Who Spoke Up?*, 329.
4. Gitlin, *The Sixties*, 409; Sale, *SDS*, 636.
5. Sale, *SDS*, 645.
6. Schultz, *The Chicago Conspiracy Trial*, 388–9.
7. Ungar, *FBI*.
8. Schultz, *The Chicago Conspiracy Trial*, 386.

21 The Miracle of Watergate

1. *The New York Times*, July 14, 2000.
2. *The New York Times*, August 27, 2000.
3. Sale, *SDS*, 10.
4. Wells, *The War Within*, 579.
5. Ibid.

Bibliography

Albert, Judith Clavir, and Stewart Edward Albert, eds. *The Sixties Papers: Documents of a Rebellious Decade.* New York, NY: Praeger, 1984.

Albert, Michael. *What Is to Be Undone: A Modern Revolutionary Discussion of Classical Left Ideologies.* Boston, MA: Sargent, 1974.

Alpert, Jane. *Growing Up Underground.* New York, NY: Citadel Press, 1990.

Austin, Alan D., ed. *The Revolutionary Imperative: Essays Toward a New Humanity.* Nashville, TN: National Methodist Student Movement, 1966.

Aya, Roderick, and Norman Miller, eds. *The New American Revolution.* New York, NY: Free Press, 1971.

Ayers, Bill. *Fugitive Days: A Memoir.* Boston, MA: Beacon Press, 2001.

Bamford, James. *Body of Secrets: Anatomy of the Ultra-Secret National Security Agency.* New York, NY: Anchor, 2002.

———. *The Puzzle Palace: A Report on America's Most Secret Agency.* New York, NY: Houghton Mifflin, 1982.

Beschloss, Michael, ed. *Reaching for Glory: Lyndon Johnson's Secret White House Tapes, 1964–1965.* New York, NY: Simon & Schuster, 2001.

Bills, Scott L., ed. *Kent State/May 4: Echoes Through a Decade.* Kent, OH: Kent State University Press, 1982.

Buhle, Paul, ed. *History and the New Left: Madison, Wisconsin, 1950–1970.* Philadelphia, PA: Temple University Press, 1990.

Chomsky, Noam. *American Power and the New Mandarins.* New York, NY: Pantheon Books, 1969.

Churchill, Ward, and Jim Vander Wall. *The COINTELPRO Papers: Documents from the FBI's Secret Wars Against Domestic Dissent.* Boston, MA: South End Press, 1990.

Cleaver, Eldridge. *Soul on Ice.* New York, NY: McGraw-Hill, 1967. Reprint, New York, NY: Dell Publishing, 1968.

Clifford, Clark, with Richard C. Holbrooke. *Counsel to the President: A*

Memoir. New York, NY: Random House, 1991.

Cohen, Mitchell, and Dennis Hale, eds. *The New Student Left: An Anthology.* Boston, MA: Beacon Press, 1967.

Dougan, Clark, Stephen Weiss, and the editors of Boston Publishing Company. *Nineteen Sixty-Eight: The Vietnam Experience.* Boston, MA: Boston Publishing Company, 1983.

Ellsberg, Daniel. *Papers on the War.* New York, NY: Simon & Schuster, 1972.

Farber, David. *Chicago '68.* Chicago, IL: Chicago University Press, 1988.

Garrett, Banning, and Katherine Barkley, eds. *Two, Three . . . Many Vietnams: A Radical Reader on the Wars in Southeast Asia and the Conflicts at Home.* San Francisco, CA: Canfield Press, 1971.

Garvy, Helen. *Rebels with a Cause: A Collective Memoir of the Hopes, Rebellions and Repressions of the 1960s.* Los Gatos, CA: Shire Press, 2007.

Gitlin, Todd. *The Sixties: Years of Hope, Days of Rage.* New York, NY: Bantam Books, 1987.

———. *The Whole World Is Watching: Mass Media in the Making and Unmaking of the New Left.* Berkeley, CA: University of California Press, 1980.

Goodwin, Richard N. *Remembering America: A Voice From the Sixties.* New York, NY: HarperCollins, 1995.

Halberstam, David. *The Best and the Brightest.* New York, NY: Random House, 1972.

Hayden, Tom. *Reunion: A Memoir.* New York, NY: Random House, 1988.

Jensen, Joan M. *Army Surveillance in America, 1775–1980.* New Haven, CT: Yale University Press, 1991.

Kaiser, David. *American Tragedy: Kennedy, Johnson, and the Origins of the Vietnam War.* Cambridge, MA: Belknap Press of Harvard University Press, 2000.

Karnow, Stanley. *Vietnam: A History.* New York, NY: Viking Press, 1983.

Klatch, Rebecca E. *A Generation Divided: The New Left, the New Right, and the 1960s.* Berkeley, CA: University of California Press, 1999.

Lynd, Staughton. *Living Inside Our Hope: A Steadfast Radical's Thoughts on Rebuilding the Movement.* Ithaca, NY: ILR Press, 1997.

McNamara, Robert S. *In Retrospect: The Tragedy and Lessons of Vietnam.* New York, NY: Times Books, 1995.

Morgan, Edward P. *The 60s Experience: Hard Lessons About Modern America.* Philadelphia, PA: Temple University Press, 1991.

Morrison, Joan, and Robert K. Morrison. *From Camelot to Kent State: The Sixties Experience in the Words of Those Who Lived It.* New York, NY: Times Books, 1987.

Pardun, Robert. *Prairie Radical: A Journey Through the Sixties*. Los Gatos, CA: Shire Press, 2001.

The Pentagon Papers. Gravel edition. Vol 3. Boston, MA: Beacon Press, 1971.

Potter, Paul. *A Name for Ourselves: Feelings About Authentic Identity, Love, Intuitive Politics, Us*. Boston, MA: Little, Brown, 1971.

Powers, Thomas. *The War at Home: Vietnam and the American People, 1964–1968*. New York, NY: Grossman, 1973.

Raskin, Jonah. *For the Hell of It: The Life and Times of Abbie Hoffman*. Berkeley, CA: University of California Press, 1996.

Raskin, Marcus G., and Bernard Fall, eds. *The Viet-Nam Reader: Articles and Documents on American Foreign Policy and the Viet-Nam Crisis*. New York, NY: Random House, 1965.

Robbins, Mary Susannah, ed. *Against the Vietnam War: Writings by Activists*. Syracuse, NY: Syracuse University Press, 1999.

Rossman, Michael. *New Age Blues: On the Politics of Consciousness*. New York, NY: Dutton, 1979.

Sale, Kirkpatrick. *SDS*. New York, NY: Random House, 1973.

Schultz, John. *The Chicago Conspiracy Trial*. New York, NY: Da Capo Press, 1993.

Sheehan, Neil. *A Bright Shining Lie: John Paul Vann and America in Vietnam*. New York, NY: Random House, 1988.

Ungar, Sanford J. *FBI: An Uncensored Look Behind the Walls*. Boston, MA: Little, Brown, 1975.

U.S. House Committee on Internal Security. *Investigation of Students for a Democratic Society*. Hearings of Ninety-first Congress. Washington, D.C.: U.S. Govt. Print. Off., 1969.

Wells, Tom. *The War Within: America's Battle over Vietnam*. Berkeley, CA: University of California Press, 1994.

Wicker, Tom. *Report of the National Advisory Commission on Civil Disorders*. New York, NY: Bantam Books, 1968.

Zaroulis, Nancy, and Gerald Sullivan. *Who Spoke Up?: American Protest Against the War in Vietnam, 1963–1975*. Garden City, NY: Doubleday, 1984.

Index

Note: CO refers to Carl Oglesby, JFK refers to John F. Kennedy, RFK refers to Robert F. Kennedy, and LBJ refers to Lyndon B. Johnson.

About the Author

Carl Oglesby was president of Students for a
Democratic Society between 1965 and 1966. His
previous books include *Containment and Change,
The Yankee and Cowboy War,* and *The JFK
Assassination.* He lives in Amherst,
Massachusetts.

Inspiring Words
FROM THE PSALMS

Presented to

Presented by

Date

Inspiring Words

FROM THE PSALMS

FOR WOMEN

Blue Sky Ink
Brentwood, Tennessee

Inspiring Words from the Psalms for Women
Copyright © 2004 by GRQ, Inc.
ISBN 1-59475-003-3

Published by Blue Sky Ink,
Brentwood, Tennessee.

Scripture quotations marked CEV are from The Contemporary English Version. Copyright © 1991, 1992, 1995 by American Bible Society. Used by permission.

Scripture quotations marked GNT are from the Good News Translation, Second Edition, Copyright © 1992 by American Bible Society. Used by permission. All rights reserved.

Scripture quotations marked KJV are from the King James Version of the Bible.

Scripture quotations marked THE MESSAGE are taken from *The Message*. Copyright by Eugene H. Peterson, 1993, 1994, 1995. Used by permission of NavPress Publishing Group.

Scripture quotations marked NASB are taken from the New American Standard Bible®, Copyright © 1960, 1962, 1963, 1968, 1971, 1972, 1973, 1975, 1977, 1995 by The Lockman Foundation. Used by permission.

Scripture quotations marked NCV are from The Holy Bible, New Century Version, copyright © 1987, 1988, 1991 by Word Publishing, Dallas, Texas 75039. Used by permission.

Scripture quotations marked NKJV are from The New King James Version. Copyright © 1979, 1980, 1982, Thomas Nelson, Inc.

Scripture quotations marked NLT are from the *Holy Bible*, New Living Translation, copyright © 1996. Used by permission of Tyndale House Publishers, Inc., Wheaton, Illinois 60189. All rights reserved.

Scripture quotations marked NRSV are from The New Revised Standard Version of the Bible, copyright © 1989 by The Division of Christian Education of the National Council of the Churches of Christ in the USA. Used by permission. All rights reserved.

Verses marked TLB are taken from *The Living Bible* © 1971. Used by permission of Tyndale House Publishers, Inc., Wheaton, Illinois 60189. All rights reserved.

Compiler and Editor: Lila Empson
Writers: Margaret Langstaff and Jan Coleman
Cover and Text Design: Diane Whisner

Printed in China. All rights reserved under International Copyright Law. Contents and/or cover may not be reproduced in whole or in part in any form without the express written consent of the Publisher.

This is My resting place forever;
Here I will dwell, for I have desired it.
I will abundantly bless her provision;
I will satisfy her poor with bread.

PSALM 132:14–15 NKJV

Contents

Introduction

The book of Psalms is an ancient collection of songs and prayers. The writers poured out their hearts and asked for help in troubled times. The psalms were pleas for rescue from pursuers,

comfort when abandoned by friends, and peace in the midst of ill health. The psalmists confessed everything—their fears, regrets, even their shortcomings—because God understands.

The psalmists asked God to teach them in his truth, to guide them, and to deliver them. And yet, every psalm ends with praise and thanksgiving for a loving God who is involved in every aspect of life. Your life. God knows your past and will walk beside you to your future. He will inspire you to become the woman he created you to be.

God already knows your questions and will place the answers in your heart. God loves you and desires to show you his ways and meet your deepest needs. Enjoy your time with him.

Teach me your ways, O LORD, that I may live
according to your truth!
Grant me purity of heart, that I may honor you.

With all my heart I will praise you,
O Lord my God.

I will give glory to your name forever,

for your love for me is very great.

PSALM 86:11–13 NLT

God's Help in Times of Need

The LORD is my strength and my shield; in him my
heart trusts; so I am helped, and my heart exalts.
PSALM 28:7 NRSV

At the end of a hectic day, do you ever feel like mumbling, "I can't do it all"? You are not alone. Being a woman today is demanding as you juggle home and work, nurture all the relationships in your life, and volunteer time, talent, and resources to causes you're passionate about. As you race to keep up, you fall behind. If you don't give your best, you fight those feelings of inadequacy.

It's okay. Remind yourself that God is ready to help. He is personally involved in every aspect of your life. He knows exactly what's up, the pressures you're under, and the decisions you're facing. He invites you to ask for his help, for insight and wisdom, and for ways to bolster your confidence.

You can live expectantly, knowing that
God will lend a hand in amazing ways
and in surprising places.

The LORD lifts the burdens of those bent beneath their loads. The LORD loves the righteous.

PSALM 146:8 NLT

God's Protection

Guard me as the apple of the eye; hide me
in the shadow of your wings.

PSALM 17:8 NRSV

The storms of life cannot be avoided. And often they come completely unannounced. When showers of troubles hit, when fears ambush and doubts plague, everything seems out of control. But just

as the mother eagle guards her young, God protects those he loves. When rough times threaten your peace, he will take you under his wing and give you strength to endure.

It's easy to slip into false thinking that God is somehow absent if disaster strikes, that you've missed his protection. Quite the opposite is true. God will never leave you

alone to face your problems. He guides you into the eye of the tornado where it is quiet and still, where you can hear his voice and feel the strength of his presence.

Whenever you find upsets in your life, you
can use these as opportunities to grow in
your trust of God.

*L*et all who take refuge
in You be glad, let
them ever sing for joy;
and may You shelter
them, that those who
love Your name may
exult in You.

PSALM 5:11 NASB

Thankfulness and Praise to God

*It is good to give thanks to the LORD, to sing
praises to your name, O Most High; to declare
your steadfast love in the morning, and your
faithfulness by night.*

PSALM 92:1–2 NRSV

When things left undone and problems not yet resolved occupy
your thoughts too much, they can distract you
from seeing the blessings in your circumstances. God is working behind the scenes
constantly, even in what looks like chaos. It's
all in how you view it. It's amazing what happens when you begin to see God in every situation and to thank him for it. It transforms
your heart.

Even if you can't see progress, thank God for what he is going to
do. Praise him for how he's growing you, building your character,
and helping you refocus your life on what's valuable in the long run.
It's like viewing life through God-colored glasses. Everything has a
rosy glow, a positive spin.

*When you begin to view life in thankfulness to
God, you find that your attitude will soon be one
of grateful appreciation for everything around you,
including the irritations and frustrations.*

I come to your altar,
LORD. I raise my voice in
praise and tell of all the
miracles you have done.

PSALM 26:6–7 NCV

God's Faithfulness

All those who know your mercy, Lord, will count on you for help. For you have never yet forsaken those who trust in you.

PSALM 9:10 TLB

The vows and promises you exchange with those you love provide you with a strong foundation on which to build your life. The faithfulness you both give and receive fills you with confidence and comforts you in your times of need. But the faithfulness of your closest family and friends appears as a pale shadow next to the splendor of God's faithfulness.

God is faithful to you no matter what. He gives you his full attention when you reach out for his love, assurance, and support. God never breaks his promises. And he is always there for you, in the depths of your despair and in the heights of your jubilation. He is there in the day-to-day of your life.

By believing this and affirming it often, you will take on a measure of his strength, and you will reflect his goodness to others.

The LORD is my rock and my fortress and my deliverer; my God, my strength, in whom I will trust; my shield and the horn of my salvation, my stronghold.

PSALM 18:2 NKJV

Seeking and Yearning for God

*Hear my cry, O God; listen to my prayer. From the
end of the earth I call to you, when my heart is faint.*

PSALM 61:1–2 NRSV

Until you place your life fully in God's hands, you will never quiet
the anxious thoughts that can cry out from
within and leave you feeling unhappy and
defeated. You can search frantically for happiness, success, and fulfillment. You can
flail about and wonder why you are never
satisfied, why you are always restless. You
may wonder why new acquisitions merely
whet your desire for more.

What you are yearning for and so
urgently trying to find has been there all the time. God alone can satisfy your deepest and most intimate longings. Without him, even the
sources of human happiness—such as children, family, homes, fond
possessions, dreams, and ambitions—invite stress and agitation
because you know one day you will lose them.

*When you make God the center of your life, you
will find true fulfillment. You can never lose him;
he will stay with you.*

I cry to God Most High, to God
who fulfills his purpose for me.

PSALM 57:2 NRSV

God's Joy and Delight in Your Life

The LORD is kind and shows mercy. He does not become angry quickly but is full of love. The LORD is good to everyone; he is merciful to all he has made.

PSALM 145:8–9 NCV

When you think of those you love—family and friends, mentors and heroes—joy and affection fill your heart. Your world is brighter and more meaningful because they are in it. You care for them and you value them. You jump at chances to nourish and sustain them, to cheer them, and to make their hearts glad. When they are happy, you are happy.

As a child of God, you mimic him in the feelings you have for your loved ones, feelings that are dim reflections of his profound delight in you as his child. He wants to see you happy and fulfilled, and he wants you to know he is the source of the abundant blessings in your life.

Your love for God will manifest itself in the affection, care, and concern that you feel for others.

Your goodness continues forever, and your teachings are true.

PSALM 119:142 NCV

God's Direction and Correction

*I will instruct thee and teach thee in the way which
thou shalt go: I will guide thee with mine eye.*

PSALM 32:8 KJV

*I*t's never pleasant when someone points out where you've messed
up. But a true friend cares enough to
risk the truth. Her words may be
tough ones, but they are always motivated by love. She has your best interest at heart. That's exactly how it is
with God. His desire is never to
trounce on you, but to bring your
heart closer to him.

Maybe you're unaware you've veered off course. Correction may
be a tug on your conscience, a gentle reminder to get back on the
right road. God desires to give you new direction, designed for you.
If you're tempted to slip into self-pity over your flubs, draw near to
God. Ask, "What do you want me to learn from this?"

*God is the best friend you'll ever have. His words
are always spiced with love.*

After you have
corrected me I will
thank you by living
as I should!

PSALM 119:7 TLB

Loving God

I love you, LORD; you are my strength.
PSALM 18:1 NLT

God's grandeur is inspiring, and his perfect goodness is imponderable. God is beyond understanding. Do you want to love him more? The first step is to make him a part of your daily life and to embrace him as your loving God.

To do that, it's important to acknowledge utter dependence on him. Look around you anywhere. Gaze at the world with new eyes, eyes full of love and admiration for God's countless wonders. You'll see constant reminders of his handiwork everywhere, countless proofs that he is greater than the most marvelous thing imaginable. Know without a doubt that you are important to God because he made you. He loves you, he protects you, and he preserves you.

You can share all your confidences with him and express all your fears. If you ask, God will help you keep his commandments.

*I*t is good to tell of your love in the morning and of your loyalty at night.

PSALM 92:2 NCV

God Listens to Your Prayers

Through each night I sing his songs, praying
to God who gives me life.
PSALM 42:8 NLT

Pulled between the demands of work and family, you have little opportunity for quiet time. The moments when you can experience God without distraction and interruption are few and precious. The faces of your loved ones are never far from your mind, reminding, cajoling, requesting. And the responsibilities of home and career follow you wherever you go.

Yet no matter how fragmented and abbreviated your prayers may become as a result, you can be sure God hears them—not only in those rare moments of peace but also during the frantic hours of activity. He hears you loud and clear, no matter how mumbled and inarticulate your message may seem.

God is quick to give you the right words to say,
the proper response to a crisis, and the kindness
and diplomacy you need to navigate your
complex and difficult days.

Morning, noon, and night
you hear my concerns
and my complaints.

PSALM 55:17 CEV

Prayer Banishes Worry and Fear

Hear my voice, O God, in my meditation;
preserve my life from fear of the enemy.
PSALM 64:1 NKJV

Worry and fear are the bane of human existence. They may be
simply irritating, or they may have the
capacity to cripple and incapacitate
you. You may have noticed that they
strike when you feel far from God. At
those times, they seem to rise up. They
crash over you when you are not paying attention to what is really important
in life. And what is really important is your relationship with God.

The more you pray, the closer you draw to God and the better
you know him. And the more you pray, the more his presence and
power surround you, lifting you up and dissolving your worries
and fears.

You can cope with whatever comes along because
you know you are shored up and strengthened with
what he has promised you. You have become
recipients of his bountiful grace.

I cry out to God Most High, to the God who does everything for me. He sends help from heaven and saves me. He punishes those who chase me. God sends me his love and truth.

PSALM 57:2–3 NCV

God Lightens Your Cares and Burdens

*Commit everything you do to the Lord. Trust
him to help you do it and he will.*

PSALM 37:5 TLB

*Y*ou may have discovered that keeping a journal is an enhancement to your spiritual life. You may not write in it every day, but you probably write often enough to record those things that are uppermost in your mind.

The act of writing down your worries and cares is liberating and exhilarating, for you are forced to examine and articulate the sources of your anxiety. When these sources are identified, analyzed, and ultimately committed to God, they lose their ability to have power over you.

*J*ournaling your worries to God is an effective discipline
for reducing stress. In a way, it is like writing God a
letter and asking him to take care of things. Once you
have done so, you can close your journal, put up your
pen, and go about the day relieved and refreshed that
you have dealt with your troubles effectively.

Why am I discouraged?
Why am I restless?
I trust you!

PSALM 42:5 CEV

Prayer Helps You Make Decisions

With my whole heart have I sought thee: O let me not wander from thy commandments.

PSALM 119:10 KJV

Throughout your life, you are presented with choices. Many times those choices are fairly easy to make, especially when they deal with simple issues of right and wrong. At other times, however, the most difficult situations you face have to do with choosing from a variety of possibilities, with varying shades of good and bad.

Fortunately, you do not have to deal with difficult choices alone and unaided. If you ask God, he will enlighten you. He will show you the way to go. He has already given you his commandments to light your way through the maze of facts and emotions.

God waits patiently for you to bring each situation before him. He is eager to help you decide and do what is right for your life and the lives of those you love.

I treasure your word in my heart,
so that I may not sin against you.

PSALM 119:11 NRSV

The Discipline of Daily Prayer

In the morning, O LORD, You will hear my voice; in the morning I will order my prayer to You and eagerly watch.
PSALM 5:3 NASB

Prayer is genuine and straightforward conversation with God about whatever is on your heart. Prayer is a simple matter of regu-

larly setting aside time to talk to God. A daily prayer habit will help you grow spiritually and draw you into a close and comforting relationship with God. Habitual prayer is exciting and unlimited when you thoughtfully and deliberately engage in it.

The regularity of prayer presents an excellent opportunity to interact with God and influence the world around you. Your prayer habit can be enhanced by finding a quiet place with a pleasant atmosphere to regularly meet with God. Keeping a Bible, journal, and other helpful books in that special place is also a good idea.

If you are faithful to make yourself available and attentive to God each day, you will reap abundant spiritual dividends.

I have complete
confidence, O God! I
will sing and praise you!
Wake up, my soul!

PSALM 108:1 GNT

The Lord Wants to Use Your Talents

Let the beauty of the LORD our God be upon us,
and establish the work of our hands for us; yes,
establish the work of our hands.

PSALM 90:17 NKJV

You are absolutely unique and irreplaceable in the eyes of God. And you have been given talents and abilities that are yours alone, whether artistic, athletic, financial, scientific, musical, literary . . . The key to achieving satisfaction and success with your talents is to place them always at the service of God.

Ask for God's direction and pray for his guidance so that you may use your gifts fruitfully and fully in his eyes. God has a specific plan for you, and he has equipped you for your journey. Your responsibility is to seek his will for you and allow him to perfect and refine your endowments until they are functioning as they were intended.

When you seek God's plan for your life, you can be
sure that he will bless the work of your hands.

Inspiring Words FROM THE PSALMS

The laws of the LORD are right, and
those who obey them are happy.
The commands of the LORD are just
and give understanding to the mind.

PSALM 19:8 GNT

Faith, Hope, and Love

Yes, Lord, let your constant love surround us,
for our hopes are in you alone.
PSALM 33:22 TLB

Your spiritual strength is founded on the marvelous triad of faith, hope, and love. Through these, God shows you how you are to behave with others. He actively demonstrates these three virtues through his own unblemished behavior toward you and everyone you love.

If you take God at his word, your ordinary, everyday life should be an acting-out of his promises to you; and your relationships with others should be energetic, vital mirror images of the trustworthy and merciful God you have come to know. Study God's Word and ask him for understanding and wisdom to grow spiritually. Have faith. Put your hope in God. And love your neighbor and your God.

Spiritual strength really is as simple as one, two,
three. You must strive for faith, hope, and love if
you want to be fully pleasing to God.

Be of good courage, and he shall
strengthen your heart, all ye that
hope in the LORD.

PSALM 31:24 KJV

Inviting God into Your Home

My soul will be satisfied as with the richest of
foods; with singing lips my mouth will praise you.
PSALM 63:5 NIV

Home is the center of family life and a reflection of who you are and who you hope to become. Home is where you are fully yourself. Home is a haven from the world and its distractions, threats, and annoyances. Just as the home is the center of family life, so God should be the center of your home.

Invite God into your home as you look to him in prayer. Invite God in as you read the Bible and apply its words to your interactions with those nearest and dearest to your heart. Invite him in as you fill your home with symbols of your faith that provide inspiration and comfort. Invite God to be head of your house.

Give God the place of honor at the heart of your
home and invite him to hold you in his will.

Thy testimonies are very sure:
holiness becometh thine house,
O LORD, for ever.

PSALM 93:5 KJV

Friends: The Image of God

*Come, let us tell of the LORD's greatness; let us
exalt his name together.*

PSALM 34:3 NLT

It has been said that a true friend is the image of God. You know it when your soul touches another and you become sisters in God. A true friend laughs with you, weeps with you, believes in you, and encourages you to pursue your dreams. With your friend, you don't have to constantly explain everything you think, feel, and need. Somehow she just knows. Your spirit is lifted just by being together.

Godly friendships are delicate, and they take work. They must be carefully tended, and when the weeds of misunderstanding crop up, take care of them right away. Let nothing come between you. Draw inspiration from your friend to keep the heavenly perspective, to think your best thoughts, and to be your best self.

*As you risk being vulnerable, you'll draw closer
to your friend and closer to God.*

*H*ow very good and pleasant it is
when kindred live together in unity!

PSALM 133:1 NRSV

God Is in the Details

I will meditate about your glory,
splendor, majesty and miracles.
PSALM 145:5 TLB

*I*sn't it marvelous? Just when you need him most, God surrounds you with reminders of his presence.

He is evident in a tear or in a far-off whistle. He is in the twinkle of a stranger's eye and in a certain shade of blue. He is in the warmth of a handshake and in the missing front teeth of a five-year-old. He is in the hum of the washing machine and in the glow of the Christmas lights. He is between the lines of handwritten letters and in the nervous laughter of teenage girls. He rises up in the aroma of freshly cut grass. He is in the invisible arc made by a hawk on a fine autumn day.

*G*od is in every sigh, whisper, and exclamation.
He is in kept promises and acts of love and mercy.

I will thank you, LORD, with all my heart;

I will tell of all the marvelous things you have done.

I will be filled with joy because of you.

I will sing praises to your name, O Most High.

PSALM 9:1–2 NLT

The Kingdom of God Is Now

Your kingdom is an everlasting kingdom, and your
dominion endures throughout all generations.
PSALM 145:13 NRSV

Heaven is usually spoken of as a faraway place that you reach only at the end of a godly life. But you would do well to remember that God's reign over all that he created is right here in the present day, before your eyes and under your nose. And you lack nothing to enter it if you only place your trust in him and in his commandments.

You don't have to wait for heaven to experience God's love and to do his will. Everything you need is available by faith and grace. God has given you the tools to know him—Scripture, prayer, communities of faithful believers, acts of love, peace, and mercy. All of these pull you toward your true center and spiritual home with God.

The foretastes of heaven are abundant if
you open your heart to see them.

The LORD is king, he is robed
in majesty; the LORD is robed,
he is girded with strength. He
has established the world; it
shall never be moved; your
throne is established from of
old; you are from everlasting.

PSALM 93:1–2 NRSV

God Brings Out Your Best

*May He grant you according to your heart's
desire, and fulfill all your purpose.*
PSALM 20:4 NKJV

You probably remember your parents telling you as a little girl,
"Always do your best." It's a message you
absorb and pass on to your own children as a
foundational principle of what it takes to get
ahead and be successful in life. At some level,
you continue to evaluate your performance
according to this standard.

But God says that the most certain way
to ensure that you are living up to your
potential is to place yourself fully in the care of God. When you
commit your ways and your abilities to him, you can be sure that he
will guide you and help you become all that you can be.

*Seek God's will in all things, pray for his wisdom
and insight into the purpose for your life, and ask
for his help in all you do.*

You guide me with your instruction and at the end you will receive me with honor.

PSALM 73:24 GNT

God Is Love

GOD sticks by all who love him.
PSALM 145:20 THE MESSAGE

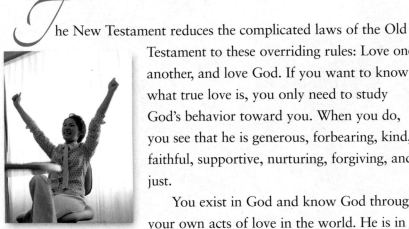

The New Testament reduces the complicated laws of the Old Testament to these overriding rules: Love one another, and love God. If you want to know what true love is, you only need to study God's behavior toward you. When you do, you see that he is generous, forbearing, kind, faithful, supportive, nurturing, forgiving, and just.

You exist in God and know God through your own acts of love in the world. He is in the face of everyone you reach out to, no matter from what station in life he or she might come. God's love is in your gentle word to a friend in pain, in the work of making a home for your family, and in the kindness you show to a stranger.

*When you live in love, you become
more and more like God.*

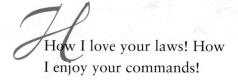

How I love your laws! How
I enjoy your commands!

PSALM 119:47 TLB

Joy: Smiling on the Inside

Make a joyful noise unto the LORD, all ye lands.
Serve the LORD with gladness: come before his
presence with singing.
PSALM 100:1–2 KJV

There is no secret formula for having a heart glad and full of joy. It comes naturally as you learn to know and trust God. Joy has nothing to do with circumstances, which are unpredictable. Circumstances rise and fall like the stock market. Joy has everything to do with your outlook. As you understand and embrace God's promises, as you put your hope in what is yet to come, a deep, inner joy that you can't explain fills you up.

Joy is a choice. You make up your mind to see God's goodness in everything, even the difficulties. You choose to believe in mysteries you cannot understand. Inner joy is the steady assurance of God's presence in your life, his plans for your future, and his power in your spirit.

Joy is contagious. It is the high point
of a God-centered life.

You have shown me the path to life, and you make me glad by being near to me. Sitting at your right side, I will always be joyful.

PSALM 16:11 CEV

God Reveals Himself in Daily Life

Those who are wise will take all this to heart; they will see in our history the faithful love of the LORD.

PSALM 107:43 NLT

Although you sometimes feel that you are alone and God is far away, God is not a distant power. He is an active presence in your everyday life. When you develop the habit of reading the tone and incidents of your days as if he shaped them, you gain real insight into how to draw closer to him.

Things don't just happen. Those things you call accidents, surprises, or discoveries are really revelations of his love and constant concern for you. If you keep your faith and trust in God, the meaning of confusing events will be made clear. If you greet each new day and expect the glory, power, and love of God to be revealed in it, your hours will be filled with joy and awe.

And this mystery will lead you ever onward toward him.

I remember the days of old,
I think about all your deeds,
I meditate on the works of your hands.

PSALM 143:5 NRSV

Your Hope Is in God

Happy are those who have the God of Israel as their
helper, whose hope is in the LORD *their God.*
PSALM 146:5 NLT

*H*ope is a quality you are so accustomed to living with that only in its absence do you truly understand its importance. Hope is what enables you to get out of bed in the morning and get your family off to school and work. Hope is the strength in your backbone that allows you to withstand storms of trouble and pain. Hope keeps you going. Those who lose hope lose the will to live.

Your ground for hope is in God's Word and in his promises, in the steadfast love he has shown toward you, and in the care and comfort he gives to you. Hope is your reliance on God's blessing and in the joyous expectation of even greater happiness.

*H*ope puts the smile on your face as you advance toward
the future with patience, courage, confidence, and stability.

*D*ay and night I'll stick with GOD; I've got
a good thing going and I'm not letting go.

PSALM 16:8 THE MESSAGE

Making the Most of Every Day

This is the day the LORD has made;
we will rejoice and be glad in it.
PSALM 118:24 NKJV

You've heard the expression *carpe diem*—it's Latin for "seize the day." While it's important to trust in the future and learn from the past, you must live life in the present. Even though the present is often difficult to take delight in, every moment focused on anything else is lost.

Someone once said that yesterday is only a dream and tomorrow nothing but a vision, but it is today well lived that really counts. Take advantage of it. Give yourself permission to grab the moment and let today be the most wonderful day of your life. Savor the miracle of the right now; relish it as its beauty unfolds in the ordinary blessings.

Today is God's gift to you so you can enjoy
him, bask in his goodness, be refreshed by his
spirit, and satisfied in his love.

I will sing praise to Your name forever, that I may daily perform my vows.

PSALM 61:8 NKJV

Patience to Wait on God

I wait for the LORD, my soul waits,
and in his word I hope.
PSALM 130:5 NRSV

No one likes to be kept waiting. *The hold button on telephones ought to be outlawed,* you may sometimes think. The line at a popular restaurant, the crowded waiting room of a doctor's office, the plumber who is late, a lunch date who keeps you waiting—these are all time wasters as far as you are concerned.

Waiting on God is a different matter. You may go through periods during which you feel he isn't listening to your prayers. Though you ardently beseech him, heaven seems to be silent. During these times, it's important to understand that the "wait" is part of the answer God is giving you.

Waiting is a necessary part of the mystery of God's plan and the degrees by which it will be unfolded to you. God answers you in his time, not yours.

Trust in him, and he will help you; he will make your righteousness shine like the noonday sun. Be patient and wait for the LORD to act.

PSALM 37:5–7 GNT

God's Infinite Forgiveness

*Order my steps in thy word: and let not any
iniquity have dominion over me.*

PSALM 119:133 KJV

Occasionally you may have a hard time apologizing when you are
wrong. You may back away from the simple
words *I'm sorry,* thinking that they are loaded
with vulnerability. You may fear retribution.
And even when you know that forgiveness will
be forthcoming, you may think it's easier to
simply let pride stand in the way.

Learning to own up to your mistakes is an
important step to maturity. That is also true in
your relationship with God. With God you can
be assured that you have nothing to fear and everything to gain, for
he has promised to forgive you whenever you come to him. Because
you are God's beloved child, you must apologize when you stray.

*You can live your life in confidence that God
wants to—and will—forgive you when you
come to him contritely.*

O Jehovah, come and bless us! . . . Satisfy us in our earliest youth with your lovingkindness, giving us constant joy to the end of our lives.

PSALM 90:13–14 TLB

The Gift of Giving

*Good people always lend freely to others,
and their children are a blessing.*
PSALM 37:26 NCV

*G*iving generously from the heart is extremely satisfying for many reasons—you're helping others, it makes you feel good—but the most important reason is that giving from your heart glorifies God. When you give freely, you are acknowledging the abundant, unreserved generosity God has poured out on you, his child.

There are many ways to give. Money is often the first thing that comes to mind. But today with your busy, even frantic, schedule, the gift of time is often an even greater sacrifice, as is the gift of your talent. No matter how you choose to give, you can always be sure that God is truly pleased and is eager to pour out his grace on you in return.

God has given you a great deal. Ask God to open your heart and open your hands to share with others.

These all look to you to give them their food at the proper time. When you give it to them, they gather it up; when you open your hand, they are satisfied with good things.

PSALM 104:27–28 NIV

Grace Sufficient for the Hour

*The LORD is gracious and full of compassion, slow
to anger and great in mercy. The LORD is good to all,
and His tender mercies are over all His works.*

PSALM 145:8–9 NKJV

Grace is God's unmerited favor, his undeserved mercy, his boundless compassion. This wondrous gift comes
to you because God gives freely, and you are
fortunate enough to be his child. And
because you are his, he loves you unconditionally.

Grace is your birthright as a child of
God. You fully avail yourself of this bounty
by placing your complete trust in him. You
have access to his grace by having confidence
in his promises. When you act on this confidence in God, you will
find that nothing is too great a challenge, that no obstacle is too
large to overcome. Nothing is impossible.

*Though you may approach a tough situation with
trepidation knowing the limitations of your own
meager abilities, you can ask for his help and be
certain that he will give it. God can do anything.*

They rise in the darkness as a light for the upright; they are gracious, merciful, and righteous.

PSALM 112:4 NRSV

Making a Sanctuary for the Spirit

LORD, *here in your Temple we meditate*
upon your kindness and your love.
PSALM 48:9 TLB

Designating a specific time and creating a particular place to meet with God can bring more focus and consistency to your quiet time.

You may want to set aside time in the morning. But any time of the day or night will work just fine, as long as the time is reserved explicitly for this specific purpose and becomes part of a daily routine.

Where you meet with God each day is also a matter of personal choice. It can be anywhere, inside or outside, as long as it is quiet, peaceful, and conducive to reflection and meditation.

Although you pray throughout the day, and even
are instructed to pray constantly, having a retreat
from the world's cares and buzz is a great boost for
your prayer life. There you can bring your heart,
mind, and soul fully to God.

I wake up early in the morning and cry out. I hope in your word. I stay awake all night so I can think about your promises.

PSALM 119:147–148 NCV

God Renews and Refreshes Your Life

With You is the fountain of life;
in Your light we see light.
PSALM 36:9 NKJV

God is the fountain of life. He is the source of all good things, and you can go to him and receive nurturing and encouragement. Day by day, for a lifetime, you have a direct line to God to refresh and regenerate your spirit.

God is the light by which you see the world and yourself and understand your reason for being. Were it not for God, you would not exist, let alone have eyes to see by his light. God discloses to you the drama of all that he has created in the light of his presence. If you stray too far from his light, you grow dim and the world is plunged into darkness.

Throughout your life, you must stay close to God in order to fulfill the purpose for which you were created.

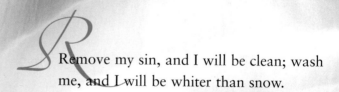

Remove my sin, and I will be clean; wash me, and I will be whiter than snow.

PSALM 51:7 GNT

Honor God by Ministering to His People

He will deliver the needy when he cries, the poor
also, and him who has no helper.

PSALM 72:12 NKJV

When you put your life in God's hands and commit to do his will,
he uses you mightily to bring comfort and peace to other people. By

helping others, you act as a conduit
for God's love among your friends
and neighbors.

There are meaning and intention
behind every circumstance you face.
Oftentimes, it becomes clear only in
hindsight. The depressed neighbor, the
neglected children of a friend, the harried checkout person at the grocery store, and the irritable plumber who comes to fix the sink all
need your loving-kindness and reassurance. These people are precious to God, and they are precious to you as well.

You can use each new day as an opportunity to do
God's work in the world, work that brings love
and peace into the life of everyone you encounter.

You do see the trouble and grief they cause. You take note of it and punish them. The helpless put their trust in you. You are the defender of orphans.

PSALM 10:14 NLT

The Divine Mystery at the Heart of Life

This is too much, too wonderful—
I can't take it all in!
PSALM 139:6 THE MESSAGE

God's power and love are too great for you to fully comprehend in this life. Great art, poetry, and music perhaps best convey God's mind-numbing majesty. When you pause from your daily routine of activities, struck by the intensity of a sunset or the beauty of a child, you catch a glimpse of the divine mystery at the heart of life. And it only whets your appetite for more. It is a glimmer of God's handiwork, vanishing as quickly as it has captured your attention.

The attitude of awe is a powerful reminder of your littleness and God's greatness, and it is your proper posture toward God and his miraculous creation.

May you reacquire the receptive mind of a child so that you will never lose the "wow" you feel for the stunning beauty of God's grandeur in the world.

God, you have taught
me since I was young.
To this day I tell about
the miracles you do.

PSALM 71:17 NCV

God Gives Abundantly

He fills my life with good things.
PSALM 103:5 NLT

God's blessings are available to you when you put your trust in him and keep his commandments. The beauty and simplicity of his abundance are so obvious, they are sometimes hard to see. His promises are everywhere in Scripture. You are God's child. If you honor and obey him, he will withhold nothing from you. All you have to do is ask.

God forgives your trespasses and provides righteousness and justice when you are treated unfairly; he is merciful and gracious; he is slow to get angry and full of unfailing love. Sin and despair are the only obstacles between you and God's many blessings. They cloud your vision and prevent you from seeing things as they are.

God understands how weak you are, and so he is eternally patient with you and sends you the grace you need to overcome your weaknesses.

*S*ee for yourself the way his mercies shower down on all who trust in him. If you belong to the Lord, reverence him; for everyone who does this has everything he needs.

PSALM 34:8–9 TLB

God's Love Makes You Wealthy

Look, here is someone who did not depend on God for safety, but trusted instead in great wealth.

PSALM 52:7 GNT

You are constantly bombarded with the message that you should want more, buy more, and have more. Doing so, you are told, will bring you happiness. Your mind is assaulted with this message every waking minute. Potential acquisitions are depicted as desirable and essential—the keys to pleasure and fulfillment. You are encouraged to acquire a bigger house and a finer car. And you are urged to use your credit cards to fill your house to the brim.

The truth is that material things can never really satisfy you. As soon as you have acquired a certain possession, the novelty begins to wear off, and you begin to yearn for something else. You must live a life in which God is the center.

God's love is the wealth you truly want, and only in him will you find peace.

We are merely moving shadows, and all our busy rushing ends in nothing. We heap up wealth for someone else to spend.

Psalm 39:6 NLT

Accepting God's Guidance

The LORD says, "I will teach you the way you should go; I will instruct you and advise you."
PSALM 32:8 GNT

When you are close to God, regularly praying, studying the Scriptures, and seeking his counsel, you are primed and attuned to the guidance he is offering for your life. You are immersed in his wisdom and his presence. And the more attention you pay to God, the more you realize that he is enveloping you and instructing you in the direction you should go.

As you quiet your mind and your heart, you will hone your senses to see and hear his will. As you attune your mind and your heart to God, your thoughts and feelings will reflect his advice in your everyday activities as well as in major decisions and challenges. God's Spirit whispers to you throughout the day, inspiring you to choose wisely and behave properly.

Your own spirit is at peace, and you receive blessings in your work and families.

This is God, our God forever and ever; He will be our guide even to death.

PSALM 48:14 NKJV

Finding Your Life in God

*O taste and see that the LORD is good; happy
are those who take refuge in him.*

PSALM 34:8 NRSV

The central questions in life—Who am I? What am I? Why was I born?—are troubling until you find the answers that ring true for you. These questions can be difficult for anyone who has no foundation in faith. Being human, you require meaning in your life, and if you do not find it, you may sometimes be tempted to feel that life is not worth the effort.

You can find the answers to these questions only as you grow in your relationship with God. For it is he who made you, and it is he who holds the key to your life.

*As you get to know God better, he reveals to
you the purpose for which you were created.
You discover that you are his child and an
heir to all his love and grace and mercy.*

He has put a new
song in my mouth—
praise to our God.

PSALM 40:3 NKJV

God's Face in the Stranger at the Door

I am your passing guest, an alien, like all my forebears.
PSALM 39:12 NRSV

As a woman, you feel compassion when you hear of anyone in need—an abandoned wife with three youngsters, perhaps, or a family homeless after a fire. God calls you to reach out beyond yourself and meet the needs of others. Scripture urges you to show goodwill to those less fortunate and relieve their distress whenever you can.

The disciples depended on Christian hospitality to survive. As they journeyed the countryside doing God's work, many people opened their homes and hearts to them. It takes only a love for others and a desire to help them be the best they can be. It may be a gift basket, a meal, or a listening ear.

Be on the lookout for people who need what you have to offer from the gifts and resources God has provided. The spiritual rewards are great.

The helpless put their trust in you.
You are the defender of orphans.

PSALM 10:14 NLT

Soul Food

*I will meditate on the glorious splendor of Your
majesty, and on Your wondrous works.*

PSALM 145:5 NKJV

When you walk through the door to your office every morning,
how do you feel? Is your desk or work area
warm and inviting? The workplace is where
you spend a large part of your life, and it
should be as conducive to peaceful, productive work as possible. Integrating your personal life into your work life can help create
a happy atmosphere. Keep in mind instead
what is truly important to you by integrating
symbols of your personal life into your work
environment.

Photos, mementos, and other objects of personal significance
warm the atmosphere and inspire a creative, enthusiastic approach to
your responsibilities. They also can help you keep things in perspective and remind you why you are working.

*These little treasures are like soul food because they
feed you emotionally and spiritually and lead your
heart back to God, the center of your life.*

O God, my heart is quiet
and confident. No wonder
I can sing your praises!

PSALM 57:7 TLB

The Value of Tradition and Ritual

*The fame of your goodness spreads across the
country; your righteousness is on everyone's lips.*
PSALM 145:7 THE MESSAGE

Y ou honor and commemorate your Christian heritage by observing little customs and rituals that are special to you and to your fam-

ily. Some of them you observe every
day; others only on special occasions
or perhaps just once a year. These
traditions are reminders of a past
shared and a future anticipated in the
steadfast love of God.

From time-honored holiday traditions of sunrise services and mid-
night vigils, to the ordinary rituals like grace before meals and
prayers and stories before bedtime, these observances reaffirm your
relationships with each other and with God. They cause you to
pause and reflect upon those things that give your life meaning. They
trigger and reinforce the values you treasure.

*As you draw together with friends and family
members on these occasions, your love for others
is refreshed and your spirit is lifted.*

A posterity shall serve Him. It will be recounted of the Lord to the next generation, they will come and declare His righteousness to a people who will be born, that He has done this.

PSALM 22:30–31 NKJV

Believe in Miracles

The Lord has done this wonderful miracle for me. . . .
I shall live! Yes, in his presence—here on earth!
PSALM 116:7, 9 TLB

Miracles happen every day. Some are extraordinary acts of God that alter the natural course of events, and some consist of situations where individuals have overcome tremendous odds to achieve their goals. But no matter how you define them, miracles do happen. No situation is so dire, no goal so remote that you cannot expect God's help and intervention on your behalf.

Miracles are unexplainable, but so are the other aspects of your relationship with God. You don't know why God loves you unconditionally and completely, but he does. You don't know why he listens to and answers your prayers, but he does. You don't know how miracles happen any more than you know how God created you in the first place.

But you don't have to understand—indeed, as a human you
are incapable of understanding—you only have to believe.

They cried to the Lord in their troubles, and he helped them and delivered them. He spoke, and they were healed—snatched from the door of death.

PSALM 107:19–20 TLB

Sinners Are to Be Helped, Not Shunned

Good and upright is the LORD; therefore He
teaches sinners in the way.
PSALM 25:8 NKJV

When you were a child, your parents warned you to stay away from "bad" companions who might cause you to stray from the

right path and participate in activities that were harmful to you and others. Certainly this is good advice for the young and easily influenced.

But you learn from Scripture that God loves all his children and wants everyone to be united with him. You also learn that you have a responsibility to be a blessing not only to those who are living a godly life but also to those who are not. You are a mirror of God's love in the world; you are to reflect and pass along the goodness and mercy shown to you.

Reach out to people who do not know that God loves
them and has a wonderful purpose for their lives.

None of us can see our own errors; deliver me, LORD, from hidden faults! Keep me safe, also, from willful sins; don't let them rule over me. Then I shall be perfect and free from the evil of sin.

PSALM 19:12–13 GNT

The Healing Power of God

O Lord my God, I cried to you for help,
and you have healed me.
Psalm 30:2 nrsv

Prayer is good medicine. It's a fact, and medical science has finally caught on and now backs up this statement of truth. Studies show that those who pray regularly and commit their welfare to God recover from serious illnesses and traumas faster than those who don't. Your outlook on life is more positive and your hope for the future is stronger than those who don't believe in God.

And as far as minor illnesses are concerned, you even get fewer colds than those who face life without the advantage of genuine faith. Prayer and thanksgiving relieve stress, alleviate anxiety, promote positive thinking, and generally foster happiness and contentment. Is it any wonder that such things contribute to your health?

When you know that God is in charge of
everything and is your guide, you are far less
likely to take yourself too seriously.

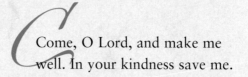

Come, O Lord, and make me
well. In your kindness save me.

PSALM 6:4 TLB

Shh, Listen

O rider in the heavens, the ancient heavens;
listen, he sends out his voice, his mighty voice.
PSALM 68:33 NRSV

Listening is the key to real communication with others. Ask yourself if this is true for you: When you ask someone a question, have you already formulated the answer that you expect to receive? When you engage in conversation or listen to music, do you have preconceived ideas of what you are going to hear? Conditioned by habit or limited thinking, expectations can drown out what is new and interesting.

When this happens, you can become a prisoner of your past experiences.

If you are to respond with your best self to the world, you have to tune up your eardrums and turn up the volume. You have to pay attention to the pauses between words, the sighs, and the tone of voice coming your way.

Eliminate the distortions, and let the true sounds
and meanings of life get through to you.

Listen to me, O my people.

PSALM 81:8 TLB

Yielding Your Spirit to God

Thy testimonies also are my delight.
PSALM 119:24 KJV

Some of your thorniest ethical quandaries occur at work. Office politics, power plays, and gossip, as well as on-the-job pressures, often bring out the worst in people. Because livelihood and financial security are involved, people can go to extremes to get the upper hand or come out on top.

But beware that you don't check your values and principles at the door when you go to work. Your values make you who you are, a child of God intent on abiding in his will at all times, on keeping his precepts in your heart. Your values are your flawless and unerring guide for your behavior. No unexpected circumstance is exempt from them. No challenge at work can overcome them.

With this in mind, you are perfectly outfitted to deal in a just and merciful manner with everything that comes your way.

What a glorious Lord!
He who daily bears our
burdens also gives us
our salvation.

PSALM 68:19 TLB

At Peace with the World

*He makes me to lie down in green pastures; He
leads me beside the still waters. He restores my soul.*
PSALM 23:2–3 NKJV

God is the restorer of your soul. There is no hardship or anxiety that can resist the refreshment and strength God gives you. Living your life with God emboldens and empowers you. Living with God enables you to conquer any sting, swipe, or bludgeon that comes your way. God has gifted you with intelligence and cunning, and he has gifted you with the privilege of resting in him and placing all your hope in him. With God, you have the possibility of succeeding at anything you do.

Those who live without God battle alone against self-doubt that undermines their best efforts. They become easy prey for despair and defeat.

*When you abide in God you are safe and secure.
You are swathed in a glow of love and peace and
able to become all that God intended you to be.*

At day's end I'm ready
for sound sleep, for you,
GOD, have put my life
back together.

PSALM 4:8 THE MESSAGE

The Forgiving Heart

Look on my affliction and my pain,
and forgive all my sins.

PSALM 25:18 NKJV

Someone once said that forgiveness is not for the forgiven; rather, it is for the forgiver. Forgiving those who have wronged you brings you to a deeper understanding of the character of God. Forgiving others is the cornerstone of your relationship with God. Holding a grudge keeps God at a comfortable distance. But when you let go of the grudge, you are restored instantly to God and you once more enjoy inner peace.

If you are struggling today, decide to release your right to be angry, your desire to judge the one who hurt you. No one is beyond God's forgiveness. That's the wonder of his mercy. Follow his example and erase the record of wrongs.

It takes courage to forgive others, and it may be the
hardest thing you've ever done. Yet forgiveness
frees you to experience amazing joy.

Create in me a clean heart, O God.
Renew a right spirit within me.

Psalm 51:10 nlt

God's Tender Mercies

The LORD is good to all; he has
compassion on all he has made.
PSALM 145:9 NIV

No one knows you like God; every secret wish, shameful weakness, latent talent, or buried pain is plainly displayed before him. And yet he loves you in the fullness of who you are, forgiving you for every sin, protecting you from every adversity. He is there like a mother to pick you up, dust you off, and kiss away your wounds. He is there like a father to guard and protect you and to hug you in his strong arms.

You may think you need more money, for instance, but God may know that what you need is to reorient your priorities. You may be disappointed because you didn't get a job or you missed an opportunity; God may know that what you want is not in your best interest.

God gives you exactly what you
need when you need it.

Hear me, O LORD, for Your lovingkindness is good; turn to me according to the multitude of Your tender mercies.

PSALM 69:16 NKJV

A Time for Rest

With all my heart, I will celebrate,
and I can safely rest.
PSALM 16:9 CEV

Rest is that marvelously restorative time when you play, leaving obligations and responsibilities on your desk for a while. You just let things happen; you don't try to make things happen. You go for undirected walks in your imagination where you are like a small child, ready for the next adventure to turn up.

For a while you let go of your cares and skip along behind God, curious and relaxed, in a little Eden of time. Who knows what will happen? You have "taken off" the ordinary and are wearing a different pair of spectacles that let you see things as if they are new. You are like a butterfly on a summer morning.

Doing nothing is an important part of life that
revives your waning spirit, and you "do nothing"
best in the security and comfort of God's love.

He lets me rest in green meadows;
he leads me beside peaceful streams.

PSALM 23:2 NLT

Joy

*You will show me the path that leads to life; your
presence fills me with joy and brings me pleasure forever.*
PSALM 16:11 GNT

Joy is the gift of the Good News. The joy of the Good News
beats ice cream, the best movie, mountain
climbing, skydiving, the Super Bowl, a
hole-in-one, a first-place victory, or a personal best. Joyful people whistle, sing,
dance, clap, smile, laugh, hoot, holler, turn
flips, hop up and down, turn somersaults,
and fly through the air in their dreams like
a superhero.

Joyful people are people on the move;
arms and legs, hearts and souls, they rip through the world, repeat-
ing everywhere what they've heard. Joy is the jubilant chorus that all
living things make while singing the praises of God. Joy is the *thank-
you, thank-you, thank-you* from the bottom of your heart that
erupts when you are put in touch with what really matters.

*Joy is the irrepressible buoyancy you feel
when you have been forgiven.*

I will be glad, yes, filled
with joy because of you.
I will sing your praises,
O Lord God.

PSALM 9:2 TLB

Heaven

Me? I plan on looking you full in the face. When I get up, I'll see your full stature and live heaven on earth.
PSALM 17:15 THE MESSAGE

The word *heaven* is used to refer to the joyous fulfillment of the purpose of your life—union with God. Certainly life offers you many fleeting fore-tastes of heaven, yet your present life is only preparation for the ultimate reward God has for you.

All the pain, care, and imperfections of your earthly life will fall away in heaven. You will be whole in your loving God. You and your loved ones—family members, friends, heroes—will be permanently reunited. All your errors will be forgiven. You will have perfect rest and happiness and complete freedom from want and anxiety. The ache at the center of your being will be filled with the perfect comfort of divine love.

Let heaven keep you going as you allow God's unbreakable promise to lead you through this life to the joy that is in him.

Inspiring Words FROM THE PSALMS

God is good, and he loves goodness; the godly shall see his face.

PSALM 11:7 TLB

Inspiring Words SERIES

This and other books in the Inspiring Words
series are available from your local bookstore.

Inspiring Words from the Psalms

Inspiring Words from the Psalms for Mothers

Inspiring Words from the Psalms for Women

Inspiring Words from the Psalms for Friends

Blue Sky Ink
Brentwood, Tennessee